Theories of the Unconscious
and
Theories of the Self

Theories of the Unconscious
and
Theories of the Self

edited by
Raphael Stern

THE ANALYTIC PRESS

1987   Hillsdale, NJ   London

The Analytic Press.

Distributed solely by

Lawrence Erlbaum Associates, Inc., Publishers
365 Broadway
Hillsdale, New Jersey 07642.

Library of Congress Cataloging-in-Publication Data

Theories of the unconscious and theories of the
  self.

  Partly based on a group of conferences and seminars
sponsored by the Association for Philosophy of Science,
Psychotherapy, and Ethics, held at the Graduate Center
of the City of New York.
  Includes bibliographies and index.
  1. Self-Congresses. 2. Emotions–Congresses.
3. Subconsciousness–Congresses. I. Stern,
Raphael, Psychotherapy, and Ethics (U.S.) [DNLM:
1. Ego. 2. Emotions. 3. Unconscious (Psychology)
BF 315 T396]
BF697.TA7   1986   155.2   85-26815
ISBN 0-88163-057-8

Printed in the United States
10 9 8 7 6 5 4 3 2 1

Contents

III   NEW APPROACHES TO THE UNCONSCIOUS, METATHEORY, AND THE SELF

Preface

This volume is the direct result of a group of conferences and seminars sponsored by the Association for Philosophy of Science, Psychotherapy and Ethics, which were held at the Graduate Center of the City of New York. The seminarists and the speakers at the conferences were asked to contribute to this volume; in addition, the book also contains invited essays. Rosemary Sand and Raphael Stern supervised the conferences for the Association. The aim of the conferences was to attempt to obtain a more unified approach to the dynamics of the unconscious, to the theory of the self, and to the emotions.

Less directly, these conferences and seminars are the outgrowth of the overall scope of the work of the Association, which has sponsored studies in linguistics, logic, semantics, mathematics, philosophy of mind, as well as in the pathologies and personality disorders – their theory and treatment. The aim of the Association has been interdisciplinary: We have assumed that an approach that invited the participation of linguists, psychotherapists, neuropharmacologists, neurophysiologists, philosophers, and mathematicians might have some hope of succeeding where others have failed.

In our work in semantics and logic, and, I think, in the present volume, we have been somewhat successful. This volume in particular, I feel, evidences a step forward, for we have begun to find ways to tie together a diverse number of topics and problems and have thus begun to uncover the beginnings of a research program.

I would like to thank the following persons and institutions for their help: Martin Tamny, Gerald Myers, the City College, and the Graduate Center.

My special gratitude goes to Pratt Institute for supporting other research that led to some of the insights developed here, for providing the wherewithal and support and facilities for completing this book, and in general for its kindness to research. In this regard I would like to thank Jack Minkoff and Carl Craycraft for their assistance.

Editor's Introduction

There are two recent trends in the philosophical study of psychoanalysis: There is the solitary researcher assiduously studying a variety of texts, and there are groups of philosophers, often working with therapists and neurophysiologists, attempting to lay the ground for a new, unified theory. The latter approach is the sort of work attempted for the last ten years by the members of the Association for Philosophy of Science, Psychotherapy, and Ethics; and this book, deriving from the last set of conferences and seminars held, is the culmination of the Association's long search, for in the present volume we begin to sketch out a research program. There are a number of people who contributed in some measure; many of the articles were requested because an author could provide some needed insight, or could close some door, or attend to some difficulty. Although, on the whole, some of the authors made rather substantial contributions in this direction, the conceptual connections that constitute the beginnings of this program are, for the most part, those worked out by the editor of the volume. This is not to say that there was not considerable help from others; it is just prudent to lay blame where it belongs. Thus, important ties of studies of mental concepts to rationality were, in their own fashion, suggested by K.D. Irani and by Joseph Margolis, both members of the Association; Gerald Myers, another member, supplied a critical link between imagination and introspection, and so also between imagination and the unconscious, and finally – given other assumptions made elsewhere in the volume – between emotions, imagination, and the unconsious.

On the whole, for the last ten years – except when we sponsored research in logic, mathematics, and semantics – our program consisted of an effort to find a set of new models for studying the unconscious, the emotions, theories of personality, and theories of the self. We thus began with this last set of conferences to firm up a concept of the emotions that ties the emotions to imagination, to intervention, to intuition, and to the unconscious, and, with this, to an account of the self. We also began to try to link this new concept to a developmental theory, and to begin to pick out the diverse idioms, languages, assumptions, and models we would need in order to pursue this research. Thus, we find throughout this book the following theme: If we are to understand the self, pathologies of the self, meanings, and the emotions, we need to adopt, at the very least, a subset of the languages of aesthetics and ethics, and to wed these to more technical languages.

To continue along these lines and suggest what we are after, Stern, in one section of this book, develops an accòunt of the emotions that ties them to the imagination, and then, relying on the work of Bowers and Myers, ties the emotions to intuition and to the unconscious as well. It is easy to see why we make this move – why we attempt to tie emotion to intuition: it enables us to account for the way the emotions process information. Intuition is needed because the emotions work out problems, difficulties, and so forth, but they do not typically think them out. At the same time, Eagle was encouraged to elaborate the years of research he has done on the unconscious. He has been at pains for some time to find a new account of the unconscious. His model and starting point is the conceptual apparatus used to talk about the self. It is easy to see, then, that, with a few adjustments in his account – and given that the self is already central in our account of the emotions – we can (through Eagle's or some analogous notion of the self) tie the emotions to the unconscious.

We encouraged Stoller's work because it enables us to develop this theory. Stoller considers the perversions, thinking of them as theater designed to humiliate. That is, the perversions are emotion-action systems at the far end of the spectrum, and they have moral and aesthetic components. This immediately permits us to extend our account in two ways: (1) So far, our account holds for healthy emotions; there are other, less healthy emotions that we find it difficult to account for; if we model our account of the latter on Stoller's study, we find that we can, for example, think of rage – which is not a perversion, but not a healthy emotion either in Stoller's terms – as theater, and as involving a desire to hurt, and as involving moral or ethical considerations; this, then, allows us to extend our account of the emotions. (2) We are also fortunate in being able to add to our account Stoller's account of pathology, for this was lacking in ours.

Because our account of the emotions involves that they also are processing information, we asked Safran and Greenberg to provide an essay concerned with information theory.

Kernberg's essay is the lead essay of the book. We very much wanted his considered view on the development of the id and about the self. His developmental views about the id, if workable, obviously provide some of the foundations we need for our theoretical account here; for in this book, everyone, or virtually everyone, notably Kuhns, uses the notion "history" as central, and one of the aims of the book is to see just how it is possible to do this, and also what the consequences are of doing so. And, of course, we also wish to see how doing so engenders problems we must solve (the section including Robinson, Caws, and Cavel explores problems with this sort of approach; in particular, in the case of Robison, with developmental accounts).

Another important feature of Kernberg's essay is his notion of the self: We are interested in the vocabulary his account of the self demands and in how the self develops. Stern's essay, in a later section, is an effort to use a different language for exploring some of the assumptions about the self, including assumptions made by others in this volume. On the whole, we encouraged the contributors to use as diverse a set of languages and approaches as they were inclined to employ in their accounts of the self.

To give an example: Modern research has focused particularly on object relations, how we acquire meanings, and how we then introduce structures over meanings. Hence, there are several ways of talking about the self: from the point of view of meanings, from the point of view of interventions, and from the point of view of emotions. These approaches are all explored in this book. They are not incompatible with one another, and one of our aims here has been to set out the tasks needed to bring these somewhat diverse styles, languages, and approaches together. Thus, there is an obvious difference between Stolorow and Atwood's approach and that of Stern—Stern uses the language of action, whereas Stolorow and Atwood use the language of meanings. Stolorow and Atwood insist that an adequate account of the self begins with a language of subjectivity; Stern insists, as do Meyers, Cavel, and Caws, that a rather diverse set of languages is needed for exploring this concept. Caws and Cavel, for example, each contribute different, important insights into the self, suggesting that both emotive and ethical languages are important for understanding the self.

Robison attempts to tie development, the growth of moral concepts, and the notion of attachment to the self. This seems to open up another, rather complex realization of what we have urged and noticed throughout the volume; namely, that not only diverse languages but diverse theories and assumptions are needed for a complete picture of the development of the self.

We have encouraged a good deal of speculation throughout the volume. We feel we now have the wherewithal to spell out in more detail a research program, but we must attend as well to the properties of these theories. One set of properties has to do with the fact that we have, in some measure, aligned ourselves with those who adopt a developmental theory. Robison's essay suggests that there are good reasons for having grave misgivings about such theories. It is not clear, however, that these reasons will remain valid when we alter our languages and assumptions to the degree that we have done by encouraging the amount of diversity found in this volume. (For example, it is not clear that they hold true for programs that require the usual vocabularies *plus* aesthetic ones, in discourse about the self.) Other properties we need to attend to are of semantic and epistemic nature – to what degree would our account, dressed up finally as theory, refer to the world as it is? Mendelsohn and Silverman provide an analysis – not for our account here, but for psychoanalytic postulates – of this kind of issue. They suggest that a cluster of studies, including outcome studies of clinical situations and subliminal research, can be performed to test psychodynamic postulates and concepts. These studies, they hope, will shed light on the different theoretical formulations of the pathogenesis and treatment of narcissism.

One or two points need clarification. There are often enough things that go on in a volume of this scope that alert someone like Kuhns to warn us that there may be two kinds of discourse involved, or that we may be using two distinct models in our work, or that we might have need of two models to further our work. What I am talking about here is the elaboration of very rich theories, in particular about the self. It is not always clear just what the properties of these theories are – are they philosophical, or are they both philosophical and empirical?

The two models people usually have in mind when they talk this way are those relevant to studies of cultures. And it does seem, as one peruses the volume, that something like two models is being employed in a number of cases.

An encouraging aspect of the volume is that philosophers have come out of their shells and begun proposing rather elaborate theories of the self. For some time now it has looked as if contemporary psychoanlysts were the only ones attempting grand theories of the self and of mind in the style of the 19th century; they seemed to be the inheritors of 19th-century philosophy. On the other hand, philosophers, busy professionalizing their own field, have for some time tended to narrow analytic studies. Indeed, philosophers have become so discrete that one hears hardly anything at all from them on matters of mind and matters of self. And so for a long time the task of framing a philosophy of mind fell to the psychologist. It appears to be the psychologist, in particular the psychotherapist, who does philosophy of mind, albeit differently from the philosopher.

This retrenchment of philosophers is not peculiar to philosophy of mind; it occurs as well in aesthetics. Indeed, artists today appear to think of themselves as epistemologists as well as artists. It is as if the great traditional areas of study in philosophy have been appropriated by other disciplines.

This is not the case here. The Association for quite some time has repudiated this approach to philosophical issues and encouraged large scale theorizing when appropriate and also attempts to combine apparently diverse models.

SELF, OBJECTS, AND THE UNCONSCIOUS:
ISSUES AND PROBLEMS

1 The Dynamic Unconscious and the Self

Otto F. Kernberg

It is at the boundaries of scientific disciplines that new developments often originate, and problems emerging at those boundaries have relevance for the central paradigms of a discipline. This holds true, I believe, for the boundary shared by psychoanalytic and philosophical inquiries into the mind-body problem, the problem of personal identity, and the limits of individual freedom and responsibility. It also pertains,moreover, to the boundaries that both psychoanalysis and philosophical inquiry share with the sociobiology of human behavior, particularly neurophysiology, neuropsychology, and the social sciences.

What follows is an outline of some questions at the level of these boundaries that I have had to struggle with in the course of my theoretical explorations of psychoanalytic object relations theory. I also present some related clinical observations derived from psychoanalytic work with patients presenting ordinary types of psychoneuroses and character pathology and with patients presenting character pathology within the borderline spectrum of personality disorders.

CHANGING VIEWS REGARDING THE NATURE AND ORIGIN OF THE DYNAMIC UNCONSCIOUS

In his two final formulations regarding the relationship between the topographic and structural theories of the unconscious, Freud (1933, 1938)

Presentation at a meeting of The Association for Philosophy of Science, Psychotherapy and Ethics at the Graduate Center of the City University of New York, May 8, 1982.

reaffirmed his differentiation between what is descriptively unconscious (that is, outside the realm of conscious thought but capable of being evoked by an effort of attention: the preconscious), from what is dynamically unconscious (that is, active in determining both intrapsychic and behavioral events without being retrievable by any effort on the part of the conscious mind). He stressed that the dynamic unconscious, thus differentiated from the descriptive unconscious or preconscious, coincided mostly, but not totally, with the structural concept of the id. Defence mechanisms of the ego, as well as the drive derivatives in the id against which they have been erected, are dynamically unconscious. What is dynamically unconscious, then, is the intrapsychic conflict between drives and defenses. Structurally speaking, the boundary between drives and defenses constitutes at the same time the delimitation between ego and id. In the course of these discussions, Freud summarized once more the functional characteristics of the primary process, characteristic of the id, and of the secondary process, characteristic of the ego. He also described the id once more as a cauldron of repressed drives, that is, an essentially unstructured compartment of the mind.

In my view, important and still unresolved problems have emerged in the application of these concepts to severe types of psychopathology. First, the question remains, what determines the dynamically unconscious nature of ego defenses? Psychoanalytic work with patients suffering from character pathology has illustrated a layering of defensive processes, so that rather than a simple boundary between ego and id, these character defenses themselves represent compromise formations between defense and impulse that present as a dynamic layering of contradictory tendencies, with a gradual veering toward preconscious and conscious "collusion" of the ego with the more superficially placed defensive processes, on one side, and a merging of the deepest layers of defensive operations with aspects of the id, on the other.

Another, more troublesome development is the observation that the repressed unconscious, the id, has more structure than is implied by its primary-process character. When the analysis of defense mechanisms permits the emergence of the previously repressed into consciousness, what we observe are not simply drive derivatives but repressed internalized object relations (Fairbairn, 1952; Van der Waals, 1952). The repressed unconscious, in clinical practice, is constituted by real or fantasied repressed internalized relationships of the patient with parental objects under the influence of sexual and aggressive drives. We never observe pure drives in clinical practice, but only drive-invested object relations.

Insofar as Freud (1923) suggested that the ego is a precipitate of the representations of instinctually invested objects by means of internalization and the superego also derives from the internalization of the demanding and prohibitive aspects of instinctually invested objects, we cannot avoid the fact that, within the clinical study of the tripartite structure (ego, superego, and id) in the course of psychoanalytic treatment, all three structures reflect vicissitudes of the drive investment of internalized object relations and are highly organized.

Even more striking is the presence in full consciousness of what ordinarily would constitute the deepest, most repressed layers of the mind in patients with psychotic and borderline psychopathology, whose defensive organization centers on the mechanism of primitive dissociation or splitting rather than repression. Freud's (1924a, b) original formulation regarding the psychoses—namely, that in the psychoses there is a rupture of the ego and a direct expression in consciousness and behavior of the conflicts between drives and external reality—was able to explain the emergence in consciousness of id material in the case of psychotic patients. The same phenomenon, however, occurring in nonpsychotic patients already troubled Freud at that time (1924b, p. 187). He then formulated the hypothesis that under certain circumstances the ego might distort itself and renounce its integrity by a process of splitting, a concept to which he returned in his 1938 paper on "Splitting of the Ego in the Process of Defense," one of his last contributions, destined to be of crucial importance in psychoanalytic theory and technique.

In the severe character pathologies that are part of borderline personality organization, the contents of the id appear in consciousness in split-off or mutually dissociated ego states, and the unconscious conflicts between ego and id in the psychoneuroses and less severe character pathologies are replaced by the expression of such conflicts in the form of alternating activation of contradictory, conscious ego/id states. Although in some patients with multiple personality, for example, repressive barriers separate contradictory personifications (reflecting an hysterical personality structure), in most patients with multiple personality the various personifications are cognitively linked, "remembered" while inactive but *affectively* split off: this is typical of borderline personality organization.

The severe psychopathologies derive from conflicts originating in earlier developmental levels than the unconscious conflicts that produce typical neurotic psychopathology. Therefore, a primitive ego organization in which the conflict between drives and defenses against them appears in consciousness reinforces the impression—already gained on the basis of the observation that the id (like the ego and the superego) contains remnants of past object relations—that the quality of being dynamically unconscious may be less central in the origin and functioning of the id than we used to think. It further suggests that the quality of dynamic unconsciousness of the id may be closely related to the consolidation of the repressive barrier that reflects the integration of the ego at a certain stage of development. In other words, both the dynamic unconscious and the ego have a developmental history in the earliest stages of which ego and id are not only undifferentiated, but are functioning under conditions different from their eventual topographic (conscious, preconscious, or unconscious) characteristics.

If this is so, it may explain the paradox that the most regressive, the most frightening and horrifying aspects of primitive aggression and primitive condensation of aggression and sexuality—in the context of loss of the differentiated capacity for object relations—are found in the behaviors, conscious wishes, and fantasies of patients with borderline personality organization, as well as in those psychotic individuals who maintain enough contact to be able to enact their psychotic wishes in external reality.

These observations led me to explore the nature of early consciousness and the conditions for the integration of the superego as the crucial structure controlling the activation of repression and related "advanced" mechanisms of defense that establish and consolidate the unconscious control of the ego over the dynamically unconscious forces of the id in its eventual (ultimate) stage.

CONSCIOUSNESS, THE SELF, AFFECTS, AND COGNITION

In addition to his hypothesis that the ego originates as a precipitate of the representations of instinctually invested objects, Freud (1923) also proposed that the ego differentiates from the id—or an original, undifferentiated ego/id—matrix, by its crystallization around the system perception-consciousness. I propose that these two formulations regarding the origin of the ego can be integrated in the understanding that the infant's perception and consciousness are particularly activated during actual interactions with mother, and that evolving instinctual investments of her will leave traces in the early ego's field of consciousness.

I shall now attempt to spell out some hypotheses regarding the early developmental stages of consciousness, their relation to the development of unconscious intrapsychic conflicts, and the crystallization of the self as an intrapsychic substructure of the ego in the process of these developments.

In clinical psychiatry, the term consciousness refers to the simultaneous availability of the following functions to the individual: (a) a clear and distinct perception of immediate, external reality (in contrast to the reduction of such awareness under conditions of somnolence or intoxication); (b) a sense of full awareness of cognitive continuity as well as differentiation of experiences under different external circumstances, which connects the present with experiences from the past (in contrast to the dissociation of states of partial consciousness in fugue states, altered states of consciousness under the influence of drugs, and certain types of multiple personalities); and (c) a clear differentiation of perceptions of immediate external reality, and of actual interactions in it from memories, fantasy, and daydreaming (in contrast to the lack of differentiation between perceptions of external reality and hallucinations, as in acute organic psychosis).

Fully developed, normal consciousness implies, first, a subjective state that can be optimally evaluated by verbal communication and, therefore, immediately raises the methodological problem of subjectivity in contrast to "objective" observation. Second, such consciousness clearly involves an awareness of one's own awareness, or self-awareness, that is, an awareness that one is experiencing mental states. There are certain clinical conditions, pathological states of consciousness, in which it becomes only retrospectively obvious that such a self-awareness was missing. Third, and less apparent but quite crucial, the mental states one is aware of experiencing imply the manipulation of symbols, that is, the use of thoughts as representing "things," (ultimately, sensorial, affective, and proprioceptive perceptions). The gradual awakening from sleep sometimes embodies all these characteristics. Successive mental states under such conditions include, first, "floating" experiences with sensorial qualities; second, diffuse thoughts and/or feelings associated with those perceptions; third, an awareness of one's experiencing such experiences; and finally, a full integration of that self-awareness into a global awareness of waking up, thus reestablishing the cognitive continuity of full consciousness as described (this view of consciousness may be compared with Rapaport's [1951, 1955] effort to relate psychopathological and psychodynamic views of consciousness).

Developmentally speaking, recent advances in the observations of infant-mother interactions, (Stern, 1985) point to the activation, within the first few weeks of life, of a capacity for discrimination of properties belonging to mother in the form of cross-modal sensorial integration, indicating that the infant is "prewired" to discriminate and begin to form distinct schemata of self and of others from the earliest months of life. In other words, the cognitive potential of infants is much more sophisticated than what traditionally has been assumed, and the same is true for the infant's affective behavior.

Affective behavior strongly influences the infant's relation with mother from birth on (Izard, 1978; Izard & Buechler, 1979). A central biological function of inborn affective patterns—with their behavioral, communicative, and psychophysiological manifestations—is to signal to the environment (the mothering person) the infant's needs and thus to initiate the communication between the infant and mother that marks the beginning of intrapsychic life (Emde, Kligman, Reich, & Wade, 1978). Recent research has surprised us with the description of a high degree of differentiation in infant-mother communications beginning very early (Hoffman, 1978). Neuropsychological theorizing now assumes the storage of affective memory in the limbic cortex, which, as direct brain-stimulation experiments indicate, permits the reactivation of not only the cognitive but also the affective aspects of past experience, particularly the subjective, affective coloring of that experience (Arnold, 1970). I have proposed elsewhere (1976) that affects, operating as the earliest motivational system, are intimately linked with the fixation by memory of an internalized world of object relations.

Although a precise timetable of developmental stages may require substantial revision in the light of contemporary infant observations regarding both cognitive and affective development, I propose the following hypotheses regarding the sequences of development leading to the gradual establishment of consciounesss as defined. In so doing, I shall differentiate the broader concept of consciousness from the intrapsychic structure of the self as derived from it.

Insofar as present neuropsychological theorizing about the nature of affects implies that the subjective quality of affects—basically, pleasure and pain— is a central feature integrating the psychophysiological, behavioral, and communicative aspect of affects, and insofar as highly differentiated behavioral, communicative, and psychophysiological aspects of affects are observable as early as the first weeks of life, it seems reasonable to assume the capacity for subjective experience of pleasure and pain to exist from very early on. In fact, granted that affective schemata as well as perceptual and motor schemas are operant from birth on, subjectivity (subjective experience of pleasure and pain) can be assumed to constitute the first stage of consciousness and, by the same token, the first stage of development of the self.

Piaget's (1954) statements, "In summary, affective states that have no cognitive elements are never seen, nor are behaviors found that are wholly cognitive" and that "affectivity would play the role of an energy source on which the functioning but not the structures of intelligence would depend" (p. 5) probably reflect generally accepted principles of psychological functioning. I suggest that affective subjectivity, the primordial experience of self, contributes to the integration—in the form of affective memory—of perceptual, behavioral, and interactional experiences, as well as the affective schemata themselves, perhaps particularly when the infant is in an extremely pleasurable or extremely unpleasurable affective state (peak affect state), which maximizes the infant's alertness and attention.

It also seems reasonable to assume that such an assembly of memory structures during peak affective states may spur the earliest symbolic activities, in that one element of such a peak affective constellation stands for the entire constellation. A light turned on in the room, for example, represents the presence of the feeding mother even before she is perceived. One could argue about exactly when simple association and conditioned reflexes are transformed into symbolic thinking—in the sense that one element stands for an entire constellation of evoked experience outside the rigid linkage of conditioned associations. In any case, it seems reasonable to assume that the earliest symbolic function, an active representation of an entire sequence by one element of it, placed outside the rigid associative chain, would occur precisely under such conditions.

Peak affective states, then, would constitute the conditions under which purely affective subjectivity would be transformed into mental activity with symbolic functions, clinically represented by affective memory structures reflecting pleasurable relations of infant and mother, in which self- and object representations, in spite of the highly differentiated, cognitive inborn schemata of them, are as yet undifferentiated. Affective memory structures derived from the unpleasant or painful peak affective states in which self-and object representations are also undifferentiated would be built up separately from the pleasurable ones.

I am thus proposing a first stage of consciousness characterized by peak affect states and the beginning of symbolization as defined. This early stage of development has essentially subjective features and cannot be considered equivalent to the observational data indicating the early capacity for cross-modal differentiation that, presumably, corresponds to "wired-in" potentials, optimally observable under experimental conditions characterized by mild or modulated affect dispositions. Subjectivity implies experiencing, and experiencing should, logically, be maximal under conditions of affective peaks. Subjectivity also implies thinking and therefore requires, as a minimum, the manipulation of symbols. That minimum, I propose, implies a breaking out from the rigid chain of conditioned associations.

There is no self-reflectiveness as yet in this first stage of consciousness; there is feeling without the awareness that it is "I" who is feeling. But "feeling always involves an affective-cognitive structure. In this earliest state of consciousness, the infant therefore would naturally organize the world of experiences into pleasurable units and painful units, based on real interactions and fantasied interactions (unrealistic distortion of perception under the impact of extreme pleasure and pain) of the infant with mother. The infant would store these units separately as "good" and "bad" affective memories (Arnold, 1970).

This early state of consciousness, which does not yet include awareness of one's awarness (or self-awareness) would correspond to the symbiotic stage of development, described by Margaret Mahler (Mahler & Furer, 1968), which takes place between approximately the second and fourth or fifth month of life. Perhaps of particular importance here is the gradual development of two parallel series of "all good" and "all bad" fantasied characteristics of this symbiotic world: The excited pleasure connected with the evoked and realized presence of the "good" feeding mother would contrast with the fantastically imagined "bad" mother under conditions of extreme frustration, pain, or rage. In this connection, that infant observation is facilitated by mildly or moderately pleasurable affect states in mother-infant interaction and that it has not focused sufficiently on the nature of behavioral developments under conditions of serious frustration may be responsible for the crucial methodological problem of relating infant observation to the subjectively painful, frightening, and enraged experiences that are so prevalent under conditions of severe psychopathology. By the same token, the transformation of painful experiences into the symbolic image of an undifferentiated "bad self-bad mother" obviously contain an element of fantasy that transcends the realistic character of the "good" self-object representations. The original fantasy material of what is later to become the repressed unconscious may reflect a predominance of aggressive imagery and affects.

Subjective experience in peak affective states may initiate the construction of an internal world that gradually separates out into a deep layer of fantastic imagery linked to internalized object relations acquired during peak states, and a more superficial layer that "infiltrates" the building up of cognitively more realistic perceptions of external reality under ordinary states of wakeful exploration of the surroundings. Eventually, symbol formation and affective organization of reality would develop in this surface layer of perception as well, transforming wired-in organization of perception into symbolically manipulated information—that is, into conscious thinking, the origin of secondary-process thinking.

The second stage of development of consciousness would begin at the fourth or fifth month of life, when both cognitive and affective development contribute to reducing the extreme nature of unpleasant or painful experiences, and when the infant gradually differentiates its perceptions of itself from those of its mother under both pleasurable and painful conditions, coincident with the onset of separation-individuation (Mahler, Pine, & Bergman, 1975). The stability of proprioceptive experiences under varying affective interactions with mother—the infant's awareness that the frightening and painful experiences of it and mother have sensoriperceptive and proprioceptive elements or schemata that coincide with some of the elated and gratifying experiences of it and mother, in short, the infant's developing sense of a body image—contributes importantly to this differentiation. I am proposing that the infant's experience of two different states of subjectivity (good and bad) as having common properties, bodily as well as intrapsychic (the two domains of affective experience), leads the infant to assign it a "seat of consciousness," in short, self-awareness. The building up of self-representations now separate from but relating to object representations implies awareness both of an interaction and of the self as subject of such interaction. The infant may now attribute a parallel seat of consciousness to the "other" person with whom it is interacting, with exactly corresponding affective experiences. Primitive projective mechanisms activated at the time of self-and object differentiation together with actual perceptions and wired-in capacities for empathic resonance, would determine such attribution of consciousness to the other person and thereby consolidate the symbiotic roots of intersubjectivity. A relation between self-representation and object representation is thus established even before the infant discovers identity of good with bad objects (=mother).

The existence of self-awareness can then definitely be assumed at this stage: now primordial experiences reflecting affective subjectivity are transformed into the self-awareness that is a correlate of differentiated self-and object representations. This self-awareness, reflecting the integration of self-representations from both pleasurable and painful peak affective experiences, is in contrast to the global, diffuse nature of awareness that preceded it, the global awareness of primordial self-experience that, in turn, has to be differentiated from the still earlier inborn schemata.

The third stage in the development of consciousness is achieved during the completion of the stage of separation-individuation, toward the end of the rapprochement crisis at the completion of the third year of life (Mahler, 1979), at which point "good" and "bad" self-representations built up under opposite affective conditions are integrated into a global concept of the self, whereas "good" and "bad" object representations are, in turn, integrated. The integration of contradictory aspects of object representations is a precondition for the related capacity for experiencing other people in depth, similarly to the deepening of self-awareness and self-knowledge achieved when self-presentations are consolidated into an integrated conception of the self. At this point, the final condition of consciousness mentioned earlier, namely, the establishment of full continuity of self-awareness, is fulfilled, and, by the same token, an integrated structure of the self emerges within the ego. Now the self as a "categorical" concept, the self as postulated by the philosophers as well as observed in the psychoanalytic exploration of neurotic and normal persons, comes into full existence.

In summary, the nature of consciousness evolves from (a) the primordial consciousness or primary affective subjectivity involved in peak affect states, to (b) the self-awareness when self-and object representations are differentiated from each other, and to (c) the consolidation of the intrapsychic structure of the self when self-representations are integrated. I may now add that the original lack of integration of contradictory ego/id states (contradictory peak affective subjectivity) is gradually transformed into an active mechanism of ego splitting that culminates in the rapprochement subphase of separation-individuation, then to be replaced, at the time of the consolidation of the self, with the development of repression and other related mechanisms.This leads to the formation of the dynamic unconscious in a broad sense, and to the id as an organized mental structure in a narrower one.

The dynamic unconscious first includes unacceptable states of self-awareness under the influence of aggressively invested relations with object representations similarly perceived as intolerable by means of primitive defensive operations, particularly projective identification. The early peak affect states under the effects of frustration activate primitive fantasies of frustrating "objects"—represented by sensoriperceptive experiences that also come to symbolize efforts to "expel" those intolerable objects—and rageful wishes to destroy the objects together with the transformation of the experience of frustration into the fantasy of being attacked and endangered. The repression of peak affective experiences of a pleasurable nature—particularly of sexually excited states related to unacceptable fantasies involving parental objects—follows the earlier aggressive wishes and fantasies of the dynamic unconscious. The unconsciously dynamic defensive functions and operations involving primitive fantasies, and the later defensive operations that secondarily reinforce repression, eventually encapsulate the deepest, unconscious layer of aggressively and libidinally invested object relations, the id in a narrow sense. The developmental sequence of states of consciousness I am proposing thus includes the consideration of repression of aspects of early subjective states and of self-awareness and the related consolidation of unconscious roots of the self in the id as well as in the unconscious ego.

The integration of the ego includes, in addition to the integration of the self, the consolidation of integrated object representations, that is, the "representational world" (Sandler & Rosenblatt, 1962). The ego also incorporates perceptive, cognitive, and psychomotor functions.

Patients with borderline personality organization, who present a differentiation between self-and object representations and the related, clinically crucial function of reality testing, have serious difficulties in integrating contradictory ego states when they are under the impact of contradictory affective qualities that, at the same time, would reflect contradictory internalized object relations as well. These patients fulfill all the preconditions for clinical presence of full consciousness, including a cognitive continuity of their contradictory ego states, but they lack a sense of affective continuity and an integrated conception of the self. This is precisely the effect of the defensive mechanism of splitting. It is as if different personalities were taking turns in these patients' relationships with significant others. They can neither state which of these is their true self nor predict their future interaction with a person who is emotionally important to them.

Psychoanalytic exploration suggests that this splitting of contradictory ego states protects these patients from the severe anxiety that is regularly activated when splitting processes are interpretively approached. Splitting also protects them from intense ambivalence, from bringing together primitive types of hatred and condensed sexual and aggressive impulses and fears, on one hand, and intense love and longing on the other, and protects them from a fear of destroying their love objects or being destroyed in turn by those whom they need and onto whom they project their aggression. These patients have self-awareness, but not an integrated conception of the self; they have full consciousness, but not a consolidated identity in the sense of cross-sectional and historical continuity of the self.

In contrast, in patients with milder character pathology and psychoneuroses whose solid repressive barriers consolidate the ego as well as the id, we observe an integrated self-concept, firmly established ego identity, and yet the shadow of unconscious influence and control over the self resulting from repressed internalized object relations—libidinally and aggressively invested—that strive for reactivation through invasion of the ego's and the self's intrapsychic and interpersonal field.

By the same token, such neurotic patients, and normal persons of course, present an integrated superego reflected in a dynamically unconscious, internalized morality as well as in a set of preconscious and conscious, abstracted, individualized, and depersonified moral standards, which is our next subject.

THE PRECONDITIONS FOR MORAL CONSCIOUSNESS

Classical psychoanalytic theory has explained how, during the development of the small child, the external demands and prohibitions of the parents are internalized into what is to become the superego. It needs to be stressed that what is internalized are not simply the parents' realistic demands or prohibitions, but unconsciously distorted and exaggerated demands and prohibitions influenced by the child's unconscious wishes and fears and projected onto the parental objects.

Jacobson (1964) outlined successive levels of internalization of superego precursors: (a) the internalization of sadistic, persecutory superego precursors that represent the remnants of "all bad" projected representations stemming from the "bad" early object relations mentioned earlier; (b) the idealized superego precursors stemming from later elaborations of "good" and idealized self-and object representations that will constitute the ego-ideal aspect of the superego; (c) the gradual integration of the persecutory and idealized superego precursors which leads to their toning down and the internalization of more realistic parental images during the oedipal stage of development. The first and second levels of internalization into the superego would extend roughly from the second to the fourth year of life; the third level from the fourth to the sixth year; a fourth level of development would be the gradual integration of all these superego constituents into the abstracted, individuated, and depersonified superego of latency and early adolescence.

What is relevant here is that the integration of good and bad internalized object relations at the time of the integration of the self-concept within the ego is parallelled at the time of superego integration. Again, the crucial issue is the establishment of an internal sense of continuity between what earlier were discontinuous, alternating mental states and a parallel sense of continuity with respect to emotional investments in others and, later, with respect to moral demands and value systems.

Clinically, one finds a spectrum of superego pathology in patients with borderline personality organization that exemplifies degrees of severity in patients' lack of superego integration and, by implication, in the stages of integration required in the internalization of moral demands and prohibitions from the parental objects. The severest form of superego pathology is represented by patients with antisocial personality disorders (formerly called psychopaths). These patients lie to the therapist, and are fully aware that they are lying. They understand the moral requirements of the therapist (or of external reality in general), to which they have to pay lip service. But they do not understand that these demands represent an authentic system of morality that other persons have internalized. Instead, moral demands from the environment are a universally accepted "warning" system, exploited by the corrupt (like the patient) and submitted to by the innocent and the sly.

These patients can lie and cheat effectively, and they do understand that they may be "caught." But they do not understand that others' experience of them as liars will affect their emotional or generally human relationships with them. Because these patients are unable to experience authentic love for others, they cannot appreciate that others may care for them and not merely wish ruthlessly to exploit and manipulate them. These patients tend to destroy the emotional relationship with the therapist without even understanding what they are doing.

Their capacity to lie effectively reflects a sort of integration of the self, an integration based, however, on the structure of the pathological grandiose self of the narcissistic personality and not on the normal integration of good and bad self-representations in the context of the integration of good and bad object representations (Kernberg, 1975, 1982). That grandiose self, which replaces the normal integration of the self-concept, is totally identified with the pleasure principle, and some of these patients present an infiltration of this grandiose self with aggression and a subsequent ego-syntonic search for the gratification of sadistic urges. There is a continuum from the passive, exploitative, parasitic psychopath to the frankly sadistic criminal, and social circumstances facilitating the expression of primitive aggression and cruelty will find a natural accommodation of these personality structures. Dicks (1972) has illustrated this convergence in sociopsychological study of SS killers.

The next level of this continuum is represented by those patients with borderline personality organization who present narcissistic personalities with antisocial features but without an antisocial personality proper; by patients with "as if" qualities; by some patients with infantile personality and chronic self-mutilating tendencies in addition to some antisocial traits; and by those patients with malignant forms of pathological narcissism, who obtain a sense of triumph by experiencing themselves above the pain of illness or death and attempt to control others by self-mutilation or suicide.

These patients manifest their superego pathology by an apparent honesty in their interactions with the therapist: they state their feelings and intentions but completely refuse to accept responsibility for their experiences and actions under different emotional states. Such patients may assure the therapist that they do not feel like cutting themselves at this moment—thereby assuring the therapist that they will not engage in self-mutilating behavior—but they cannot be sure that they might not feel otherwise later when they might engage in self-mutilating or suicidal behavior. Or such a patient may, with a sense that she is being totally honest and realistic, tell a man that he is her only and total love in life, knowing that she may say exactly the same thing to another man when she is in a different affective state later on, and will again feel that she is being entirely truthful.

That patient is not consciously lying in the ordinary sense of the word but is obviously dishonest in a deeper sense, namely, in refusing to accept any responsibility for the reliability of her feelings, intentions, and actions. In fact, it is striking how easily some of these patients, who usually have a history of manipulative, controlling, and exploitive behavior with others, are able to "brainwash" the therapist with the logic of their bland, cavalier dismissals of a sense of personal responsibility and concern for themselves and for others. Clearly, these patients show a cognitive continuity of their mental states, while maintaining an affective discontinuity that protects them from anxiety or guilt, and from any identification with moral values. They simultaneously illustrate the defensive use of the mechanism of split-

ting and the nature of the totally self-centered behavior that one can observe in children before superego integration has taken place. But, in
additon, they show a severe deterioration in their human relations.

The normal small child who has just attacked mother, destroyed objects,
and been defiant and negativistic may come back to mother a short time
later with a big smile and asking for some gratification. Such discontinuity
between good and bad object relations may be challenged by mother's
pointing out that she is still upset by the child's behavior and that the child
has to consider her feelings as well and his own and must not deny what
has occurred by a sudden shift in attitude. In other words, the normal
establishment of continuity between ideal and rageful states in interpersonal interactions between child and parents fosters a sense of responsibility
and concern for self and others in the child, while raising the question of
the endangerment to the loving aspects of object relations by the activation
of unavoidable aggression in them.

The therapist's task, in fact, is precisely to interpret the splitting operations that maintain the borderline patient's denial of responsibility and to
confront the patient with a corresponding rationalization of his dishonesty
in relating to self and others. In contrast, however, to the normal relation
between mother and small child, borderline patients cannot understand
that they are being loved and cared for rather than simply being controlled
by the other person; nor are they able to experience ambivalence and
gratitude. Their denial of responsibility for their actions serves the unconscious—and conscious—purpose of allowing them to attack others and to
avoid the painful awareness of their aggression. What mother can achieve
in a short time with her normal child may take the therapist of borderline
patients many months or years.

The problem in these cases lies in the splitting of good and bad internalized object relations, which protects the patients from intolerable ambivalence but at the cost of making unavailable to them the capacity for
deep investment in others as total objects—and in themselves as integrated
individuals. The lack of integration of moral demands, the inability to
tolerate guilt feelings, are the consequence, at the levels of superego development, of the lack of integration of the self in the "categorical" sense—
the lack of an integrated sense of identity. Under these conditions, the
idealized superego precursors are totally split off from the persecutory
ones, and the third level of superego internalization of more realistic parental demands and prohibitions is missing. Here the integration of the self
in the therapeutic process must precede the integration of more normal
superego functioning. Under optimal circumstances, guilt is first experienced and tolerated in the transference.

The next level of superego pathology found in the majority of patients
with borderline personality organization without the antisocial, narcissis-

tic, "as if," and self-mutilating features mentioned before, is reflected in the following characteristics. The patients are aware of strong and contradictory urges that they cannot control and spontaneously express concern that in mental states contradictory to the present one they may feel or act in ways that would be unacceptable now. Clinically, this condition may be illustrated by patients with dissociated, severe suicidal tendencies who are nevertheless concerned about this suicidal potential and are willing to ask for help when they feel threatened by such powerful impulses. That these patients can feel concern for themselves and others and can tolerate guilt feelings when they act aggressively against those they love indicates both a beginning stage of internalization of superego functions and a much stronger capacity for an emotional investment in others; this capacity suggests a favorable prognosis.

These patients also show the beginning of what may be called authentic personal feedom. Freedom, clinically speaking, implies the capacity to make moral and rational decisions about one's actions, as opposed to being dominated by inner needs and impulses beyond one's control. In contrast to the absence of freedom of the impulse-ridden person (who, however, frequently may experience himself "free" in the sense of experiencing no internal constraints on his actions, and who has no sense of choice), freedom implies the awareness of intrapsychic conflict, the availability of alternative courses of actions, and the mastery to execute the chosen course of action.

Under conditions of still more advanced superego pathology, namely, that of patients with neurotic personality organization and a well-integrated but excessively severe and sadistic superego, unconscious guilt may be reflected in a different kind of restriction of individual freedom: a regressive deterioration into moralistic attitudes, overconventionalism, and an adherence to a conventionalized sense of morality that reflects the contents and rigidity of unconscious infantile morality. Paradoxically, some borderline patients at a stage of improvement may have more internal freedom than some severely restricted neurotic patients. It should be kept in mind, however, that the psychoanalytic resolution of neurotic superego pathology—that is, of unconsciously determined guilt feelings related to a repressed, infantile morality originally directed against unacceptable infantile wishes—leads potentially to the highest degree of moral integrity and internal freedom.

In concluding this analysis of superego pathology, we may state that the development of the superego depends on the development, quality and depth of internalized object relations and the corresponding integration of the self as a psychological structure.

From a different perspective, this description also illustrates the complex relation between the self as an intrapsychic structure rooted in subjectivity, on one hand, and the interpersonal, psychosocial nature of object relations, the actual relation between the self and significant others, on the other hand, in determining, shaping, and expressing what might be called the subjective, existential self and its moral dimension. This leads us back to the general methodological problem of the definition of self as an intrapsychic structure versus its definition as a psychosocial, behaviorial given.

SOCIAL AND EXISTENTIAL DIMENSIONS OF THE SELF

A few operational definitions may help to differentiate semantic problems from substantive issues in this field. Character refers to the overall, dynamically determined integration of component character traits, that is, the individuals' habitual modes of adapting himself to his internal and external reality. The more normal the character, the more flexible are its component traits and, paradoxically, the more difficult it is to define. In contrast, the more pathological the character, the more that fixed and rigid, defensively structured character traits predominate and the more clearly does character appear organized in clusters of traits or constellations that are reflected clinically in pathological character structures, such as the obsessive personality, the narcissistic personality, the hysterical personality, and the like. Character traits and constellations are reflected mostly in behavior, but secondarily also in how the individual organizes perception and subjective experience.

Self-representations refer to a person's subjective experiences of himself in relating to others, both actually and intrapsychically. Self-representations are normally integrated into a cohesive concept of the self; in short, they are "the self." For practical purposes, in the case of less severe types of neurotic character pathology and in normality, this concept of the self controls the ego's conscious and preconscious, self-reflecting, self-aware, self-evaluating functions. In contrast, in patients with severe psychopathology, those presenting borderline personality organization, the defensively motivated mutual dissociation or splitting of contradictory self-representations prevents such an integration of a normal self and is reflected in the syndrome of identity diffusion. Identity diffusion is also characterized by a lack of integration of object representations into total or global conceptions of significant others in the patient's life.

By the same token, in the case of the severe character pathology characteristic of borderline personality organization, instead of the inhibitory character traits and reaction formations predominant at less severe levels of character pathology, sharply contradictory character traits influence the patient's behavior, with alternating activation of such contradictory character patterns and related contradictory self- and object representations.

These contradictory character traits reflect the splitting of self- and object representations, or, rather, of contradictory units of self- and object representations, and contribute, in turn, to maintaining splitting operations.

With some oversimplification, one might say that character reflects the predominantly behavioral aspects of ego functions; self-representations and the self, the more subjective ones; and that these behavioral and subjective aspects of ego functions acquire dynamically determined, particularly rigid and repetitive characteristics when there exists severe psychopathology or, more generally, significant ego weakness.

I trust these definitions already indicate a general trend of my argument, namely, my conviction that the separation between subjective, "existential" self-experience and psychosocial manifestations of the self as character is artificial. The experiences of self and others strongly influence the behavioral patterns expressing these experiences in relating to self and others; and characterologically fixated patterns of interactions, in turn, influence self-experience, actual interactions, and the experiences of others.

I think that the strength of psychoanalysis as a research tool derives precisely from its combining the analysis of the patient's subjective experiences as (a) communicated to the therapist and (b) as experienced in a transitory, empathic trial identification with the patient by the analyst, with (c) the analyst's observations of the patient's patterns of interaction with him that reflect the patient's characterological style, and (4) the analyst's own exploration of the nature of the emotional interactions that are activated by the combination of his experiencing the patient's subjectivity and behavior. Contemporary understanding of countertransference includes the diagnosis of the patient's dissociated, repressed, or projected object representations activated within the subjective experience of the psychoanalyst in interactions with the patient.

In short, the combination of direct observation, empathy, countertransference analysis, and the study of the "ambience," or "analytic space," provides a broad basis for psychoanalytic investigation (Kernberg, 1980). In addition, by sharing with a patient his observations of him by the analyst creates a further dimension of integration of subjective experience and objective observations. Without underestimating the enormous difficulties and limitations inherent in obtaining a deep understanding of another person (and of oneself, for that matter), I think we are probably justified in reformulating the relationships between unconscious motivation, the self concept, and character along the following lines.

First, the dynamically unconscious roots of the self correspond, as was described earlier, to dynamically unconscious experiences of early objects. The id contains primitive fantasies and experiences of the earliest objects, primarily those influenced by peak affect experiences, particularly of a frustrating and aggressive nature. Second, the id also contains the experiences of relations with object representations influenced by extremely pleasurable, particularly sexually tinged, affective conditions. In both cases, the primitivity of the repressed internalized object relations also implies a blurring of the boundaries between self and object, the remnants of an early state of development before the differentiation of self-/from object representations.

Third, insofar as the earliest pleasurable peak affect experiences of an undifferentiated self and object representation under the condition of an "all good" object relation may be considered a core self experience, the awareness of self and of others is intimately linked in the area of self-experience that will be incorporated into ego functions and structure as well. While affectively modulated experiences may foster the mapping out of areas of differentiation between self and objects from early on, a core of fused or undifferentated primitive experiences is rooted in the early ego as well as in the id.

Peak affect experiences thus originate a core structure of intersubjectivity, both in the earliest identification with an object of love (an introjective identification) and in the earliest identification with the object of hatred eliminated onto the periphery of a self-experience (a projective identification) that, later on, is dissociated, projected more effectively, and, eventually, repressed.

Intersubjectivity, therefore, whether incorporated into the self-experience or rejected by projective mechanisms, is an inseparable aspect of the development of normal identity. The psychoanalyst, by the same token, by means of concordant identification, that is, empathy with the patient's central subjective experience, and by means of complementary identification, that is, empathy with what the patient cannot tolerate within himself and activates by means of projective identification, may diagnose the patient's world of internalized object relations, which is part of his or her ego identity.

The subjective experience of the self, with its component aspects of self-awarenss or self-reflection, its sense of subjective lateral and sequential continuity, and its sense of responsibility for its actions, is more than a simple fantasy. It constitutes an intrapsychic structure, that is, a dynamically determined, internally consistent, stable frame for organizing psychic experience and behavioral control. It is a channel for various psychic functions that actualizes itself in these functions, a substructure of the ego that gradually acquires supraordinate functions within the ego. It represents an intrapsychic structure of the highest order, whose nature is confirmed by its behavioral consequences, its expression in character formations, and by the dimension of human depth and moral commitment in relations with others.

At the completion of the development of consciousness and of the self, the concept of consciousness, the self, and the person tend to converge. It is important, however, to keep in mind that, from a developmental viewpoint, the origins of the self include transitory, highy subjective, and diffuse and contradictory ego states; in other words, that it is an emergent structure within the original ego/id, and later the ego, which gradually evolves into a central position within the intrapsychic world and the total personality. One might say that the puzzling recognition that one is a different person under different affectively charged circumstances is the basis of the development of the categorical self. The analysis of the structural properties of intrapsychic experience, and of character patterns linked with the corresponding analysis of the subjective states accompanying and underlying them, is a new road to the relation between unconscious motivation and unconscious conflict, on the one hand, and conscious self-experience on the other.

The dynamic unconscious does not simply lie in the dark corners of psychic experience; it is manifest in observable behavior, the meaning of which may be less available to the subject than to the observer. The dynamic unconscious, we might say, is active both at the level of observable, interpersonal dynamics of behavior and in the repressed fantasies that emerge in the course of psychoanalytic exploration. The relation between the dynamic unconscious and consciousness is complex; the concept of the ego's differentiating from the id (or from an original undifferentiated ego/id matrix) by its crystallization around perception-consciousness needs to be expanded with the concept that the light of consciousness not only illuminates the derivatives of the unconscious but also helps to shape them. Primitive stages of consciousness enter into the intrapsychic structures of the original ego/id matrix, and the dynamic unconscious is constituted by the repressed remnants of these earliest intrapsychic experiences.

This is true from the earliest presymbolic schemata that will remain descriptively unconscious, to the emergence of primitive behavior patterns reflecting the interaction of the ego/id matrix with the environment, to the simultaneous enactment of drive derivatives in consciousness and the gradual creation of unconscious fantasies regarding such enactments, to the dynamically unconscious, repressed meanings of symptomatic acts. There is an intimate relation between conscious and unconscious elements throughout the entire sequence of intrapsychic developments.

I propose, in short, that primary-process fantasy emerges out of the state of primordial consciousness, at a point when the manipulation of symbols outside the rigid chain of conditioned associations becomes possible. Such primary-process fantasy influences the perception of reality under varying conditions of the development of consciousness and self-awareness, and the gradual differentiation of reality increases the cleavage between fantasy and the development of cognitive-affective, symbolic structures to deal with reality.

The dynamic unconscious is pushed deeper into the psychic apparatus, a development that culminates with the establishment of repressive barriers that simultaneously signify the mutual rejection and the consolidation of the id and the ego. The dynamic unconscious of both the neurotic patient and the normal person is the end product of a long evolution of psychic functioning, within which the qualities of consciousness and the dynamically unconscious are more closely interwoven that is apparent from observing these people. But the eruption of the dynamic unconscious into consciousness is not reserved to patients with severe character pathology or the psychoses. Interpersonal behavior in small, unstructured groups, and to a greater extent even in unstructured large groups that temporarily eliminate or blur ordinary social role functions, may activate, sometimes in frightening ways, the primitive contents of the repressed in the form of fantasies and behaviors shared by the entire group. This leads us back to the question of the ultimate nature of the motivational forces of the dynamic unconscious and to the psychoanalytic theory of drives.

THE ORIGIN AND STRUCTURE OF DRIVES AS MOTIVATIONAL FORCES.

Here I shall summarize my conclusions from previous work in this area (Kernberg, 1981).

In my view, affects are the primary motivational system in that they are at the center of each of the infinite number of gratifying and frustrating concrete events the infant experiences with its environment. Affects link the series of undifferentiated self-object representations so that gradually a complex world of internalized object relations, some pleasurably tinged, others unpleasantly tinged, is constructed. But even while affects are linking internalized object relations in two parallel series of rewarding, pleasurable, or gratifying and painful, aversive, or frustrating experiences, the corresponding "good" and "bad" internalized object relations are themselves being transformed. The predominant affect of love or hate of the two series of internalized object relations becomes enriched, is modulated, and becomes increasingly complex.

Eventually, the internal relation of the infant to mother under the sign of "love" is more than the sum of a finite number of concrete pleasurable affect states. The same holds true for hate. Love and hate thus become stable intrapsychic structures in the sense of being two dynamically determined, internally consistent, stable frames for organizing psychic experience and behavioral control, in genetic continuity through various developmental stages. By that very continuity, love and hate consolidate into libido and aggression, which in turn, become hierarchically supraordinate motivational systems, expressing themselves in a multitude of differentiated affect dispositions under different circumstances. Affects, in short, are the building blocks, or constituents, of drives; affects eventually acquire a signal function for the activation of drives.

The term *drive* for these overall, hierarchically supraordinate motivational systems, aggression and libido, fits Freud's original intentions remarkably well. Freud perferred *Trieb,* best translated as drive, precisely because he conceived of drives as relatively continuous psychic motivational systems at the border between the physical and the mental, in contrast to instincts, which he viewed as discontinuous, rigid, inborn behavioral dispositions. In light of the prevailing concepttion of instincts in biology (Tinbergen, 1951; Lorenz, 1963; Wilson, 1975), the term *instinct components* for inborn perceptive, behavioral, communicative, psychophysiological, and subjective experiential patterns—that is, affects) seems appropriate, in contrast to the term *drives* for the motivational systems, libido and aggression. Here Freud's concept of psychological drives in contrast to biological instincts fits contemporary biological developments very well indeed (Kernberg, 1976).

Libido and aggression manifest themselves clinically in a range of concrete affect dispositions and affect states, so that we can trace the vast array of affect states and their corresponding object relations to aggression, libido or—at later stages of development—condensations of these two drives.

Again, it needs to be stressed that drives are manifest not simply by affects, but by the activation of a specific object relation, which includes an affect and wherein the drive is represented by a specific desire or wish. Unconscious fantasy, the most important being oedipal in nature, includes a specific wish directed toward an object. The wish derives from the drive and is more precise than the affect state, an additional reason for rejecting a concept that would make affects rather than drives the hierarchically supraordinate motivational system.

We can now reformulate the developmental history of the self by stating that the origin of the self derives from self-experience and self-representations under the impact of both aggressively and libidinally invested states of merger; and the eventual integration of such contradictory self-representations into an integrated self-concept, and, in the process, from the corresponding integration of the derivatives of libidinal and aggressive drive investments as well. The self as defined is thus invested with both libidinal and aggressive drive derivatives that are fused or integrated in the context of the integration of their component self-representations.

I trust that my hidden intention has become apparent, namely, my wish to offer a psychoanalytically influenced approach to the mind-body problem in the following terms. Inborn, wired-in affective, perceptual, cognitive, and behavior patterns determine the early interaction of the infant with his human environment, particularly mother. The subjectively painful and pleasurable aspects of peak affect states accelerate the organization of subjective experience itself and the early activation of the capacity for symbolic thinking. The organization of drives, internalized object relations, intrapsychic structures, the self and character, and developing systems of internalized morality gradually reflect the emergent autonomy of purely intrapsychic structures and functions, while these structures still maintain a permanent relationship with physiologically activated affect states at any stage of development. In turn, the constant intervention of psychosocial environmental structures on the manifestations of character, the behavioral aspects of identity and the self, influence the functioning and ongoing restructuring of the tripartite psychic apparatus.

The genetic predisposition to major affective disorders and the related hypotheses regarding alterations of serotonin and/or catecholamine metabolism in patients suffering from these disorders illustrate the influence of neurochemical predispositions on the development of abnormal affective reactions. The triggering of severe mood swings in response to psychosocial trauma and the modification of depressive-masochistic character patterns by their psychoanalytic exploration in the transference illustrate the psychological influence on intrapsychic structures in the same area of mood disturbances. Intrapsychic structures originate from neurophysiological substrates in their interaction with the psychosocial environment, but gradually they evolve into an emergent autonomy and self-regulation while still interacting on their boundaries with biological and psychosocial structures and functions. This conception seems to me to correspond most closely to the conception of emergent interactionism within philosophical theorizing. But here my contribution must end with a question mark, and philosophical inquiry must take over.

REFERENCES

Arnold, M. B. (1970), Brain function in emotion: A phenomeno-logical analysis. In: *Physiological Correlates of Emotion*, ed. P. Black. New York: Academic Press, pp. 261–285.

Dicks, H. (1972), *Licensed Mass Murder: A Socio-Psychological Study of Some SS Killers*. New York: Basic Books

Emde, R. N., Kligman, D. H., Reich, J. H., & Wade, T. D. (1978), Emotional expression in infancy: I: Initial studies of social signaling and an emergent model. In *The Development of Affect*, ed. M. Lewis & L. Rosenblum. New York: Plenum Press, pp. 125–148.

Fairbairn, W. D. (1952), Theoretical and experimental aspects of psycho-analysis. *Brit. J. Med. Psychol., 25:* 122–127.

Freud, S. (1923), The ego and the id. *Standard Edition,* 19:3–66. London: Hogarth Press, 1961.

―――― (1924a), Neurosis and psychosis. *Standard Edition,* 19:147–153. London: Hogarth Press, 1961.

_____ (1924b), The loss of reality in neurosis and psychosis. *Standard Edition*, 19: 183–187. London: Hogarth Press, 1961.

_____ (1933), New introductory lectures on psycho-analysis. *Standard Edition*, 22:3–184. London: Hogarth Press, 1964.

_____ (1938), Splitting of the ego in the process of defence. *Standard Edition*, 23:273–278. London: Hogarth Press, 1964.

Hoffman, M. L. (1978), Toward a theory of empathic arousal and development. In *The Development of Affect*, ed. M. Lewis & L. Rosenblum. New York: Plenum Press, pp. 227–256.

Izard, C. (1978), On the ontogenesis of emotions and emotion-cognition relationships in infancy. In *The Development of Affect*, ed. M. Lewis & L. Rosenblum. New York: Plenum Press, pp. 389–413.

_____ & Buechler, S. (1979), Emotion expressions and personality integration in infancy. In *Emotions in Personality and Psychopathology*, ed. C. Izard. New York: Plenum Press, pp. 447–472.

Jacobson, E. (1964), *The Self and the Object World*. New York: International Universities Press.

Kernberg, O. (1975), *Borderline Conditions and Pathological Narcissism*. New York: Jason Aronson.

_____ (1976), *Object Relations Theory and Clinical Psychoanalysis*. New York: Aronson.

_____ (1980), *Internal World and External Reality*. New York: Aronson.

_____ (1981), Self, ego, effects and drives. *J. Amer. Psychoanal. Assn. 30*, 893–915.

_____ (1982), An ego psychology-object relations theory approach to the narcissistic personality. In *Psychiatry 1982: Annual Review*, ed. L. Grinspoon. Washington, DC: American Psychiatric Press, pp. 510–523.

Lorenz, K. (1963), *On Aggression*. New York: Bantam Books.

Mahler, M. (1979), *Selected papers of Margaret S. Mahler*. New York: Aronson.

_____ & Furer, M. (1968), *On Human Symbiosis and the Vicissitudes of Individuation*. New York: International Universities Press.

_____ Pine, F., & Bergman, A. (1975), *The Psychological Birth of the Human Infant*. New York: Basic Books.

Piaget, J. (1954), *Intelligence and Affectivity*. Palo Alto, CA: Annual Review Press, 1981.

Rapaport, D. (1951), States of consciousness. In: *The Collected Papers of David Rapaport*, ed. M. M. Gill. New York: Basic Books, 1967, pp. 385–404.

_____ (1955), Cognitive Structures. In: *Contemporary Approaches to Cognition*. Cambridge: Harvard University Press, 1957, pp. 157–200.

Sandler, J., & Rosenblatt, B. (1962), The concept of the representational world. The *Psychoanalytic Study of the Child*, 17:128–145. New York: International Universities Press.

Stern, D. N. (1985), *The Interpersonal World of the Infant*. New York: Basic Books.

Tinbergen, N. (1951), An attempt at synthesis. In: *The Study of Instinct*. New York: Oxford University Press, pp. 101–127.

Van der Waals, H. G. (1952), Discussion of the mutual influences in the development of the ego and id. *The Psychoanalytic Study of the Child*, 7:66–68. New York: International Universities Press.

Wilson, E. O. (1975), *Sociobiology: The New Synthesis*. Cambridge, MA: Harvard University Press.

2 The Unconscious and the Archaeology of Human Relationships

Althea J. Horner

I come to my thoughts about mental development and the nature of the unconscious as a biological scientist. The marriage between biology and philosophy may appear strange and unnatural, but insofar as all aspects of being are integrated within a cohesive self in healthy development, a person's biology, psychology, and philosophy must inevitably and permanently be wedded.

Since that which we call the unconscious cannot be directly perceived, it must be considered a theoretical construct. Adler (1980), referring to the "electron" in nuclear physics and to the "black hole" in astronomy, notes that modern science legitimately and validly deals with objects that lie outside the range of ordinary experience because they cannot be directly perceived. He includes the unconscious in psychology as another example of such a legitimate and valid object of study (p. 67). He reminds us of Ockham's assertion that "we are justified in positing or asserting the real existence of unobserved or unobservable entities if—and *only* if—their real existence is indispensable for the explanation of observed phenomena" (Adler, 1980; p. 98).

Strachey (1957) wrote that the basis of Freud's repression theory of hysteria and the cathartic approach to treatment "cried out for a psychological explanation," noting that it was "only by the most contorted efforts that they had been accounted for neurologically" (p. 164). The neurological explanation disappeared in Freud's "Interpretation of Dreams" (1900); and what Freud had written previously about the nervous system was now translated into mental terms. Strachey says that here "the unconscious was established once and for all" (p.164).

Freud (1915) saw the difficulties of psychophysical parallelism as insoluble, the physical characteristics of "latent mental states" being totally inaccessible to us. "No physiological concept or chemical process can give us any notion of their nature" (p. 168). "But," he adds with respect to these latent mental states, "we know for certain that they have abundant points of contact with conscious mental processes." Setting his role as neurologist aside, he says that "every endeavor to think of ideas as stored up in nerve cells and of excitation as travelling along nerve fibers, has miscarried completely" (p. 174).

Despite findings of recent brain research, such as the functioning of the neurotransmitters, we are really no further than Freud in our understanding of the physical correlates of what we call "mind." But, as long as we speak as scientists, we must assume that, like the "black hole," they are there. Since they are still unknowable at this point in time, the use of the theoretical construct we refer to as the "unconscious" allows us to bridge what is unknown with what is known.

From an "object relations" point of view, we seek to discover the nature of the content of the unconscious that most directly affects the experience of the self, the experience of the other, and the complex relationships between them.

A developmental approach to the understanding of these experiences of self and other, (experiences that include ideas, perceptions, feelings, wishes and impulses) has taken us back further and further in the life of the child, with most recent research highlighting the interactional basis of their evolution from the start of life. As genetically patterned as the hunting and mating behaviors of other species is the neonate's readiness to respond to, as well as to initiate, that interaction. And built into the healthy central nervous system is the readiness to respond to patterns and actively to construct and synthesize new patterns.

The patterning of the mental schema we call "self" and the patterning of the mental schema referred to as the "object" take place in predictable, hierarchical stages. We use the term "object" rather than "mother" because this particular mental schema is in part *created* by the child in accord with its own limited mental capabilities and unique experience of the early caretaking environment. In a way, the child creates a kind of metaphor for the significant other from its interpersonal experiences. This metaphor, in turn, reciprocally shapes the child's perception and expectations of the interpersonal environment, along with the child's behavior towards it. Herein lies the relevance of unconscious mental schemata for conscious experience and behavior, and for the psychological treatment of disturbances in that sphere.

It is the child's ability to synthesize patterns out of experience and to register, as memory, those which occur repeatedly and regularly that leads from a *process* of interaction to what we call psychic *structure*—that is, to the enduring memories that will build and evolve over time to form the mental schemata of self and object. These patterns are built up out of the child's entire universe of experience, including what originates from within its own body as well as what originates from the external world with which it interacts.

The failure to distinguish between *process* and *structure* has led to some popular misconceptions about attachment, or what is being referred to as "bonding." Rather than being understood as a process that leads eventually to structure, attachment is being understood as an *event*. Parents-to-be, as well as delivery-room personnel, espouse what might be characterized as the "epoxy theory of attachment," believing that this is an event that takes place immediately in the first minutes of life, analogous to the imprinting of Lorenz's ducks (1935).

But we are not ducks, and although attachment-seeking behavior begins in the early hours of life with the maintenance of eye contact by the baby, the actual structuring of the enduring mental tie with the primary caretaker takes several months to develop fully. During this time, the child builds or synthesizes the experience of himself or herself in such a way as to include the primary caretaker and the salient qualities of their interaction.

That the expectant mother who wants her baby is bonded to it long before it is born is clearly evident in the grief of women who miscarry. Because of the faddish furor with respect to the critical nature of bonding and the near hysteria surrounding it, some women who are unable to deliver by natural childbirth, or who for some reason are unable to have immediate "skin to skin" contact with their new baby, are inflicted with undue anxiety or guilt about themselves as mothers or about the future of their child.

As the child negotiates a series of developmental processes, beginning with the process of attachment, each stage brings him to a higher level of structural organization. The schemata of self and object—referred to as self-/ and object representations in psychoanalytic terms— become increasingly complex and increasingly differentiated from each other. At the same time, disparate aspects of the organization of the self become increasingly integrated within a single self-schema, while a similar process takes place with disparate aspects of object representation. Gradually, a single integrated self-representation evolves, as does a single, integrated object representation. Each level of psychic organization determines to a large extent the nature of the child's experience of himself and of the other, along with the interaction between the two. The individual's psychic organization is not directly observable, and, for the most part, it remains beyond conscious awareness, although what derives from it is conscious. Edith Jacobson (1964) defines identity as the conscious experience of the self-representation.

From the object relations point of view, the unconscious is highly organized, being characterized by a discoverable structure with its own dynamics, comparable to the dynamics of conscious experience. Discovering the link between them in the course of psychoanalytic therapy is the first step towards the remediation of pathological development and its consequent pathology of structure. Sandler (1981) notes that "every wish comes to include a representation of the person's own self and a representation of the object who also has a role to play in the fulfillment of the wish. The wish contains representations of self and object in interaction (p. 183). The fact that such wishes are rooted in unconscious structure is what makes them so tenacious, to be acted out over and over even when the relationship may appear to the observer to be highly unsatisfactory.

Elsewhere (Horner, 1979, 1984) I have described the stages and processes in the development of early object relations and have related the pathology of each of the developmental way stations to specific pathology of the personality. Particularly relevant to this discussion is the work of Mahler (1968; Mahler, Pine, and Bergman, 1975), as well as that of Bowlby (1969), Winnicott (1965) and Kohut (1971). Each of these developmental stages, which are defined in terms of the nature of the self and object representations and their relationship to one another, leaves its traces in the unconscious, and even in the fully evolved individual they may be reactivated under stress and regression, or in dream or fantasy.

THE PREATTACHMENT STAGE

At birth the child is in a state of what Mahler (1968) refers to as "normal autism" (p. 7). This term has been criticized because the newborn is clearly not in a chronic withdrawn state, as in pathological autism. Indeed, the child actively seeks contact from the very start. Here again the distinction between process and structure is important.Despite the immediate activation of the process of attachment, there is as yet no enduring, structured internal mental representation of the object. The experiences and their patterning and resultant memory traces are yet to come. Some might argue that the innate preference for the pattern of a facial configuration over a geometrical or other nonhuman-type pattern (Fantz, 1966) indicates an innate object structure from the start. However, although the precursors of self-/ and object representations may be present at birth in terms of preference, readiness, and potential, the cognitive development that is necessary for the structuring of mental schemata and for the development of structure, as we use the term, has not yet occurred.

The most clearly stage-related pathology is that of early infantile autism, in which the child remains at this infantile stage of life and makes no move

towards attachment. Along with the absence of attachment-seeking behavior, there appears to be a basic cognitive defect in these children that
interferes with the organizational processes themselves. Before these discoveries, the mothers of such children were branded "icebox mothers,"
with the assumption that the failure of attachment in these children was
the direct consequence of the failure of the mother to facilitate the process.
In situations in which the environment is grossly pathological, disrupting
the organizing capacities of the child, there may be a retreat into secondary
autism. Autistic withdrawal in response to severe stress in an adult suggests that the failures of the environment date back to the earliest months
of life.

THE PROCESS OF ATTACHMENT

Over the earliest months of life we see the innate attachment-seeking
behavior of the infant interacting with maternal behavior and response in a
manner that, optimally, brings about the subsequent stage of normal symbiosis (Mahler, 1968) when the child has synthesized the experience of
himself or herself in such a way as to include the primary caretaker and the
salient qualities of their characteristic interaction. It is here that the basis for
an affectional relationship and for what Erikson (1950) calls "basic trust" is
laid down. The mother's emotional availability and her capacity for empathic response are essential to this process.

At the most primitive level, failure of attachment may carry with it
severe deficits in the early organization of the self. The failure to develop
an attachment and to achieve a satisfactory symbiosis because of environmental factors, such as institutionalization or an unstable foster-home situation, may lead to the development of characteristic disturbances, such as
the inability to keep rules, lack of capacity to experience guilt, and indiscriminate friendliness with an inordinate craving for affection and no ability to make lasting relationships (Rutter, 1974). Also, the "affectionless
psychopath" (Bowlby, 1946) is characterized by the failure to develop the
affectional bond that goes with attachment.

There may be a disruption of attachment due to separation and loss.
Subsequent development depends upon the availability of a satisfactory
substitute attachment object. Such interruption may lead to a lifelong
schizoid detachment. Rutter says that "many (but not all) young children
show an immediate reaction of acute distress and crying (. . . the period of
'protest'), followed by misery and apathy (the phase of 'despair'). There
may be "a stage when the child becomes apparently contented and seems
to lose interest in his parents ('detachment')" (p. 29). Rutter concludes that

this syndrome is probably due to the disruption or distortion of the bond-ing process itself.

Bowlby (1960) notes that the persistent longing of a young child for the lost love object is often suffused with intense generalized hostility. He writes, "There is no experience to which a young child can be subjected that is more prone to elicit intense and violent hatred for the mother than that of separation" (p. 24). The detachment is not permanent if the separa-tion is not too long, but, Bowlby states, there is reason to believe that with prolonged and repeated separations during the first three years of life, detachment can persist indefinietly.

The quality of the child's experience during the attachment process, and during subsequent separations and losses in the first three years of life, builds into the inner world of the unconscious characteristic feelings and expectations about the interpersonal world that will color all later develop-mental stages as well as future interpersonal relationships.

STAGE OF NORMAL SYMBIOSIS

Midway between the process of attachment and the separation-individua-tion process (Mahler, 1968), stands the primitive mental structure, the un-differentiated self-object representations. Because of immature cognitive abilities, the undifferentiated images of the self and object are not yet integrated into a single image. Instead, they are organized on the basis of the predominant feelings that go with the interactions between the self and the other. The good self-/ and object images are linked by posititive feeling and mood. The bad self-/ and object images are linked by negative feelings and mood. Not until the cognitive development that will come towards the end of the second year of life will the disparate images be integrated into single cohesive representations of the self and of the other. The persistence of this split into adult life leads to an inability to hold on to relationships. When the other fails to be all good because of a failure to meet the wishes or needs or demands of the self, he or she then becomes all bad and is discarded, or becomes the object of intense hatred.

Insofar as the primary caretaker has been able to lend herself to the child's unfolding, the experience vis-à-vis the other is part of the child's positive and trusting experience of the self. Herein lies the archaic uncon-scious basis for the experience of oneness that at times comes with a loved other. But whatever the ecstasy of that experience, it also may carry a charge of anxiety at the felt loss of separateness of the self.

The bipolarity of experience—that which is directed towards the self and that which is directed towards the other—exists from the beginning of life. It starts with the infant's alternating attention to what is happening within its own body and to the interpersonal environment that it seeks to engage. All through life, these conflicting pulls will be felt in one way or another, the intensity of the conflict dependent upon the security of the sense of self and the security within the interpersonal situation. The conflict is often expressed as that between "being myself" (identity) and "being in a loving relationship" (intimacy) (Horner, 1978).

No sooner is the symbiotic structure established intrapsychically with the organization of the undifferentiated self-object representations, than the child moves towards a new process, that of separation and individuation (Mahler, et al., 1975).

HATCHING: THE BEGINNING OF SEPARATION

Mahler (1968) emphasizes the importance of the optimal symbiosis for subsequent differentiation of the self-schema, or self-representation, from the object representation. "The more the symbiotic partner has helped the infant to become ready to 'hatch' from the symbiotic orbit smoothly and gradually—that is, without undue strain on his own resources—the better equipped has the child become to separate out and to differentiate his self representations from the hitherto fused symbiotic self-plus-object representation" (p. 18).

During this process the mother functions as a frame of reference, a point of orientation for the individuating child. If this security is lacking, there will be a "disturbance in the primitive 'self-feeling,' which would derive or originate from a pleasurable and safe state of symbiosis, from which he did not have to hatch prematurely and abruptly" (p. 19). That is, while the self-representation remains intertwined with the object representation, the loss of the object and the sense of connection with that person evoke a sense of disorganization and dissolution of the self of which the object and the sense of connection are still a part.

When the unconscious psychic structure is dominated by this picture, the person may experience severe separation panics. These separations can be due to the break in the emotional connection with the significant other just as much as to an actual physical separation. It is this sense of inner connectedness which remains critical, and which is so insecure.

THE PRACTICING PERIOD:
SECOND STEP IN SEPARATION AND INDIVIDUATION

From about ten months of age until approximately sixteen months, the child's focus shifts increasingly to those functions which develop as a consequence of the maturation of the central nervous system, such as locomotion, perception, and the learning process. These are referred to as the autonomous functions of the ego. The child is also increasingly confronted with the experience and awareness of separateness from mother. Her ready availability when the child needs her, and the pleasure he or she derives from the mastery of new abilities make these small separations tolerable for the child. With the culmination of the practicing period around the middle of the second year, the toddler appears to be in an elated mood.This accompanies the experiences of standing upright and walking alone. This peak point of the child's belief in his or her own magic omnipotence, Mahler (1968) tell us, "is still to a considerable degree derived *from his sense of sharing in his mother's magic powers*" (p. 20).

At this point in development, the inner representation of self and other are still in great part undifferentiated, and it is the *anlage* of a pathological structure that is referred to as the "grandiose self." If things go wrong in the child's subsequent relationship with his caretakers, at a time when he child has come to realize how relatively helpless and dependent he or she really is, the grandiose self is a defensive fall-back position. The adult that the child becomes can deny anxiety and dependency wishes as long as this inflated omnipotent self is in charge. The other is no longer of any emotional consequence. Of course, the person must go to great lengths to protect this illusion, and if it is threatened, as by poor grades in school, or the loss of a job, the reaction will be severe, with the development of symptoms such as depression or suicidal behavior. Sometimes others must be debased or demeaned to protect this state of being.

Echoes of the practicing period and its magic omnipotence in the unconscious sometimes lead to persisting beliefs about the magical nature of one's abilities. Learning to walk and talk does indeed come as by magic, unlike the conscious effort one must make to learn the vocabulary of a foreign language at school. I have worked with some patients who were clearly of superior intelligence and to whom early learning was effortless throughout the grade school years; paradoxically, they were far less secure about their abilities than people of lesser innate ability. They did not connect their abilities with that sense of conscious effort which gives one a feeling of some control over what one can and cannot do. What comes by magic can also disappear by magic—one cannot rely on it.

THE RAPPROCHEMENT PHASE AND THE RAPPROCHEMENT CRISIS

At around the age of 18 months, the toddler becomes increasingly aware of his or her separateness from mother and mother's separateness from him or her. The child's experiences with reality have counteracted his or her overestimation of omnipotence, self-esteem has been deflated, and the child is vulnerable to shame. Furthermore, through dependence on the object, who is now perceived as powerful, the child is confronted with the relative helplessness of the self. There is an upsurge of separation anxiety and depressed mood. If the other uses power in a benign and helpful manner, that power is the basis for the child's sense of security. If, on the other hand, parental power is experienced as against the self, as something that is not only given but also withheld, the child learns to both hate and envy the power and will develop techniques to control it. Behind such controlling behavior lies insecurity and anxiety

The major concern of the person who struggles with issues associated primarily with this stage of development is the loss of the support, love, and approval of the other that is feared to result from the assertion of one's own wishes or feelings. Still vulnerable to feelings of helplessness and shame, the person tends to idealize the other and see that person as having the power to protect the self from these painful feelings. The other may be a parents, or perhaps a spouse or friend. This persisting dependent way of seeing the self and the other and the expectations and demands that go with it, puts a strain on interpersonal relationships. Although the other may be idealized, he or she is also envied and feared and is blamed when things do not go well.

The rapprochement crisis is the developmental switch-point that marks the shift from a sense of omnipotence to a sense of helplessness—from a sense of perfection to a sense of shame. When prior development has not gone well, the conscious awareness of the reality of separateness and the loss of omnipotence may be very traumatic. If there are deficits in the structural organization of the self- and object representations, either as the result of unfavorable circumstances and experience or as the result of some deficit in the child's synthesizing capabilities, these deficits become evident at this time. The child, and the adult he or she becomes, is unable to negotiate the developmental demands, and symptomatic behavior develops, such as anxious clinging.

The response of the environment to the child's growth has to allow for the child's strivings towards autonomy that conflict with the intensely felt dependency needs. The term "rapprochement" suggests the alternating moving away from mother and the return to her for emotional refueling. Healthy parents do not have a need for the child either to stay dependent and helpless or to be completely self-reliant. They can shift their way of relating to the child, being empathically in tune with the child's conflicting impulses and needs. Echoes of the rapprochement crisis are heard in adolescence, and the setup in the unconscious left over from this early childhood phase of development will affect the manner in which the young person negotiates the later developmental tasks. Anxiety over self-assertion, or at the prospect of moving out of the parental home, may come from the activation of unconscious rapprochement factors. The sense of self and other is still being determined by the nature of the unconscious self- and object representations that were in existence at that early time and are still making themselves felt.

THE ACHIEVEMENT OF IDENTITY AND OBJECT CONSTANCY

With the development of language, the concepts of "Mama" and "Baby" are established at the start of the rapprochement period. This conceptual capability has organizing and integrating effect. Unintegrated islands of disparate self-representations, and of disparate object-representations, become unified cognitively and structurally under each specific label, or symbol. There is a single self who may be good or bad, happy or angry, and a single object who may also be experienced in a number of different ways. This cognitive and structural integration sets the stage for an integrated sense of self, or identity, and an integrated view of the other. Although the child may be angry at the mother for some felt deprivation or failure of empathy, she is still the mother who is loved and valued in her own right, and not only for what she can do for the child's self. In the earlier stage of development, before the cognitive achievement that brought the recognition that there is really just one self and one emotional mother, the self- and object representations were split on the basis of the quality of feeling and emotion that went into the interaction. Mother was all good, idealized, adored; or she was all bad and hated. The self in interaction with her was also split. With integration, the complex, differentiated self and the sense of having a single identity come into being and provide a foundation for an unfolding individuality. In healthy development, with a more realistic picture of the other, relationships are increasingly defined on the basis of here-and-now interaction, although certain wishes, attitudes, and expectations, as well as the quality of emotion, are still colored by the forgotten past.

Although archaic self- and object representations persist in the unconscious, their impact is mitigated by the ascendency of reality-dominated perception and thought. The unconscious images may appear in dreams or in fantasy or may be recreated in artistic productions. The fairy godmother and the wicked witch of the fairy tales of childhood strike a familiar chord in children and adults alike, resonating with the now unconscious split images that dominate the earliest months of life. At times we may yearn for the blissful oneness of symbiosis, of chafe under what feels like engulfment in a relationship. But by and large, our reality perceptions keep us firmly rooted in our own individuality and that of the other.

IDENTIFICATION AND EMOTIONAL AUTONOMY

With the final stages of differentiation of self from object, certain identifications with the object remain as part of the self. The baby needed mother to comfort it and relieve its anxiety. Now the capacity to comfort the self and to relieve one's own anxiety with a variety of psychological mechanisms, is part of the self, derived from what once came from outside. This transformation can be observed in process in the toddler's relationship with his teddy bear or Linus blanket—the so-called "transitional object" (Winnicott, 1951).

The parents' "Good for you!" which reflected their pleasure in the child's accomplishments now is voiced by the part of the self referred to as the "superego" (Freud, 1923), which is composed of both the ego-ideal and the conscience. Not only does the superego criticize the self for transgressions, it also praises when one lives up to one's ego-ideal, and is the source of a healthy and secure self-esteem. These identifications allow the person to do for the self what once could be done only by parental figures; they are necessary to the development of full emotional autonomy.

AND NOW THE ETERNAL TRIANGLE

With the full differentiation of self from object, there is also a firmer differentiation of mother from father. The parents no longer can function interchangeably as "the object." The individuality of each parent is recognized and valued differentially. This is the point at which the conflicts of the Oedipus complex (Freud, 1913) come to the fore. What was a dyadic view of the interpersonal world now includes *two* significant others. A two-way competitiveness within the triangle generates new wishes, anxieties and defenses. The child wants to be preferred by mother over father and by father over mother. Along with envy, the child now experiences jealousy of a rival who is also loved; an uncomfortable ambivalence is generated. The relative ease or difficulty of this period will be strongly influenced by prior development and by the nature of the inner, unconscious representational world. The oedipal period tends to overlap with the latter part of the rapprochement phase of the separation-individuation process, so that rapprochement anxieties are aggravated by oedipal strivings. The child's ability to negotiate this troublesome period will also be affected by parental attitudes towards the child, who now presents the parents with an increasingly complex little person. The anxiety-generating wishes and feelings of the oedipal period may be repressed, taking their place in the unconscious along with the archaic images of earlier development.

THE UNCONSCIOUS AND PSYCHOANALYSIS

The consistent and predictable presence of the primary mothering person throughout the early months of life ties the infant's experience together in a particular way. It is through her that the child's body, impulse, feeling, action, and eventually thought become organized as part of the self and integrated not only with each other but also with external reality, of which she is a representative. She is a bridge between the child's inner world of experience and the outer world of reality. The mothering person not only mediates the process of organization and reality-relatedness, but her image is part of what is organized and is the basis for the development of object-relatedness as well. Thus, her role in the evolution of the self- and object representations is critical. When early development within the maternal matrix goes well, the outcome is the achievement of a cohesive, reality-related, object-related self.

Character pathology results from failures in this process of organization and may take the form of deficits of cohesion or integration, deficits of reality-relatedness, or deficits of object-relatedness. With the interruption or distortion of the development of early object relations, the individual does not arrive at the healthy outcome of the separation-individuation process—namely, a well-secured identity, object constancy, and the structuring of the superego that regulates self-esteem.

The therapeutic matrix can be viewed as analogous to that provided by the good-enough mother of the early years. It is a relationship within which repair of the defects of character structure, of the unconscious representational world, may take place. Within an accepting, understanding, and safe relationship, various split-off aspects of self can be experienced, expressed, and integrated. The therapeutic matrix facilitates the attachment process, which will eventually provide the basis for the internatlization of maternal-therapist functions, responses, and interactions—for the further integration of the self within a context of human relatedness. The therapeutic matrix facilitates differentiation, the structuring of the boundaries of the self, the achievement of identity coupled with the achievement of object constancy, and the structuring of a guiding and loving superego. With structural repair and growth, the archaic images of the self and object, which had been played out in adult interpersonal relationships, will loosen their grip on the individual's life and will fade into the realm of the unconscious.

With a secure sense of identity, the person can explore the repressed, unconscious conflicts of the oedipal period without undue anxiety, and thus can finally renounce the wishes of childhood, being free to find suitable adult love objects and to strive for mature goals.

REFERENCES

Adler, M. (1980), *How to Think about God.* New York: Bantam Books.

Bowlby, J. (1946), *Forty-four juvenile thieves: Their character and home life.* London: Baillere, Tindall & Cox.

_____(1960), Grief and mourning in infancy and early childhood. *The Psychoanalytic Study of the Child,* 15:9–52. New York: International Universities Press.

_____ (1969), *Attachment and Loss, Vol. 1: Attachment.* New York: Basic Books.

Erikson, E. (1950), *Childhood and Society.* New York: Norton.

Fantz, R. L. (1966), Pattern discrimination and selective attention as determinants of perceptual development from birth. In: *Perceptual development in children,* eds. A. J. Kidd & J. L. Rivoire. New York: International Universities Press.

Freud, S. (1900), Interpretation of dreams. *Standard Edition,* 4 & 5. London: Hogarth Press, 1953.

_____ (1913), Totem and taboo. *Standard Edition* 13:1–161. London: Hogarth Press, 1953.

_____ (1915), The unconscious. *Standard Edition* 14:166–204. London: Hogarth Press, 1957.

_____ (1923), The ego and the id. Standard Edition 19:12–59. London: Hogarth Press, 1961.

Horner, A. (1978), *Being and Loving.* New York: Schocken Books. New York: Aronson, 1986.

_____(1979), *Object Relations and the Developing Ego in Therapy.* New York: Aronson.

_____ (1984), *Object Relations and the Developing Ego in Therapy* (2nd ed.). New York: Aronson.

Jacobson, E. (1964), *The Self and the Object World.* New York: International Universities Press.

Kohut, H. (1971), *The Analysis of the Self.* New York: International Universities Press.

Lorenz, K. (1935), Der Kumpan in der Umwelt des Vogels. Berlin: *Journal für Ornithologie,* 83:137–213, 289–413. Trans. in. *Instinctive Behavior,* ed. C. H. Schiller. New York: International Universities Press, 1957.

Mahler, M. S.(1968), *On Human Symbiosis and the Vicissitudes of Individuation.* New York: International Universities Press.

Mahler, M. S., Pine, F., & Bergman, A. (1975), *The Psychological Birth of the Human Infant.* New York:Basic Books.

Rutter, M. (1974), *The Qualities of Mothering: Maternal Deprivation Reassessed.* New York: Aronson.

Sandler, J. (1981), Unconscious wishes and human relationships. *Contemp. Psychoanal.* 17:180–196.

Strachey, J. (1957), Editor's note. *Standard Edition,* 14:164. London: Hogarth Press.

Winnicott, D. W. (1951), Transitional objects and transitional phenomena. In: *Through Paediatrics to Psychoanalysis.* New York: Basic Books, 1975, pp. 229–242.

_____ (1965), *The Maturational Processes and the Facilitating Environment.* New York: International Universities Press.

II STRUCTURAL QUESTIONS: INTROSPECTION, FEELINGS, AND THE SELF

3

Commentaries: Philosophical and Research Perspectives

EDITOR'S INTRODUCTION

This volume as a whole presents a research program. Starting with efforts to provide accounts of the emotions, we found that we could not provide such accounts fully and successfully unless we brought in accounts of the self as well. To this end we invited Kernberg and Horner to present their accounts of the self and the links they felt their way of conceptualizing the self had to developmental theories. The first two papers, then, discuss the notion of the self and the idea of the development of a self. In this and later chapters, we will examine the links of the self to still other concepts. On the whole, the most fundamental link is that of the self to interventions and the emotions. This requires that we turn to models from ethics and aesthetics, a view that is confirmed by Caws and Cavel—we learn from each that if we want to talk of the self, we need models from both of these disciplines.

Caws, for example, is interested in a theory of subjectivity and suggests that for a complete concept of the self we need to bring in language about feelings and language about motivation. Cavel explores the relation between ethical concepts and the integration of the self.

At the same time, if we are interested in developmental theories we should also attend to their difficulties. Robison examines this class of theories and suggests that they do, indeed, present problems.

Kuhns brings to bear a rather different set of worries. His work, on the whole, tends to probe the question of how one discipline resonates with another; and in the present paper he investigates how one tradition, science, resonates with another trying to discover "laws of the mind." Kuhns suggests that the psychoanalytic theories presuppose developmental theories. He cites Dilthey as suggesting that one might use empathy to move from the individual maturational process to history, or from the self to history. But what can this mean? This sort of thing has meaning only if we have a clearly specified class of developmental theories and if we understand the complex properties of such theories. If this is so, however, Robison's critique is suggestive, for one senses here that even properly formulated developmental theories are rather loose. One gets the feeling that the realm of discourse involving such theories is rather different from the languages involved in other areas, such as the sciences. It is conceivable, then, if we combine Robison and Kuhns that the appropriate set of languages for such theories includes both technical and nontechnical ones, languages from technical disciplines and, for example, the languages used in aesthetics. Kuhns suggests something like this when he cites two traditions, the nineteenth-century one and that of the twentieth century, as somehow both being operative when we think in psychoanalytic terms (or perhaps he means to suggest that more attention should be paid to both).

LINKING DEVELOPMENTAL THEORY TO DEVELOPMENTAL RESEARCH
Esther Robison

In addition to philosophers, developmental psychologists and psychoanalysts have found the origins and development of moral behavior a compelling focus of study. Developmental achievement in infants is marked by the emergence of a capacity to tolerate more complex stimulation (both internal and external) without behavioral disorganization and the capacity for regulated behavior.

To explain this phenomenon, the developmental psychologists present us with a schema of preset stages proceeding in stepwise fashion; each new level represents not merely a change in behavior but a structural change that can be achieved only after the preceding stage has been mastered. Each level is then stable and irreversible. In object relations theory, the notion of a facilitator is critical, a person who shapes adaptational behavior. As Horner states in this volume, the patterning of experience from the process of interaction creates psychic structure, and the developmental process of differentiation is affected by maternal stimulation. A failure of attachment (to achieve a satisfactory symbiosis) may lead to characteristic disturbances, with an inability to keep rules, lack of the capacity to experience guilt, indiscriminate friendliness, and inordinate craving for affection as consequences. The central operator in this model is the process of identification with the mother.

Developmentalists who are interested in moral development stress the link between responsive and reciprocal mothering and the feeling of control and competence engendered by a predictable and responsive human environment, i.e., the interactional element that promotes agency, mastery, and relatedness. Since these developmental processes are assumed to be affected by the type, quality, and amount of care and stimulation from the caretaker, the child's degree of organization and capacity for self-regulating behavior should be linked to specific maternal interventions. For these developmentalists, such as Kohlberg, identification is a constellation of attitudes in which provision of role-taking opportunities, particularly in moral discussion, is pivotal for the development of moral judgment.

Clearly, what is common to developmental theories and psychoanalytic theories of moral development is the importance of human attachment, but we have no evidence about the specific interactive processes through which these attachments take place, or what constitutes their structure.

It is generally agreed that a person (mother) at the earliest stages of an infant's development, by selecting and structuring the sensory environment, regulating behavior stages, and providing routine care, shapes the infants adaptational behavior. There is a literature that supports a system of mutuality, reciprocity, and responsiveness as the model of successful mothering (Ainsworth, 1964; Schaffer,1977). But research has yet to specify what aspects of this pattern (or whether any aspects) of good mother–child interaction are necessary for normal moral development. It might be more fruitful to look at the other side of the coin: deviant mothering. We do know that positive forms of mothering, such as warmth and an absence of harsh punishment, do not assure normal moral development. And we also have evidence that bad or conflictual relationships between mother and child produce disturbances in development that impede or disrupt such development (Steele and Pollack, 1968).

What we do not know is whether these effects are cumulative or reversible, nor whether it is the specific maternal behaviors that are responsible or other negative influences in these children's lives; nor do we know for sure what specific dynamic is operative, that is, which theory accurately accounts for the outcome.

The significant role accorded to parent-child interaction, even in the presence of other influences, in all psychoanalytic and developmental theories of moral development suggests an empirical account of the process from a longitudinal perspective would lend clarity to unresolved issues.

If, for example, the pattern that Kernberg describes is a form of deviant behavior that represents a departure from normative development, then looking at deviant groups such as abusive mothers may serve to single out some of the specific patterns and mechanisms that can give rise to problems having their basis in early exchanges between mother and child.[1]

I am suggesting that a natural laboratory for the examination of the pathogenesis of severely impaired object relations exists among the population of mothers who are known to engage in various forms of child maltreatment. While the literature indicates that abusive mothers do not show any single distinct personality profile, research has shown they do show a cluster of characteristics behaviors and attitudinal postures toward their children that differentiate them from normal mothers (Spinetta and Rigler, 1972; Fontana and Robison, 1984).

Similarly, abused children evidence an array of behaviors indicative of an impaired sense of social attachment, namely, poorly regulated behavior, maladaptive ways of handling separation anxiety, poor impulse control, impaired tolerance for handling frustration, inferior school performance, and during adolescence delinquent behavior. Since these patterns often encompass a range of undesirable and social pathological behaviors, they present an interesting negative model from which to sort out differential results.

Investigators who have examined the effects of abuse and neglect and other forms of maltreatment on the development of abused children have found that although maternal abuse is presumed to have a major contributory role in the child's development, the consequences to children (although negative) are varied. There is no direct relationship between abuse per se and specific developmental outcomes, nor is there evidence to support how abusive interaction effects moral development. One initial research task is to sort out the long-term effects from the short-term effects and then to trace the longitudinal course of long-term affects.

The data from interactional studies that focus on such connections are sparse. One series of studies beginning in 1979 (Egeland) identified four patterns of maltreatment: physically abusive, neglectful, psychologically unavailable, and hostile/verbally abusive. In a longitudinal study of the developmental consequences of different patterns of maltreatment, children were compared at ages at which critical developmental issues are negotiated: 3, 6, 12, 18, 24 and 42 months, and 56 months.

Children of the psychologically unavailable mothers were most damaged, but each group of abused children showed distinct clusters of maladaptive behavior in comparison with children in the control group. The former were distractable, impulsive, low in ego control, and inflexible in

---

[1] If, Kernberg is not describing a deviant character type within a normative population but the structure of an emergent personality prototype, the possibilities for understanding the etiology of such a structure lie outside the approach offered.

problem-solving tasks. No differences were evident in the three- and six-month old infants, but differences began to emerge at twelve months. At that age, all of the maltreated children showed a continual pattern of declining functioning. However, it is not until the child is four and a half or five years old that one can point to a pattern of characteristics that correlate with maternal attitudes. One interesting finding, which perhaps lends some support to the notion of pathological identification, is that physical abuse appears to soften the negative impact of maternal indifference. This is supported by the less anxious attachment and less impaired coping skills of physically abused children whose mothers were not deemed also "unavailable." The latter group of children showed declining skills in all areas.

Models for conducting longitudinal research on mother-child interaction are difficult to implement. Issues to be dealt with involve mechanics (population attrition), contamination, logistics, cost, and methodology (naturalistic standardized settings, validity of indices, selection of appropriate measures, etc.).

The biggest problem is that interaction (interdependent action) is difficult to describe. What are described are actions of individuals, because it is difficult to translate concepts into interactional units. Another problem is selecting the dimension of behavior to be studied. Some dimensions usually studied are the vocal dimension, the visual (looking, gazing), and the linguistic dimension. Category systems encode content; if they presuppose a particular conceptual system, then there can be some difficulty in establishing whether translation from concepts to measures are accurate. This presents a real problem if one's study is inconclusive; then it is difficult to establish whether the fault is in the theory or in the measure.

Another problem is the choice of statistical model in measuring reciprocity. There is a great deal of rich and suggestive research on the infant-mother interaction, particularly the mathematical regularity noted in their visual and vocal exchanges (Stern, 1974). This regularity permits the establishment of probability functions for communication patterns from which marked deviations can be precisely predicted. But the mathematical models used for measuring reciprocity in infant research become less applicable as the child moves beyond infancy when internal language and memory serve as links in responding to past nonimmediate events.

For example, initiating, responding and termination—commonly used categories in interaction research, represent some of the complexity and difficulties in applying the model. A specific act, while apparently an initiation, may also be a response to an act that occurred earlier, or a response may be unobservable.

Certainly, most communication patterns are not immediate, quid pro quo reactions, as is assumed in models used in mapping infant-mother communication. Correlational analysis, which is a summary statement rather than a process model, is also deemed to be an inapplicable model because it loses the temporal dimension. It has been argued, however, that even when behavior is viewed as a continuous exchange between organism and environment, their correlations should emerge at the aggregate level rather than in momentary events. Restricting one's methodology in examining reciprocal influences to conditional probability analysis not only is an unnecessary restriction, but may distort the concept of reciprocity as it actually occurs through events in time (Baum, 1973).

The mechanical and conceptual difficulties in trying to render an accurate account of interaction between mother and child have been documented. Many methodological problems are shared by all research dealing with interaction, but some are particular to the mother and very young child.

The research tools are available, and studies can be done on a small scale with small populations if they are carefully designed. Despite the difficulties, longitudinal studies focusing on mother-child interaction, taking into account other intervening variables, hold forth a possibility for assessing the value of various developmental approaches as explanatory tools for moral development.

References

Ainsworth, M. D. (1964), Patterns of attachment behavior shown by the infant in interaction with his mother. *Merr. Palm. Quart,* 10:51–58.

Baum, W. M. (1973), The correlation based law of effect. *J. Exper. Anal. Beh.,* 20:137–153.

Egeland, B. (1979), Preliminary results of a prospective study of the antecedents of child abuse. *Internat. J. Child Abuse & Neglect,* 3:209–278.

———— et al., (in press), The developmental consequences of different patterns of maltreatment. *Internat. J. Child Abuse & Neglect.*

Fontana, V., & E. Robison (1984), Observing child abuse. *J. Pediat.,* Oct. 655–660.

Schaffer, R. (1977), *Mothering.* Cambridge, MA: Harvard University Press.

Spinetta, J. J., & Rigler, D. (1972), The child-abusing parent: A psychological review, *Psychol. Bull.* 77:296–304.

Steele, B. F., & Pollack, C. B. (1968), A psychiatric study of parents who abuse infants and small children. In: *The Battered Child.* R. B. Helfer & C. H. Kempe, Chicago: University of Chicago Press, pp. 103–147.

Stern, D. N. (1974), Motherhood/Infant at Play: The dyadic interaction involving facial, vocal and gaze behaviors. In: *The Effects of the Infant on Its Caregiver.* ed. M. Lewis & L. A. Rosenblum. New York: Wiley

GOVERNING OF THE SELF: LAWS AND FREEDOM
Richard Kuhns

Of the several philosophical traditions in which psychoanalytic theory stands and to which it has made significant contributions, the essay by Kernberg amplifies two. Psychoanalytic theory as established by Freud participates in (1) the tradition of those nineteenth-century disciplines we refer to as the social sciences, in which the question of the possibility of social and psychological laws is still debated; (2) the tradition of philosophical ethics, in which the question of freedom and responsibility remains central. In both traditions the effort to formulate a method for the establishment of lawlike relationships has been of deep concern, and that search itself has led to a philosophical question: If lawlike relationships are established for human conduct—whether individual or group—are these laws part of a general natural science, which would include the sciences of nature, or are the laws part of a related, yet distinct discipline, the science of human action and culture?

The distinction I refer to has been formulated by the terms *Naturwissenschaft* and *Geisteswissenschaft,* introduced by Dilthey (1985). But the lawlike relationships established in the social sciences might constitute a third realm between nature and culture; and of the social sciences, psychology has had an uncomfortable situation: is it itself natural, cultural, or social? Psychologists today take different views of their discipline; some would have psychology as a part of the natural sciences, or, if not there, to be abandoned; some would give it a separate and distinct location in the spectrum of inquiries; and some would insist that the study of mind, action, and social conduct must be a part of the cultural sciences. In order to locate the philosophical contribution of Kernberg's essay, I shall begin with the claim that psychology does establish laws, in some sense; and then, in the light of that claim, I will consider, briefly, the related issues of freedom and responsibility.

In vain the Sage, with retrospective eye,
Would from the apparent What conclude the Why,
Infer the Motive from the Deed, and show,
That what we chance'd was what we meant to do.

—Alexander Pope

Methodological Implications of Kernberg's View.

Since the Enlightenment, philosophical attention to the formulation of a "science of mind" has been constant.And since the Enlightenment, there have been two points of view about where a science of mind might discover its laws. One point of view is represented by a predominantly historical outlook; the other, by a psychological outlook. One begins with history and moves to individuals, the other begins with individuals and moves to history. Freud represents the latter approach, and Kernberg's observations, like Freud's, begin in the clinic; indeed the most striking part of Kernberg's presentation is his description of the stages of development of the narcissistic personality. The philosophical value of Kernberg's description is its relevance to history and to ethics.

There is a common methodological theme in the psychoanalytic and historical avenues to the understanding of ourselves in the present: both require moving back through the stages of development, reliving, as it were, the stages antecedent to the present. The historical method "relives" earlier forms of cultural life; the psychoanalytic one "relives" earlier forms of maturation of the individual. Both methods emphasize growing up, but the historical one seeks growing up as a civilization; the psychoanalytic one, growing up as a fully adult individual. Both seek understanding; but in different paths.

The Enlightenment historian, using anthropology and history to see how the self arrived at its present form and received its accumulation of cultural modes of functioning, moves from history to the self. The psychoanalytic approach studies developmental stages of the individual and reads from self to history. Self-understanding follows from attention to different observable conditions: the historical method attends to stages of social growth, culminating in the present condition of the individual in culture. The psychoanalytic method observes the psychosexual stages of development and tries to become conscious of "intrapsychic conflict."

In making self-understanding their goal, both methods share an important means, though referred to by different names. If we look at the historical approach, represented by the philosopher Dilthey, we see that the move from history to the self requires a means of empathy, *Einfühlung,* feeling into the stages of human history of the past, and of cultures other than our own. Dilthey continued and elaborated the Enlightenment search for lawlike relationships in human conduct and in history, but he insisted that the method and the outcome established a separate science to which he gave the name *Geisteswissenschaft.* In contrast, the natural sciences did not require the special method of empathetic understanding, but through sense observation and the laboratory discovered the laws which obtain in the natural order. Psychoanalytic theory straddles both the natural and the cultural sciences, though it is clear that Freud sought a science of mind based upon the natural sciences. It is questionable whether the psychoanalytic mode of inquiry and of theoretical explanation realizes Freud's intention, and it seems to me it draws on the traditions of both cultural and natural sciences. Kernberg's paper describes developmental sequences assumed to be expressible in lawlike formulations, and at the same time it makes clear that the discovery of lawful relationships depends upon a clinical method that has important similarities to the method of empathy (*Einfühlung*), which was explored by Dilthey as the method appropriate to the cultural sciences. Kernberg's presentation clarifies the necessary, close dependence of the developmental stages of maturation and its pathologies, as we now understand them, upon transference and countertransference. However, it should be kept in mind that within psychoanalytic discussion today there is disagreement on the role, function, and conceptual status of the transference-countertransference relationship. For purposes of the discussion here I shall treat this relationship as a central part of psychoanalytic method.

Psychoanalysis is a clinic-situated inquiry, put into effect by two individuals with the goal of understanding neurosis and psychosis, and with the aim of bringing about cure. Kernberg calls psychoanalysis a "research tool" whose focus is on subjective experience, and that experience is given conscious articulation through a method that employs "empathic trial identification with the patient by the analyst," and "the analyst's own exploration of the nature of the emotional interactions that are activated by the combination of his experiencing the patient's subjectivity and behavior. Contemporary understanding of countertransference includes the diagnosis of the patient's dissociated, repressed, or projected object representations activated within the subjective experience of the psychoanalyst in his interaction with the patient."

Kernberg's formulations provide the theoretical framework in terms of which he, as a clinical psychoanalyst, attempts to cope with his patients' narcissistic character disorders. These formulations are:

1. The id is structured, and the means of this developmental structure is internalized object relations.
2. There is ego from the earliest stages of consciousness.
3. Affects are basic units out of which drives develop.
4. A consequence of 1., the id has a history (as does the ego).
5. Freedom is defined as awareness of inner conflict.

These five postulates, derived from clinical observation, function as directives for further clinical inquiry. They are at once postulates and hypotheses; together they structure Kernberg's contribution to psychoanalytic theory and clinical procedure. Kernberg makes it clear that the clinical inquiry, which culminates in his remarkable descriptions of stages of pathological development, derives from his work as a clinical psychoanalyst with his patients. Therefore, the generalizations I have listed are derived from controlled conditions peculiar to this analyst-patient relationship, within which transference and contertransference play an essential part. And in the cultural sciences as Dilthey conceived them, there are strong affinities between empathy and transference-countertransference. I think a further exploration of the cultural sciences and the contribution of psychoanalysis to our understanding of the cultural sciences will demonstrate the usefulness of the transference relationships to social and historical inquiry. I have attempted to work out the structure of the transference relationships in the cultural sciences in my study *Psychoanalytic Theory of Art:*

A Philosophy of Art on Developmental Principles. (Kuhns, 1983). It seems to me that Kernberg's paper offers suggestions about the ways in which a science of psychological development in culture might be worked out.

Central to Kernberg's presentation is the developmental history of the id as it has been described since Freud's investigations; to that, Kernberg adds ideational contents derived from close scrutiny of object relations and the attendant process of splitting. The paper offers the working analyst and the theorist a developmental description of id and ego formation. Stages of id development, as outlined in the paper, are arrived at through the therapeutic method under the controlled conditions of interpreted transference and countertransference.

Foundational to an id psychology is Kernberg's theory of object relations, so vividly presented in the descriptions of "splitting" as a part of the developmental process in id and ego formation. The discovery of the stages of id development, Kernberg suggests, is a product of the therapeutic method under the controlled conditions of interpreted transference and countertransference. Thus, when psychoanalysis is put into the perspective of a possible cultural science, it appears that there is a method, underlying both the therapy and the theoretical directives for investigation, that seeks law-like regularities of psychic development, and requires therapeutic sensitivity to the transference-countertransference relationship. Kernberg assumes that the therapeutic sensitivity constitutes a method for treatment and for discovery in the clinic.

It is this process which has brought Kernberg to the hypothesis he repeats in the next paragraph: "The id contains primitive fantasies and experiences of the earliest objects . . . [and] the experiences of relations wih object representations . . . ." But as we read Kernberg's description we are compelled to ask a question about the location of the object relations. Is it claimed that the object relations are internalized in the developing id, or is the claim that, though they are assembled in the id, and assembled from the earliest stages of development, they are *experienced* in the ego? We are not clear about the exact stages of development and the dynamic interrelationship of id and ego in object relations theory. I now refer to the "theory" because Kernberg moves rapidly from clinical observation to theoretical formulation without carefully drawing the distinction, and without explaining to the reader how the theory is related to the clinical observations.

It is clear that Kernberg lays claim to a systematic mode of inquiry, and of cure, that straddles the two kinds of inquiries described above as the "natural" and the "cultural" sciences. Insofar as the transference-countertransference relationship is the central methods, we are in the domain of the cultural sciences; insofar as the model is the search for and discovery of causal relationships, the ideal remains—as it was with Freud—the natural sciences. It seems to me that this synthesis of methods and practices characterizes disciplines that are closely related to psychoanalysis—that is, history and philosophy. If this is correct (I am aware of how arguable these comments are), then there are contributions that philosophy and psychoanalysis have to offer to each other, and I shall, in the following section, discuss one such exchange in the area of moral theory and action.

> Oft in the Passions' wild rotation tost,
> The spring of action to ourselves is lost.
>
> —Alexander Pope

Contribution to Moral Theory

Methodological reconsiderations lead to cultural reconsiderations, especially in the realm of morality and political theory. A philosophical use of psychoanalytic theory can well begin with conduct on the level of moral deliberation and choice, and then move on to the wider social and political scene. Traditional moral theory, whether utilitarian or deontological, assumes a paradigm of rationality, a capacity in the individual not only to reason clearly, but also to test ends and goals while exercising self-control.

Kernberg's presentation casts into doubt several of the assumptions philosophers make when formulating moral theory. If Kernberg is correct in his descriptions and diagnoses, we ought to reconsider our common moral expectations, for we may be faced with a widespread incapacity to be moral. Kernberg compels us, as moral theoreticians, to ask if the superego pathologies may not be endemic to our culture, and if so, what philosophy should do in response—if indeed it should take notice at all of psychoanalytic data. I suspect the pathologies Kernberg describes are widespread, and if that is so, our moral theory fails to take into account one kind of incapacity to be moral. (Traditional moral theory has dealt repeatedly with other forms of incapacity.) Since superego pathologies are so very difficult to cure, and the developmental defects are so crippling to the persons affected, we are in a difficult cultural situation, and I should like to explore briefly the implications for moral theory of an endemic superego pathology.

Full adult functioning, which includes moral maturity, retains remnants of early, immature stages of development; thus we are never completely free from superego conflicts. Kernberg's paper makes it pessimistically clear how difficult it is, in many cases, to overcome these conflicts. When the clinical prognosis is combined with Kernberg's Spinozistic ideal of moral freedom as awareness of internal conflict, we are brought up short as moral theorists: internal conflicts generated by both familial and cultural conditions may then be writ large, as Plato would have said, in political life. And if the narcissistic superego pathologies are endemic, difficult to root out, then we may be coming into—indeed, may have arrived at—a period of severe social dislocation.

To assess and to provide a social therapy for this condition, philosophy requires a mode of analysis like that brought by psychoanalysis to the treatment of the individual. And it is here, once again, that the ideal of a cultural science may be of help, for the cultural sciences stress subjectivity, work in terms of criteria of subjective awareness, and give access to modes of conduct that are similar to those that the analyst treats. Just as the psychotherapist must possess a method to understand, and then address, and then "cure" the patient, so the student of social ways and goals requires a method of inquiry, and a vocabulary to use in prescriptions for improvement. Moral theory and social science then ought to take into account a subjectivity of the sort Kernberg spells out for us. Transference and countertransference have their place in cultural sciences.

In my own reflections on psychoanalytic theory of culture, I have extended, broadened, and exploited the concepts of transference and countertransference to apply to cultural objects, their interrelationships, and the ways the participants in a tradition relate to the cultural objects of the tradition. There is a broad area of social and moral theory to which the concepts transference and countertransference can be extended. And in our effort to understand the developmental pathologies as they affect the moral life, our incapacities as moral agents become clear when we look at our conduct through the paradigm of inquiry and attempted cure that Kernberg supplies.

For example, there is clearly a solipsistic condition generated by many of the pathologies Kernberg describes. To put the beliefs of the narcissistic personality in philosophical terms, the claim of the narcissistic person, so well expressed by the philosopher Wittgenstein (1961) in his private ruminations, is this: "If what I feel is always *my* pain only, what can the supposition mean that someone else has pain?" (p. 84). Nagel, in his *The Possibility of Altruism* (1970), glosses the passage as follows: "His [the solipsist's] view is that pain, something with which he is familiar, cannot be conceived apart from its relation to his own consciousness" (p. 107). This fits very well the description Kernberg has given us of the superego pathologies. But to the philosopher, solipsism is a form of argument, and to the psychoanalyst it is a prevalent condition blocking full adult functioning. The inability to make judgments about other persons is a common defect, a lack far more serious and debilitating than we realize from philosophical argumentation, although the philosophical argument expresses conditions of crippled conduct that we can now see in a clinical light.

We can compare the developmental phases of Kernberg's clinical spectrum to philosophical inadequacies that seem congruent with arrest in development and to the splitting to which Kernberg makes reference. Extreme isolation of persons, as solipsism defines it, is a clinical reality to which a therapy other than philosophical argument must be applied, and towards which, if we accept Kernberg's view, the perversion is recalcitrant. We as philosophers can and do seek "cure" for our logical diseases, but however we insist, as Nagel does, that "one's basic practical principles must be universal" (p. 107), we see the practical difficulty for the narcissistic person to entertain and to act in conformity with universal principles. One wonders if a logical clarification in the manner of moral theory would work where psychoanalysis fails!

The pathologies described by Kernberg are precisely those conditions which are called "dissociations" by Nagel, and they are, Nagel makes clear, responsible for defects in judgment, for if I (the moral agent) cannot generalize, and include others in my judgments, I cannot logically make the judgment about myself. Here philosophy contributes clarification to psychoanalytic struggles with sick people; and as a matter of clinical observation, there are many people with character disorders who cannot bridge the void between themselves and others.

The implication for philosophical reflection on the moral life is that the concept of rationality must be set into a psychologically realistic world of persons, many of whom are morally incapacitated, as Kernberg's descriptions make clear. We are morally complex beings because we are not simply constructed logical beings; rather we are, as Stuart Hampshire (1975) has pointed out, beings within whom "the traditional scheme, which distinguishes the lusts from thoughtful desire, may turn out to be much too simple, and to reflect too grossly simple moral ideas" (p. 44).

So we as philosophers, given our growing awareness of complexity due to the contributions of psychoanalysis, must reconsider the impact of the character pathologies Kernberg presents to us. His dictum of rationality, deeply Spinozistic in tone and idea, accords with the philosophical dictum; but sets the definition in a clinical-pathological framework that lacks a sociopolitical dimension: "Freedom, clinically speaking, implies the capacity to make moral and rational decisions about one's actions . . . . freedom implies the awareness of intrapsychic conflict." Yet it does not follow from this that rational choosing will be realized where there is insight, for insight reveals unresolvable conflicts, and the course of conduct to be undertaken requires morally defensible goals. Clinical insight means little without political education, and it is in the placing of the individual in a larger social context, with full awareness not only of "the possibilities of altruism" but also of the necessity of altruism, that a moral reality can be realized. Insight "on the couch" must be translated into action in the sociopolitical world of communal life.

Kernberg concludes his reflections on freedom with the psychoanalytic observation that "the development of the superego depends on the development, quality, and depth of internalized object relations and the corresponding integration of the self as a psychological structure." The very concept of internalized object relations is one that philosophy finds hard to incorporate into its mode of moral reflection as it has grown up in the West, and yet there are, again, means of bridging the two modes of thinking that can be helpful in both directions. To the psychoanalyst, defects in object relations are both the cause and the symbolic expression of narcissistic pathology. Restoration to full object relations implies cure; but, again, cure for the sick person is not full; nor is it moral until the person acts in the shared world. As Kernberg says, the self has to place itself in the context of "the interpersonal, psychosocial nature of object relations, the actual relation between the self and significant others . . . ." My contention here is that full restoration of object relations includes more than the parental and body objects that the psychoanalyst deals with in the process of bringing unconscious material into consciousness. In addition, object relations have a cultural dimension, and if that is not realized ("restored" is the wrong word), then the person remains crippled, in a moral sense that should be explored by philosophy.

The assault upon superego pathologies requires two waves: the first, an assault on the unconscious psychosexual stages of development, as psychoanalysis undertakes it; the second, an assault on the conscious inheritance of a cultural tradition, whose existence, power, and normative content is far from obvious. The second wave requires development of ego capacities, and of the most advanced id stages that the society is able to enforce through education and the model of political altruism. Cultural regeneration must be waged alongside the clinical one if the superego pathologies are to be overcome, for by "overcome" I mean not simply freedom from internal conflict, or awareness of internal conflict, but, most important to the social life we lead, the freedom to act on behalf of others.

As we read Kernberg's paper, that outcomes seems a lorn hope; for narcissistic personality disorders are widespread and deeply rooted, and therefore our cultural future is dim indeed. I read Kernberg's paper with a pessimism that is far deeper than that generated by Freud's "Civilization and its Discontents" (1930) because it arises from the inadequacy of object relations in the person as a familial and as a cultural participant. We are witness to a process of splitting that is far more debilitating, morally speaking, than the conditions Freud foresaw at the end of World War I. The danger he diagnosed was the result of civilizations' repressions on the individual, whose instinctual life was thereby crippled and his capacity to realize himself fully diverted into neurosis and psychosis. Kernberg's diagnosis goes into the family as such, a condition far more debilitating, and a condition prior to that of integration into civilization. Object relations theory, therefore, opens up to our awareness both a psychosexual and an infantile fixation that make it seem almost impossible to free the entrapped person suffering from superego pathologies to function fully in the political realm.

Psychoanalytic discussions that assume Kernberg's position see objects as parts of self and mother, generated through the peak good-bad object experiences of early months and years. Human beings, it is to be remembered, grow up as well in a realm of *cultural objects,* and it is my contention that the role of cultural objects has not been thoroughly explored by psychoanalysis. Yet Kernberg is well aware of this dimension of maturation when he remarks tht the integration of the ego includes "the consolidation of integrated object representations, that is, the 'representational world'," and I take the term "representation" to include not only percepts and the conceptual system expressed by the individual's conduct, but also the shared objects of the cultural tradition. In asserting that the integration of the ego follows from (a) the maturational process of the individual and (b) the cultural integration of the individual with the group, I am urging that psychoanalytic inquiry be directed to the cultural as well as the psychological foundations of mature functioning. When we take both into account, it will be clear that the preconditions for mature moral consciousness lie in the two foundations just mentioned: in the private, familial, mother-child phase of development, and in the public, group, child-society phase of development. The two, of course, are interwoven.

When maturation is considered in this dual perspective, we are brought to ask, can our *cultural* tradition and environment take any of the blame for the prevalence of the borderline psychopathologies that are endemic today?

Kernberg's description of the borderline personality needs a further dimension to be complete; the superego pathologies represent cultural as well as psychosexual impoverishments. Both private, familial and public, cultural objects are inadequately integrated into the person. To be sure, the borderline pathology cannot be repaired on the cultural level without first undergoing superego reparation; yet one that is initiated, mastery of the representational world that is cultural must be undertaken as a further developmental goal.

Although my belief that there are causally significant cultural factors in the etiology of borderline pathologies complicates diagnosis and cure, it seems to me essential to psychoanalytic therapy that the cultural dimension be explored once again, as it was by Freud in his late, speculative essays. Philosophy, as a contributor to the process of cultural analysis (along with anthropology and sociology), can join psychoanalysis in carrying out this process. In assuming a cultural as well as a psychosexual perspective, we broaden therapeutic goals, which puts greater demands on therapy than we ordinarily recognize; but it is not too great a burden if once again we pick up leads that have been given to us in the tradition.

One psychoanalyst who attempted to expand psychoanalysis in the direction of cultural representations was D. W. Winnicott (1965) who saw that therapeutic intervention had a public responsibility in the development of the person. Although his work focused on objects in a person's early years, it readily is extended to the cultural life as a whole. I would add to his explorations Kernberg's suggestions of moral responsibility and freedom, because the maturational process as we come to understand it today expresses a serious moral lack. Philosophically, this condition leaves a deeply troubling, unanswered question: what kinds of objects and object relations are necessary to full cultural functioning? Could it be that the prevalence of the narcissistic personality is caused in some part by the loss of the cultural tradition from which moral representations are derived? Narcissistic personalities have been cut off from the tradition through the maturational deflections we have been examining; can we imagine, and structure in therapeutic reality, a means to reparation that will help the psychoanalytic discipline to become a truly reconstructive force in our moral lives?

References

Dilthey, W. (1985), *Poetry and Experience, Vol. V, Selected Works.* Princeton, NJ: Princeton University Press.
Hampshire, S. (1975), *Freedom and the Individual,* Expanded ed. Princeton, NJ: Princeton University Press.
Kuhns, R. (1983), *Psychoanalytic Theory of Art: A Philosophy of Art on Developmental Principles.* New York: Columbia University Press.
Nagel, T. (1970), *The Possibility of Altruism.* Oxford: Clarendon Press.
Winnicott, D. W. (1965), *The Maturational Processes and the Facilitating Environment.* New York: International Universities Press.
Wittgenstein, L. (1961), *Notebooks, 1914–1916,* trans. G. E. M. Anscombe. New York: Harper Torchbooks.
Freud, S. (1930), *Civilization and its Discontents. Standard Edition,* 21:64–145. London: Hogarth Press, 1961.

A RESPONSE TO OTTO KERNBERG'S "THE DYNAMIC UNCONSCIOUS AND THE SELF"
Marcia Cavell

Dr. Kernberg mentions three philosophical problems: mind-body, freedom, and personal identity. There is a fourth, the problem of "other minds," to which he implicitly refers in speaking of "a methodological problem involving subjectivity," and a fifth, of his title, namely, "the self." I will flesh out the particular concept of self to which I think he alludes, and suggest why philosophers, as well, have thought it the focus of a number of specifically human capacities. This will bring me to brief commentary on the other philosophical problems he mentions.

About the self: Dr. Kernberg describes normal adult consciousness as involving an "awareness of one's awareness," or "that one is experiencing mental states." I would underline the word 'mental'; that is, in such awareness one knows one's mental states *as* mental. One is not immersed in the world, in this sort of reflexive self-consciousness, but aware *that* one sees it through the medium of one's awareness, which points to a definition of self as a being who is aware of itself as a locus of consciousness, therefore able to refer to itself as an "I" (or its linguistic counterpart). Neither Hartmann's (1964) concept of self nor the common psychoanalytic ones of self as a structure of self-representations quite gets to the peculiarity of the self as the referent of "I". Nor does the term "self-consciousness" do so, since a baby may have, as Kernberg says, some sense of self from the start. Furthermore, a child can recognize itself in a mirror before it behaves in ways that would lead us to attribute to it a full-fledged reflexive self-awareness.

Something of what is implied by this self-awareness Descartes succinctly indicated when he said, "I think therefore I am." *When* I am aware of the contents of my mind—and of course I am not always—I am aware of some of my thoughts under a minimally adequate description; for example, as thoughts of Jane. I know that my thought is not Jane herself, nor any other kind of thing-versus-thought, a distinction which Bion (1977) has greatly clarified; and I know myself as the subject of my thoughts, or as the one thinking them. Furthermore, I know that the word "I" is a pronoun whose logic is such that it can be used by anyone; that it refers to whoever uses it as ineluctably as it does to me when I speak of myself; and that it is systematically linked to second- and third-person pronouns.

All this requires a complex affective-cognitive learning, which centrally includes processes of identification, separation, and individuation, among them perhaps what Abelin (1975) has referred to as "early triangulation," the discovery that "there must be an I [a subject] like him [a subject] wanting her" (pp. 293–294). One might read this as the question: How many persons must one *know* there to be in the world for there to be *one* person who conceives of himself or herself *as* a self? And the answer is at least three. (If this is so, it means that one's knowledge of the reality of other persons—what philosophers call "the problem of Other Minds"—can only be called into question by someone who is as certain of this knowledge as he or she is of his or her own mind. That is, the concept of self in virtue of which one can ask questions and pursue the truth contains as part of its structure the knowledge that at least two other persons exist in the world.

Kernberg says: "I shall differentiate the broader concept of consciousness from the intrapsychic structure of self as derived from it." May I understand "intrapsychic structure of the self" to mean: structure of consciousness—call it schema or concept—in virtue of which one can speak in the first person? It is important to note, by the way, that this structure of consciousness need not itself be a content of consciousness, and almost certainly is not (see O'Shaughnessy, 1972). Recognizing this helps avoid the infinite regress of self-conscious selves that the concept of reflexive self-consciousness seems to generate. In part, this is because the phrase "self-consciousness" is deceptive. When I say, "I am thinking of Jane," I am not aware of my *self* as a content of consciousness along with other contents (O'Shaughnessy, 1972) but of my thoughts as mine. If this still seems circular, a way out is provided by a continuum that Kernberg's article suggests to me. I propose that we distinguish three different senses of self. There is an un-self-conscious self—say a self in sense one—before there is a self which can be reflexively self-aware and which in virtue of that awareness, can sometimes take responsibility. Call this responsible self a self in sense two. Then I suggest that being able to speak in the first person is the precondition for a progressively more integrated consciousness. So self-consciousness does not constitute a self in a third sense, but precedes it. This third-sense self is a spectrum, a progression towards an ideal and unachievable limit of integration, in which there are more and more areas of one's activity for which one can take responsibility.

It is this connection between responsibility and having a concept of self that makes the latter so important. For example, recognizing some of my desires as desires, and as mine, is what allows me to reflect on them, then to decide that I will act on some, and not on others. Reflexive self-consciousness makes the difference between volitional behavior in a weak sense and those specific volitions we speak of as choices. Similarly, it is in virtue of reflexive self-consciousness that we can take responsibility for our beliefs, doubt the veracity of some, measure them against evidence, and work towards a coherent body of truth that we acknowledge as having a claim on us in community with others. (Incidentally, the root of "responsibility" is related to "respondeo", "I respond" or "I answer," so that the idea of communication, and therefore of community, is implied by the notion of self as responsible agent.)

Now I come to what I take to be a larger issue in Kernberg's paper. He suggests that subjectivity characterizes consciousness from the start. If he means that there is some vague sense of self, he is probably right. But the methodological problem which he says he finds in knowing another's subjective state is that it "can be optimally evaluated by verbal communication," which suggests that by "subjectivity" he means something more specific, namely, subject as a fledgling thinker, not, for example, subject as a fledgling doer. And here, I think, is where the Cartesian model betrays us. Descartes captured the concept of self as articulately thinking subject; and he was right to make this a defining feature of the self that can be a responsible agent. But in ignoring the developmental question of how a child arrives at this concept, he overlooked the roles of both action and other persons in the sense of self. Articulate self-consciousness is only one of a variety of forms of consciousness; and as Kernberg, among others, has helped to show, it is a climactic moment in intersubjective processes. The answer to the problem of other minds lies in the prehistory of self-conscious thought, specifically in these early interpersonal relations that, according to object relations theory, are needed to structure the self. So while it is natural to assume that the subject of *self*-consciousness begins as a subject of consciousness, this assumption may be unhelpful to Kernberg's own concerns. For one thing, it tends inadvertently to equate consciousness with the self-conscious and speakable, and to emphasize it at the expense of the unconscious. For another, it leads to talk of objects as endopsychic structures rather than as external ones, which they obviously also are. The world is mediated through our consciousness of it. But both philosophy and psychoanalysis risk interpreting this to mean that the only world each of us can know is in his or her own mind.

I think, then, that it makes for more coherence to assume sentient action and desire-to-act, rather than consciousness generally, as primary to the sense of self. Consider the three philosophical problems Kernberg has mentioned in this light

(1) Mind-body: Rooting the self in activity allows us to account for our knowability not just as objects but as subjects. We are subjects in relation to the objects on which we act, as well as in relation to our ideas (which philosophers sometimes call "intentional objects"). And unlike the thoughts I am conscious of, what I am doing, and even what I am trying to do, is often apparent, to others sometimes even more than to myself. Descartes taught us to think of mind as something to which only one's self has access. But it is only self-conscious thoughts that are uniquely known to me in an immediate way, and these are only a fraction of the mind. Volition is a psychological category. But the desire to lift my arm, say, is not a kind of mental pebble, embedded in my mind; normally, it is continuous with my lifting my arm. Of course, conflicted or inhibited desires, or ones we consciously decide not to gratify, may not get expressed; or not in transparent ways. But this does not imply that volitions are in principle invisible.

(2) Freedom: Taking activity as basic allows for a spectrum of volitional activity (see O'Shaughnessy, 1980), beginning perhaps with what Piaget

calls a circular reaction. In that innocent conversion from organism being activated to organism enacting its own schema, from passivity to activity, we get the rudiments of what will later become choice.

(3) Personal identity: Taking activity as prior to what I call a self in sense (2) permits us to make sense of notions like "splitting" and "repression," which otherwise lead to paradoxical questions like, Who is doing the splitting?; for there can be an organism that structures experience and defends itself against attack—a self in the first sense mentioned above—though there is no reflexive self-consciousness, or a self in the second sense.

This brings me again to the methodological problem that Kernberg mentions. He says: "Fully developed, normal consciousness . . . implies . . . a subjective state that can be optimally evaluated by verbal communication and therefore immediately raises the methodological problem involving subjectivity in contrast to 'objective' observation." If the methodological problem here has to do with our knowledge of other minds, I have already suggested that focusing on the development of the mind at earlier stages than Descartes does, will show not only that there is no impassable barrier between being a self and knowing other selves, but also that, on the contrary, they are inextricably entwined.

In any case, what is "unobjective" about speech? Kernberg puts the word "objective" in quotes, so perhaps he agrees that standards of objectivity must be relative to the kind of object in question. Furthermore, there are a million ways of evaluating a person's subjective state other than through his verbal communications, most obviously through his actions, which I assume is why Kernberg himself says that the distinction between "subjective . . . and psychosocial manifestations of the self . . . is artificial."

Even when someone does speak, we have the task of knowing what the speaker means. To accomplish this task, we consider the rest of the speaker's behavior and that the person is saying what he or she says now, in this manner, and so on. Then there is always the question of whether or not the speaker is telling the truth, to us or to himself. Perhaps Kernberg wants to suggest—it seems to be so—that the articulateness of human consciousness is what allows this consciousness to be devious, and requires that we decipher what it says.

A more specific problem apropos of "other minds" is explaining the phenomena of empathy. Two suggestions emerge from what I have said. First, understanding you does not mean knowing the thoughts of which you are consciously aware in the immediate way that you do. It cannot mean this, since you are a person separate from me in virtue of the fact that your access to some of the contents of your consciousness is direct in a way that my access to the contents of your consciousness can never be. Second, if the root experience of the self is in sentient doing, the reciprocity between activity and passivity helps to explain how we come to know what the other is doing and suffering. When I hit someone, I learn what happens when someone is hit. One way a baby comes to know itself, Winnicott suggests, is in the mirror of its mother's face, as the one eliciting a particular response from her. In general, where the object I act upon is another person, action itself implies that array of phenomena called "identificat- ion." And there are a number of other phenomena, brought to light by psychoanalysis, suggesting that before one comes to know one's own mind as one's own, one has already, in a sense, been in the place of the other. I am thinking particularly of "splitting" and "projective identifica- tion." So that, as Kernberg himself might say, one comes to own one's mind through object-relational processes, and through learning to know another as separate from one's self.

References

Abelin, E. (1975), Further observations and comments on the earliest role of the father. *Internat. J. Pshcyo-Anal.* 56:293–302.
Bion, W. R. (1977), *Learning from experience.* In *Seven Servants.* New York: Aronson.
O'Shaughnessy, B. (1972), Mental structure and self-consciousness. *Inquiry,* 15:30–63.
O'Shaughnessy, B. (1980), *The Will,* Vols. I and II. Cambridge: Cambridge University Press.
Hartmann, H. (1964), *Essays on Ego Psychology.* New York: International Universities Press.
Winnicott, D. W. (1971), Mirror-role of mother and family in child development. In: *Playing and Reality.* New York: Basic Books.

HOW THE BODY BECOMES A SELF:
A RESPONSE TO KERNBERG
Peter Caws

In thinking about the mind/body problem, it is helpful to treat it not as one problem but as two, both amenable to resolution—the first, by showing that it is not a problem; the second, by showing that it is really a different problem. The two problems are what I call the mind/live-body problem and the mind/dead-body problem. The mind/live-body problem is not a problem because mind (i.e., thinking, wondering, hoping, fearing, etc.) is just one of the functions of the live body, like breathing or digesting, although the bodily system it relies on—the nervous system, including the brain—is rather more complicated than the respiratory system or the diges- tive system. The mind/dead-body problem *is* a problem all right—how can these inanimate bodily materials possibly come to be endowed with feel- ing, consciousness, purpose, and so forth? But it is really just another version of the dead-body/live-body problem: how can these inanimate materials be an organism at all? For if they are living human organisms, complete with sense organs, brain, and so on, then that organism, assuming it to have come to maturity in a social setting, will have feelings and be conscious and purposive.

That mental events should be bodily functions among others (note that there is not some *other* bodily function with which they are identical, as the proposed solution to the mind/body problem known as the "identity thesis" seems to require) is so obvious and plausible that it seems at first surprising that anyone should ever have thought otherwise. But it takes time for reflexive truths to establish themselves: the one thing the eye cannot see is the seeing eye. Thinking bodies, when they think of themselves as thinking, can easily fail to notice or remember that they are bodies. But we do not know any cases of *disembodied* thinking (what we might think of as the content of disembodied thought is, of course, necessarily embodied in *us*), and so far we do not have examples of thinking as otherwise embodied than in nervous systems. (I leave aside the question as to whether all these nervous systems are organic.) Of course, mind is not the only bodily function, and it would be reasonable to make a working distinction between mind and the rest of the body, its other, merely somatic functions. The trouble with the expression "psychosomatic" is that the "somatic" is redundant, all psychic functions being necessarily somatic in their way (since they cannot be disembodied); however we cannot as yet treat neuroses in the same way as other bodily diseases, at least not without running the risk of unacceptable subjective costs (neurosurgery and mind-altering drugs may result in unwelcome changes in the patient), and this seems to legitimize a distinction between psychiatry and the care of the bodily body, as it were, although it is becoming increasingly clear that this boundary is constantly being crossed and recrossed.

Psychiatry attends to what may go wrong with the development and adequate functioning of the mature individual, apart (insofar as this distinction can be maintained) from what may go wrong with his or her body. (What "adequate" involves depends on what the individual wants to be equal to; it is a private choice as long as it does not have unacceptable social consequences.) Like the other branches of medicine, psychiatry looks to a basis of scientific information about the organism and its parts, but (again, as in the other branches) the success of its clinical practice is often independent of the question whether that scientific basis is correct. The special difficulty of the scientific basis of psychiatry is that the ascent from mechanisms to symptoms is longer and more complex, by several orders of magnitude, than the comparable ascent in any other medical specialty. Also the identification of the symptoms themselves, because of the vagueness of the notion of "adequate functioning" referred to earlier, is far less clear-cut. While in most of medicine, as in science generally, it is reasonable to look for explanations of the abnormal behavior of wholes in terms of nonstandard arrangements or functionings of their physical parts (note that this is possible even if we do not yet fully understand the *normal* behavior of the wholes, in terms of *standard* arrangements and functionings) this approach is as yet unavailable for most neurotic or psychotic symptoms, even though these may be relieved by surgery or medication.

Historically this has led to an interesting inversion of comparative priorities in the work of some important thinkers. Carnap (1928), for example, started out in *The Logical Structure of the World* to reconstruct scientific knowledge phenomenologically, but soon gave up the attempt in favor of physicalism. Freud, on the other hand, started out in the "Project for a Scientific Psychology" (1895) to reconstruct mental processes physically, but soon gave up the attempt in favor of a clinical approach. The result was that his hypotheses remained mentalistic and did not bridge, as he had hoped they would, the opposition between mind and body. The preceding paragraphs, however, were intended to convey my own conviction that this is not a true opposition as long as the body is alive and fully functioning; whether the hypotheses are couched in the earlier topographical terms or the later so-called structural ones, they are hypotheses about the functioning of a complex organism, not about events in some domain of nonmaterial substance. It is a question of starting from what is accessible, and trying to account for it by fitting it into whatever intelligible and testable system we can devise.

The suggestion has sometimes been made that "mind" might be regarded as a hypothesis, like "force" in physics, from the postulated existence of which various observable consequences would follow, but this move really is not necessary. As far as that goes, the status of "matter," for example, is only hypothetical, but physicists do not need to postulate it (confusion arises because of the alleged convertibility of matter and energy, but actually the terms of that equation are *mass* and energy); what they postulate are, among other things, particles, fields, and probability distributions. What Freud postulated were repressions, drives, and so on, as well as the structural components of the "mind," an expression which he used in its ordinary, informal sense. I assume in what follows, then, that the mind/body problem, in so far as there is such a problem, is not one of finding a correspondence between two different domains, but, rather, one of filling in the gaps in an essentially continuous story which is played out in the only domain there is, and which will take us, when it is finished, from the ultimate constituents of matter to autonomous agents capable of work and love. In terms of what we know so far, no higher ascent is possible.

One of the most obvious ways of attempting to tell this story is developmentally, and that is where Kernberg's paper comes in. Freud's developmental account (1940), summarized at the end of his life in "An Outline of

Psycho-Analysis," began, as everyone knows, with a chaotic and unstruc-tured id partially differentiated into the ego, from which system the super-ego detaches itself under influences from without, the whole passing through the various phases of sexuality. This represented a first approxima-tion in the light of his clinical experience. However, what is striking about it is its third-person character, the absence of attention to what we think of as the *subject*, and at the same time the very sparse attention given to the *contents* of psychic states. Kernberg and others have helped to alleviate the second lack of attention by the development of object relations theory; in "The Dynamic Unconscious and the Self," Kernberg takes an important step toward alleviating the first.

In thinking about subjectivity, from a philosophical point of view, I have been mainly interested in the conditions of its manifestation, which I locate developmentally at the point where the organism is able to be aware of the matching of internal representations, deriving from the external world or from its internal state. This conclusion is arrived at from purely structural considerations, beginning from merely reactive organisms (which match an internal state with an external state), ascending through sensitive organisms (which match an internal state with an internal repre-sentation of an external state) and conscious organisms (which match an internal representation of an internal state with an internal representation of an external state) to emerge in full subjectivity with an organism that can apprehend and follow the sequence of these conscious (although not neces-sarily deliberate) matchings, thus matching two or more internal represen-tations of internal states, and thereby acquiring selfhood and a personal history. The concept of "matching" invoked here is a development from some ideas originally due to the structural linguistics of Saussure (1916). As used developmentally it suggests a *requirement* (the primitive organism *must* match its internal state to the salinity of its ambient fluid, say, and will move about at random until it has done so), which shows up in conscious subjectivity as a requirement of intelligibility or significance.

While this ascent yields a self-aware subject, however, it does not yield one who is motivated to do anything *except* organize the contents of his or her thought in intelligible or significant patterns. What is needed is an account of the differences between *observing* a discrepancy between an actual state and a required state, and calmly taking action to bring them to coincidence, and *feeling* such a discrepancy, feeling panic or compulsion, and impulsively taking action—which may, or may not, overcome the discrepancy, or which may, if it does overcome it, have the effect of open-ing up another discrepancy in some other department of thought or feeling. What my account fails to recognize, I think, is that the earlier, simply reactive behavior pattern will still be there under the more advanced and reflective layer, *and that there is no reason why conscious subjectivity should not be fully aware of this.* The self has more to contend with than just its higher-level reflective functions.

All this seems banal enough—indeed, how could anyone be so dumb as to forget that we are aware of bodily states as well as mental ones? Well, it was not exactly that I forgot it, it was that I was concentrating on what *distinguishes* full conscious subjectivity from mere sensitivity or awareness, which many organisms have to which we might hesitate to attribute subjective selves. Now, it seems to me that this over-intellectualizing of subjectivity is analogous to Freud's concentration on what we might call the "erudite" functions of the unconscious, its deviousness and cleverness. The id may be "rude," but the defense mechanisms that join it in the dynamic unconscious are refined, even literate. What Kernberg suggests is that the cunning of repression is not the only weapon the self has at its disposal in dealing with psychic conflict, but that it is capable of admitting to consciousness, without screening by the secondary process, the rudest contents of the id, provided it can get rid of them again when necessary, and that this purge is achieved in some pathological cases not by censorship but by sidestepping across a split in the ego, into another self, as it were.

Kernberg's image of splitting reminds me of the chopsticks one sometimes gets in Oriental restaurants, that are still joined at the bottom and need to be broken apart. Normal selves (or normally neurotic ones), we might say, are not split at all; either they can face the contents of the id without repression, or else they censor them according to the old topographic scheme. True multiple personalities may be split all the way to the bottom,or at least far enough down to make reintegration impossible. Between these two extremes, different degrees of splitting represent more or less grave character disorders. The interesting cases that Kernberg cites are those of patients with borderline personality organization in which there is cognitive continuity but affective splitting, and part of the importance of his paper lies in his connection of this pathology to concepts of morality and responsibility in dealings with significant others.

There is an interesting connection here with the work of Sartre, in particular his notion of bad faith (Sartre, 1943, ch. 2). Sartre was always critical of the Freudian unconscious, insisting on the transparency of the subject to itself, down to the lowest depth of what Freud would have called the id. He was not entirely successful at sustaining this heroic self-knowledge as a consistent position, but one can understand his impatience with what he saw as the exploitation of the unconscious as an excuse for behavior that would otherwise be judged immoral; the censor, he felt, has to make a *conscious* appraisal of what it is censoring, and must know why it is doing so—in other words, the self is in collusion with its unconscious, its defenses are not involuntary but deliberate, and, if they lead to harmful consequences for others, it has no excuse. When Kernberg says of his inconsistent patient—who professes total love to different men at different times, knowing that she does this, yet each time believing herself to be truthful—that she is "not consciously lying in the ordinary sense of the word, but [is] obviously *dishonest* in a deeper sense" (my emphasis), he seems to be acknowledging something like Sartre's transparency; splitting as a defense looks like a classic case of bad faith.

This part of Kernberg's work, while welcome (because rare) in an analytic context, seems to me relatively unproblematic, and it is clearly anchored in long clinical experience. What I find really interesting and challenging is his reversal of the image of splitting into a developmental account of the process of integration of object relations at progressively higher levels under the influence of primary interactions in early childhood. The final pages of his essay constitute, in my view, a brilliant account, from the psychoanalytic side, of the sort of ascent I have tried to describe in structural terms. One difference is that my account is primarily phylogenetic, whereas his is clearly ontogenetic; as such, it offers a plausible explanatory mechanism for the succession of stages—in terms of peak affect states, for example— which is lacking in my merely descriptive sequence.

It would be tempting to explore here a version of the recapitulation hypothesis, and connect the sequence, as Kernberg almost seems willing to do at the end, to brain development. One problem to be dealt with would be the apparent anomaly that arises from the fact that the limbic system forms before the cortex, just as affective relations are established before symbolic ones; and yet Kernberg's cases seem to show that it is easier to maintain cognitive than affective continuity. Perhaps that is why they showed up as cases; the assumption that the integration into a consistent and stable system of the "good" and "bad" internalized object relations follows the sequence of brain development may hold in normal cases but be violated in pathological ones.

Kernberg's developmental picture constitutes, I believe, a major contribution to the work of filling-in that I alluded to above; the gaps that remain in that account are perceptibly narrowed by this contribution. The questions his paper leaves me with are not questions of substance so much as questions of philosophical attitude. Why should this admirable work be considered a contribution to the solution of the *old* mind/body problem? Why does Kernberg, in closing, invoke a view such as emergent interactionism (the interactions here being between the mental and the physical, and not between the self and the other)? Why consider that intrapsychic structures somehow *detach* themselves from their neurophysiological substrates? That such structures are emergent I readily grant, but nothing except old philosophical prejudice stands in the way of our taking them as emergent properties *of* the very physical bodies which, by virtue of that emergence, become the selves we are.

References

Carnap, R. (1928), *The Logical Structure of the World,* trans. R. A. George. London: Routledge & Kegan, Paul, 1967.

Freud, S. (1895), *The Origins of Psycho-Analysis,* trans. E. Mosbacher & J. Strachey. New York: Basic Books, 1954.

———— (1940), *An Outline of Psycho-Analysis.* New York: W. W. Norton, 1949.

Saussure, F. de (1916), *Course in General Linguistics,* trans. W. Baskin. New York: Philosophical Library, 1959.

Sartre, J. -P. (1943), *Being and Nothingness,* trans. H. Barnes. New York: Philosophical Library, 1956.

4 Intuition and Discovery*

Kenneth S. Bowers

The notion of the "unconscious" is a source of continuous fascination and threat. It is fascinating because it signifies something unknown about ourselves that renders us more mysterious and unfathomable than our (often mundane) appearance would suggest; it is threatening because the absence of consciousness implies to most people an absence of control—the quintessential hazard and indignity. Add to the above the fact that the Freudian unconscious is rooted in elemental forces of sex and aggression (together with more or less tenuous defenses against them), and we have a traditional notion of an unconscious that is as threatening and fascinating as Count Dracula.

In a recent book entitled *The Unconscious Reconsidered* (Bowers and Meichenbaum, 1984), various psychologists reflected on the notion of the "unconscious" in light of recent advances in their special areas of interest (e.g., developmental psychology, biopsychology, information processing, etc.). Interestingly, the contributors by and large either did not highlight the importance of sex and aggression in their accounts, or simply ignored them altogether. Instead, unconscious perception and thought emerged as an intrinsic property of mental functioning. For example, I argued in my chapter (Bowers, 1984) that "unconscious influences on human thought and action precede particular theories of 'unconsciousness' in somewhat the same way that thinking precedes any particular theory of thought" (p. 227).

---

*This paper is based on an address invited by the University of Waterloo Arts Faculty Lecture Committee, and delivered in the Humanities Theatre, University of Waterloo, Ontario, Canada, on February 24, 1981.

A related theme that emerged in the book was the importance of unconscious perception, as distinct from unconscious drives and motives. In Bowers' (1984) terminology, perception can occur without noticing (i.e., without consciousness of what is perceived), and furthermore, what is noticed need not be comprehended or understood. According to this view, determinants of thought and action that are not noticed or appreciated as such are, in effect, unconscious influences. This possibility of being unconsciously influenced and informed by one's environment is especially congenial to the notion of intuition, which serves as the main topic of this paper.

It is perhaps worth pointing out that the notion of unconscious processes in the service of intuition implies that people are often in closer touch with reality than they are able to represent in consciousness. Thus, while the unconscious of a Freudian kind may sometimes wreak havoc with the reality testing of an emotionally or psychologically disturbed person, part of the burden of the present paper will be to indicate how it is possible for unconscious processing *qua* intuition to extend and enhance our knowledge and control of the world, and hence of ourselves.

INTUITION OVERLOOKED AND UNDERDONE

Intuition is not one of psychology's shopworn, research-fatigued concepts.This fact of course does not prevent psychologists and lay people alike from invoking intuition, hunch, and a variety of even less precise synonyms (e.g., "feel" and "sense") in order to identify a stage of knowledge acquisition in which relevant evidence is either unavailable or insufficient to justify some claim or course of action.

Psychology has not, however, been entirely mute about intuition. Jerome Bruner (1961), for example, in summarizing a Woods Hole conference on education, defined intuition as "the intellectual technique of arriving at plausible but tentative formulations without going through the analytic steps by which such formulations would be found to be valid or invalid conclusions" (p. 13). In what is perhaps the most ambitious research program on the topic to date, Westcott (1968) states that intuition involves *"reaching conclusions on the basis of little information which are ordinarily reached on the basis of significantly more information* (italics in original; p. 71). In other words, for Westcott, as for Bruner, intuition involves "going beyond the information given."

For both Bruner andWestcott, intuition is something to celebrate, because it implies that people have at least the possibility for transcending the available evidence, thereby arriving at judgments that may be correct even though they are not yet proven.There is, however, a darker side to intuition, which is particularly evident in the recent writings on social cognition. In the studies reported by Ross (1977) and later Nisbett and Ross (1980), intuition looks more like a source of systematic error than a presentiment of valid knowledge. Indeed, intuition is the source of the now famous "fundamental attribution error," whereby dispositional attributions are allegedly invalidated by the recurrent finding that situational constraints are more powerful determinants of human action than are enduring characteristics of persons.

The notion of intuition that I wish to develop in this paper borrows liberally from both of the above perspectives on intuition and will, I hope, resolve at least some of the apparent contradictions between them. In particular, I will argue that intuition presupposes the possibility of mistakes and, indeed, depends on this possibility for its very existence. On the other hand, I will propose that intuition involves not simply going beyond the information given, but as well implies sensitivity and responsiveness to information that is not consciously represented, but which nevertheless guides inquiry toward productive and often profound insights.

The paper consists of three parts. First, I will try to show just why mistakes are an inevitable part of human conduct and inquiry and that the inevitability of mistakes is absolutely crucial to the notion of intuition conceived as responsiveness to unnoticed or tacit information. Second, I will try to show, by evidence and various illustrations, how people are in fact responsive to and influenced by information they do not consciously notice. Finally, I try to clarify how thinking is not just influenced, but often genuinely informed by tacit considerations that are not well represented in consciousness.

THE LIMITATIONS OF INTROSPECTION

Much of the inspiration for the first part of this paper comes from an article published by Nisbett and Wilson in 1977. Their thesis was a highly provocative and controversial one. In essence, they argued that people have no privileged introspective access to the causes or determining conditions of their behavior. In other words, people do not necessarily discover the truth about why they have done something merely because they honestly search their memories, thoughts, and feelings for the answer. Racking one's brain in this fashion can most assuredly lead to a conviction of having acted for this reason, rather than any other, but this conviction does not automatically authenticate the resulting explanation. Although this inward searching, or introspection, does not necessarily lead to valid insights about the causes of one's behavior, it does typically lead to reasonable-sounding, plausible explanations. However, as Nisbett and Wilson (1977; see also

Nisbett and Ross, 1980) demonstrated in a series of experiments, the plausible accounts that people offer for their actions frequently turn out to be inadequate or even badly mistaken.

Consider just one of the many illustrations that Nisbett and Wilson put forward in support of their controversial thesis. An experiment was set up in a shopping mall in which passers-by were to judge the quality of five pairs of nylon stockings lined up in a row. After finally selecting the one pair of stockings that seemed superior to the others, the subjects were asked why they chose that particular pair of stockings as best. Not surprisingly, the subjects offered a variety of plausible-sounding reasons—that is, just the sort of reasons one would offer in justifying a choice of this kind. People would point to the fact that the stockings they had selected were of finer fabric, softer to the touch, lighter and more flattering in color, and so on. In point of fact, however, the stockings were all identical, so that the apparent basis for discriminating the pairs of stockings was more in the eye of the beholder than in the stockings beheld. Moreover, there was a very strong tendency for people to select as superior the pair of stockings that was farthest to the right in the line of the five pairs they were to judge. In other words, the experiment seemed to demonstrate that participants in the experiment were in fact strongly influenced in their judgments by the position of the selected stockings relative to the remaining pairs.

What is even more interesting is how people in the experiment reacted to any suggestion by the experimenter that the position of the stockings might have had something to do with their selection of it as superior. People did not look embarrassed and say, "how obvious, now that you've pointed it out." Rather, they vigorously denied any such possibility. The reason for such a reaction is not hard to understand: the relative position of the stockings seemed irrelevant as a reason for selecting them as superior, and it seemed incredible to suppose that the experimenter would even make such a suggestion.

In sum, the participants in this study offered plausible but erroneous explanations for their choice of stockings, consistently overlooked the influence of its position on their selection, and rejected out of hand the experimenter's suggestion that the stockings' position may have had something to do with the selection of a particular pair of stockings as superior.

It is true that this particular experiment, like many others that Nisbett and Wilson report, is problematic in a variety of ways (Smith and Miller, 1978; Ericsson and Simon, 1980; White, 1980). But I think their basic point—that people often misunderstand the basis for their actions—survives the criticisms that have been leveled against them (Bowers, 1981). To press the point home, however, I would like to give another example of how subjects are prone to give mistaken accounts of their behavior—this one from my own laboratory.

The experiment involved an attempt to alter people's preferences for paintings (Bowers, 1975). Each of the many trials of the experiment involved presenting postcard reproductions of two paintings—one a landscape, the other a portrait. On each trial, the person was to select which of the two paintings he or she preferred. For the first twenty trials, I said nothing, so that the person's natural preferences for either portraits or landscapes would emerge. For the next ninety trials, however, I systematically reinforced or approved the kind of painting that the person had liked least during the first twenty trials. I particularly want to mention the results of one pilot subject in this study.

This young lady demonstrated a distinct increase in her selection of landscapes over the ninety reinforced trials. Later on, when the experiment was over, I asked her whether she had preferred landscapes or portraits. She acknowledged that, on the whole, she had preferred landscapes. When asked whether she had noticed my tendency to approve some of her choices, she acknowledged that I had approved her selection of landscapes. Finally, I asked her if my approval of her choice of landscapes had had any influence on her preference for them. She was quite indignant at the suggestion, and said, "Of course not. I selected the landscapes because I liked them best. Besides, you only approved my selection after I made it, so that what you said couldn't possibly have influenced my choice." Clearly, the subject was proceeding on the assumption that causes must precede their effects and that each trial was completely independent of those preceding and following it. Note that such a view is not irrational but is simply uninformed by thousands of experiments showing the very considerable impact of reinforcement on subsequent behavior.

Another intriguing finding emerged from this study: When subjects had been previously informed about the impact of reinforcement on behavior, they were much less influenced by it. In other words, when people realized that my approval was an attempt to alter their preferences, they simply did not show the reinforcement effect. Thus, a person's awareness or consciousness of potentially controlling factors in the environment can undermine and neutralize the power of such variables to control thought and behavior (Brehm, 1966). This is an important point to which we shall return later on.

Neither the ingenuous young lady in my painting preference experiment nor any of the participants in the study on stocking preferences were well informed about why they behaved the way they did. In other words, the determining influence of specific factors or variables, such as the position of stockings or contingent reinforcement, are not necessarily and automatically as self-evident to introspection as they are influential (Bowers, 1981, 1984). Indeed, if the determining conditions of our thought and action were necessarily as self evident to introspection as they are influential on our behavior, psychologists would be out of business. For it is surely the business of psychology to discover by systematic investigation what is not self-evident, namely, the importance of particular factors or variables as causes or determinants of behavior.

To summarize, the work of Nisbett and Wilson (1977) has demonstrated that people do not necessarily have direct introspective access to the determinants of their behavior. This seems to me an entirely plausible conclusion. Just think of all the times that you have asked yourself, "Now why in the world did I do that?", "What possessed me to stay so long at the party when I knew I had to get up early in the morning?", "Why in the world did I snap at my wife?", "Why am I feeling so grouchy?" or, "Why was I so cruel to that person whom I don't even know?" The problem of understanding one's own behavior was, of course, recognized by the Biblical Paul, when he stated in his letter to the Romans: "I do not understand my own actions. For I do not do what I want, but I do the very thing I hate."

Paul's comment readily captures the puzzlement we all occasionally feel about the why's of our behavior. What it does not reveal as clearly is how prone we are to be perfectly satisfied with an erroneous understanding of our own action. We have seen how people can misunderstand their preferences for stockings or paintings without having the least idea that they have overlooked important influences on their selection. Freud saw this point exactly, many years before Nisbett and Wilson made it a current topic of debate. As part of an extended footnote to his case history of Frau Emmy von N., Freud stated:

> There seems to be a necessity for bringing psychical phenomena of which one becomes conscious into causal connection with other conscious material. In cases in which the true causation evades conscious perception, one does not hesitate to attempt to make another connection, which one believes, although it is false [Breuer & Freud, 1895, p. 125].

It is not difficult to understand why both Freud and, much later, Nisbett and Wilson, have been taken to task for their respective positions. In both cases, the authors have proposed that much of what activates human thought and behavior is essentially outside awareness. For Freud, the important determinants were typically intrapsychic, that is, sexual and aggressive instincts sublimated or transformed in various ways, which rendered the original impulses virtually unrecognizable to all but the most dedicated psychoanalyst. For Nisbett and Wilson, on the other hand, the important determinants are much more apt to be environmental features and events that are unrecognized by the person for their coercive power. I dare say that Freud would consider Nisbett and Wilson's account trivial and superficial, whereas Nisbett and Wilson would consider Freud's views as obscenely indifferent to the pervasive impact of the environment on behavior (Nisbett and Ross, 1980, chapter 10).

Whatever arguments these authors from two eras might have with each other, ordinary folks find *both* versions of unconscious influence profoundly disquieting. For as soon as we admit that our conscious experience may be misleading or downright mistaken in its views of the why's and wherefore's of our own behavior, we seem to open up a Pandora's box of alternative possibilities. Indeed, once we give up the anchoring influence of conscious experience as the best indicator of why we behave the way we do, then *anything* is possible. The simple buying of a cigar can be fraught with libidinous implications, and buying a particular car can be evidence for a subtle but successful sales gimmick rather than the exercise of the consumer's informed choice.

To save us from such an unflattering view of ourselves, we may persist in believing that we have direct introspective access to at least some of the determinants of our behavior and that we can therefore know with absolute certainty just why we do at least some things. My position is this: it is no doubt the case that we can know with virtual certainty why we do some things; the question remains, however, whether or not this knowledge is the result of direct introspective access to the causal connection linking our thoughts, actions and feelings on one hand, to their determining conditions on the other.

The problem here is easiest to illustrate with observation of external events, rather than with introspection of internal events. Consider that whenever a pencil is released from someone's grip, it falls. It is a most reliable finding, for the pencil *always* falls when released. On the other hand, it never falls down if it is not released. The conclusion seems clear: letting go of the pencil causes it to fall.

But what is it that we see here? We see two events: the release of the pencil and its fall to the ground. We do not, however, see the necessary causal connection between these two events. Even though it may seem as if we perceive the causal connection between two events, what we have recognized, ever since Hume, is that causal connections are inferred, not observed. And our inferences are based not only on the events we observe, but on our understanding or conceptualization of the events in question. Consequently, as far as pencils are concerned, it is clear to a contemporary audience that letting go of one does not cause it to fall: gravity does. But gravity is an extraordinarily abstract concept that cannot be perceived directly. And I suspect that it is precisely because Newton's theory of gravitation is so abstract and so unavailable to immediate perception that it took us so long to understand how it could fill the gap between letting go of an object and that object's fall to the earth.

Although the above example is instructive, it is not unique; the causal connection between events is always an inference based on some sort of conceptual understanding of the events under consideration. When the theory is in some sense sufficient, so too is the causal explanation. When the theory is incorrect, the causal inferences will also be erroneous.

As with observation, so with introspection. If we have an informed understanding of our behavior, chances are we can offer a correct account of it. But this understanding is not based on direct and introspective access to the necessary connection between action and its causes or determinants. Rather, it is based on some formal or informal conceptualization or understanding of the behavior in question. It is for this reason that a psychotherapist can recognize far sooner and better than a ten-year old patient why the child, for the first time in years, has begun wetting the bed at night. The child is simply too young and unsophisticated to realize that the father's abandonment of the home has something to do with these enuretic episodes, whereas to an experienced therapist, the connection between these two events may be quite compelling. Moreover, competent therapists are in a better than average position to understand their own personal problems. Here again, however, a therapists's success would not derive from direct introspective access to the links connecting personal problems to their determining conditions, but from his or her relative psychological sophistication. And, surely, therapists may well be wrong in trying to understand their own difficulties. This is, of course, the implication of Nisbett and Wilson's provocative thesis regarding the limitations of self-knowledge. Mistaken accounts about our behavior are always possible because (a) introspection does not have privileged access to the causal links connecting action with its determinants, and (b) there are always limitations and inadequacies in our understanding and sophistication about what the truly important causes of our behavior might be.

ERROR AND INTUITION

I emphasized at the beginning of this paper that the possibility for making errors in accounting for our behavior is critical to the notion of intuition that I wish to develop. It is now time to explain why this is so. Notice that whenever a person submits a partial or incorrect explanation of his or her behavior, some truly influential factors remain undetected or unappreciated and are therefore, in an important sense, unconscious influences on behavior. In their paper, Nisbett and Wilson (1977) stressed that people are unable to identify such unconscious influences, the end result being that people end up looking somewhat stupid.

There is, however, another side to this coin. That people can be mistaken in identifying the truly influential factors operating on their thought and behavior means that human behavior and thought are sensitive and responsive to information that is not consciously perceived. Whereas Nisbett and Wilson have emphasized the *inability* of people to identify and appreciate the truly controlling factors that unconsciously influence their thought and action, I would like to stress the *ability* of persons to be influenced and informed by factors that are not explicitly represented in conscious awareness. In fact, what I am calling intuition is precisely this possibility for being tacitly informed by considerations that remain outside of conscious awareness (Polanyi, 1964). So, if it is true, as Nisbett and Wilson imply, tht people seem rather stupid for being unable to provide valid accounts of their behavior, it is also true that they are smarter and more intuitive in their thought and conduct than is implied by their inability to articulate the basis for what they think and do.

And notice this: If through observation or introspection we necessarily had direct and automatic access to the causal links connecting our action to its determinants, we could never be mistaken in explaining why we did something. We would know absolutely everything about our own behavior, even as we were behaving. More generally, if the causal connections between events of any kind were necessarily and automatically accessible to observation or introspection, we would know everything about anything we could see and observe. In such a world, it would be absurd to talk of hunches or intuitions, because such words presuppose that we do not explicitly know about all the determinants of our thought and action. In other words, intuition is incompatible with introspective or observational access to causal necessity. In turn, lack of such access means that we are in constant danger of making errors whenever we try to explain why things happen the way they do. Therefore, the possibility for making errors of explanation is necessary to the concept of intuition that I am proposing.

That we can make errors and are responsive to unconscious influences only makes intuition possible; it does not guarantee the emergence of a genuinely creative insight into the nature of things. In fact, unconscious influences—that is, influences that are not well represented in consciousness—can have a profoundly disquieting impact on behavior and thought. In the next section, I provide a few examples of how information that is not consciously represented can have a potentially adverse impact on thought and behavior. I reserve for last the potentially benign and instructive role of tacit information.

UNCONSCIOUS INFLUENCES

I once had a graduate student come to me in a state of profound unease because of something he had just done out of some sense of compulsion that he did not understand at all. Upon awakening one morning, he had called up his girlfriend and cancelled their date with apologies but with no satisfactory explanation, not even one he could give himself. Since he liked the woman, he was both puzzled and ashamed of his action and more than a bit worried about behaving in such an inexplicable manner. Several days later, he showed up with an unusual resolution of the puzzle. He had been walking across the campus, when "like a bolt out of the blue," a dream came back to him that he had had the night before cancelling the date. He had dreamt that he was already out with his date, was driving down a highway, and had a terrible automobile accident he had survived but in which his date had been killed. He had no memory of the dream upon awakening—only an absolute, compulsive need to cancel the date. In this case, the recall of the dream was an occasion of considerable relief, since the person considered it a satisfactory explanation to an otherwise inexplicable action. But recall of mental events that have led to inexplicable actions is by no means certain or even typical. And the absence of such spontaneous recall for disturbing events of this sort can conceivably escalate further into a real crisis.

To illustrate, Levinson (1967) reported a case of a woman who emerged from surgery with an inexplicable depression. She was weepy and almost completely disconsolate. No one could unearth what the problem was, which was certainly psychological, since nothing about the operation itself should have precipitated such an emotional crisis. Finally, an expert in hypnosis was brought in and, through various means, was able to get the woman to recall many of the events of the surgery. The big surprise came when the woman blurted out with considerable distress: "The surgeon says it might be malignant." Upon checking, it was discovered that the surgeon had in fact made such a remark during surgery when he ran across an unexpected lump in the woman's mouth. Even though the woman had been under general anesthesia throughout the operation, she had somehow registered, unconsciously as it were, the emotionally traumatic information tendered by an unsuspecting surgeon.

Subsequent experimentation on state-dependent learning (Overton, 1977) has indeed shown that people can, in fact, process and register information while they are deeply asleep (Oswald, 1962; Evans, 1979) or unconscious from the effects of general anesthesia (Levinson, 1967; Bennett, 1985), and that they remain totally forgetful of this information after awakening. If the information received in such an unconscious state has personal significance, it can have considerable impact, either of negative or a positive kind. For example, in one study it was found that tape-recorded messages of a quick and benign recovery delivered to surgical patients under general anesthesia led to a speedier release from the hospital than was true for control patients exposed to tape-recorded music (Pearson, 1961; Bennett, in press).

While both of the examples I have given so far involve the impact of information on sleeping or unconscious persons, this is in no sense critical to the notion that people can be influenced by external or internally generated information that they do not consciously notice. Let me give you two examples from literature to make my point.

That doyen of the unconscious, Fyodor Dostoyevsky, early in the *Brothers Karamazov,* describes a picture by the Russian painter Kramskoy, called "Contemplation." According to Dostoyevsky (1950):

> There is a forest in winter, and on a roadway through the forest, in absolute solitude, stands a peasant in a torn kaftan and bark shoes. He stands, as it were, lost in thought. Yet he is not thinking; he is "contemplating." If anyone touched him he would start and look at one as though awakening and bewildered. It's true he would come to himself immediately; but if he were asked what he had been thinking about, he would remember nothing. Yet probably he has hidden within himself, the impression which had dominated him during the period of contemplation. Those impressions are dear to him and no doubt he hoards them imperceptibly, and even unconsciously. How and why, of course, he does not know either. He may suddenly, after hoarding impressions for many years, abandon everything and go off to Jerusalem on a pilgrimage for his soul's salvation, or perhaps he will suddenly set fire to his native village, and perhaps do both. There are a good many "contemplatives" among the peasantry [p. 150].

Obviously, we have here a case of internally generated preoccupations that are dissociated from consciousness (Janet, 1901; Hilgard, 1977) but which can nevertheless have a potentially catastrophic impact on behavior. I will only add that though the content of such preoccupation, reveries, or contemplations may not be in principle unconscious, it is often the case that people simply do not pay any attention to their thoughts and thus do not notice them consciously. Having thoughts or perceptions does not entail noticing the thoughts or perceptions one has (Lundh, 1979; Bowers, 1984). This state of affairs is easily illustrated by a commonplace example from everyday life. Most people have had the experience of reading a book and suddenly realizing that nothing of the material has registered for a considerable period of time. The reader has been lost in thought, as it were. What is perhaps less often noticed is how difficult it can sometimes be to recover the thoughts one had during the reverie. We often lose the thoughts we have been lost in (Varendonck, 1921). Nevertheless, as Dostoyevsky implies, such lost or unconscious thoughts may occasionally have considerable impact on one's conscious thought and behavior.

Whereas we have so far emphasized the potential influence of thoughts and fantasies that are, in effect, unconscious, the next illustration from the pen of the early-nineteenth century essayist and critic Hazlitt points instead to the impact of external influences that initially are not well represented in consciousness. Hazlitt describes in this quotation an Englishman who has been charged with treason, but who had evidently managed to escape to a leisurely retirement in Wales. According to Hazlitt (1821),

> He had ordered his breakfast, and was sitting at the window in all the dalliance of expectation, when a face passed of which he took no notice at the instant—but when his breakfast was brought in presently after, he found his appetite for it gone, the day had lost its freshness in his eye, he was uneasy and spiritless; and without any cause that he could discover, a total change had taken place in his feelings. While he was trying to account for this odd circumstance, the same face passed again—it was the face of Taylor the spy; and he was no longer at a loss to explain the difficulty. He had before caught only a transient glimpse, a passing side-view of the face; but though this was not sufficient to awaken a distinct idea in his memory, his feelings, quicker and surer, had taken the alarm . . . though he could not at all tell what was the matter with him. To the flitting, shadowy, half-distinguished profile that had glided by his window was linked unconsciously and mysteriously, but inseparably, the impression of the trains that had been laid for him by this person;—in this brief moment, in this dim, illegible shorthand of the mind he had just escaped the speeches of the Attorney and Solicitor-General over again; the gaunt figure of Mr. Pitt glared by him; the walls of a prison enclosed him; and he felt the hands of the executioner near him, without knowing it till the tremor and disorder of his nerves gave information to his reasoning faculties that all was not well within . . . . In other words, the feeling of pleasure or pain, of good or evil, is revived, and acts instantaneously upon the mind, before we have time to recollect the precise objects which have originally given birth to it [p. 658–659].

This quotation illustrates better than anything I could have devised how we can be affectively responsive to information that has not yet been consciously perceived (Simonton, 1980; Zajonc 1980).

These examples from literature are, I think, compelling illustrations of how people can be influenced by naturally occurring information that is not consciously recognized or appreciated as an important influence on their feelings and behavior. However, when the tacit influences on thought and action are not spontaneous, but planned by some sort of external agency (advertising or otherwise), we have the possibility for subtle but effective control over a person's thought and action (Bowers, 1978). We have already seen how the woman in my landscape-portrait experiment remained unappreciative of the controlling impact of my approval for her selection of landscapes. Let me provide one more illustration of considerably greater moment.

Near the end of Lyndon Johnson's presidency, his press secretary, George Reedy, was present at the Cabinet meetings in which the conduct of the Viet Nam war was being discussed. He was impressed with how

Cabinet members would consistently discount the eloquent and reasoned attempts of George Ball to persuade the Cabinet to wind down the war. By contrast, however, Mr. Reedy later

> saw Clark Clifford change President Johnson's mind and not once dissent in the process. I think I was one of the few people in the room who caught on to what Clifford was doing. In fact, Clifford did not draw any conclusions. He would get up at cabinet meetings and go on with long, rambling, apparently aimless briefings in which he would merely sum up the world situation and leave it at that. But what he was doing was subtly planting in the minds of the people around the table and in the mind of the President a set of facts and a series of predicates upon which one could come to only one conclusion. When President Johnson said that Clark Clifford had not changed his mind on Viet Nam, I think Mr. Johnson was being honest. I don't think he knew Clifford was changing his mind [Reedy, 1971: p. 13].[1]

I will only add to Reedy's observation that if President Johnson had been aware of the subtle machinations of his new Secretary of State, he might have been much less susceptible to their influence, just as many of the subjects in my painting-preference experiment were resistant to the effect of reinforcement when they appreciated it as an attempt to influence their selection of preferred paintings.

Such anecdotal accounts of subtle influence that is not consciously appreciated have the advantage of being graphic and vivid. Nevertheless, they are not scientifically controlled observations and therefore possess limited evidential value. There has been no difficulty, however, in demonstrating some of these subtle influences in the psychological laboratory. One of the best examples of how information can influence people unawares was demonstrated in an investigation conducted by MacKay (1973). He presented a series of ambiguous sentences to experimental subjects to see how they would interpret them. For example, consider the sentence, "They threw stones toward the bank yesterday." The word "bank" in this sentence is ambiguous: it is not clear whether it refers to a bank where money is kept or to a river bank. Each such ambiguous sentence was presented by tape recording to only one ear of a person through a pair of headphones. On the other ear, single words were presented that removed the ambiguity of the sentence. For example, at the exact instant that the word "bank" was presented to the right ear, the word "river" or "money" was presented to the left ear.

---

[1]The subtleties of language and paralinguistic communications are becoming more and more recognized by professional psychotherapists as important, if implicit, factors in the effective mobilization of the patient's resources (e.g., Bandler and Grinder, 1975).

It is very difficult to listen to the information on both ears at the same time, and since the subjects were asked to concentrate on the right ear, where the sentence was presented, they did not pay much attention to the left ear, where the single word was presented. As a matter of fact, when subjects were later asked to recall the words on the unattended left ear, they found it virtually impossible to do so. Nevertheless, there was a distinct tendency for subjects to interpret the ambiguous sentences in a way that was influenced by the single word that they could not recall. For example, subjects who were presented with the word "river" on the left ear tended to understand the ambiguous sentence "They threw stones toward the bank yesterday" as meaning that the stones were thrown at a river bank rather than at a money bank. In contrast, people who had been presented with the word "money" on the left ear when attending to this sentence interpreted it to mean that stones were thrown at a place where money is kept.

Thus, under controlled experimental circumstances, we have evidence that something not consciously noticed or recalled has a definite impact on conscious interpretation of the ambiguous sentence (see also Lundh, 1979; Bowers, 1981, 1984). Or, if I may phrase this finding somewhat differently, our conscious experience can be influenced by tacitly or unconsciously perceived events that we do not notice or recall.

In this ambiguous-sentence experiment, there was nothing novel or inventive about the person's interpretation of the sentence, and in this sense it can be argued that the experiment was merely an example of how a person's perceptions can be biased by influences that are not experienced consciously. In the next experiment, however, a very good case can be made that an unnoticed event does not merely bias, slant, or influence one's thinking in a certain direction, but genuinely informs thought in a manner that helps in the solution of a challenging problem. In effect, the results of the following experiment constitute a point of entry into the third and final section of this paper, wherein it is proposed that intuition consists precisely in being implicitly or tacitly informed by considerations that are not consciously noticed or appreciated as important conditions of insight, invention, and discovery (Polanyi, 1964).

ON BEING IMPLICITLY INFORMED

The experiment in question was conducted by Maier (1931) and is known as the string-pendulum problem. Basically, the problem consisted of having people figure out how to tie two strings together that were hanging from the ceiling. Since the strings were too far apart to be grasped at the same time, the issue was how to get hold of both strings in order to tie them together. There were several different ways of solving this problem, but the one Maier focused on involved tying a pair of pliers to one of the strings, and swinging it toward the stationary string. Meanwhile, the person could go to the stationary string, bring it as close to the swinging string as possible, and simply await its arrival.

About forty percent of the participants in this experiment solved the problem spontaneously, that is, without any intervention on the part of the experimenter. It is the results of 23 subjects who did *not* solve the problem "spontaneously" that we will focus on here. After these people had tried in vain for about ten minutes to solve the problem, the experimenter provided a clue. The clue involved the experimenter casually bumping into one of the strings, thereby setting it into motion. The experimenter did not call the person's attenion to the moving string, or in any way announce that it constituted a clue to the solution of the problem. Nevertheless, an average of 42 seconds after the clue was administered, the subjects suddenly achieved the solution to the problem by tying a pair of pliers to one of the strings and swinging it toward the stationary string. What is fascinating is that 15 of the 23 subjects who solved the problem after being exposed to the bumped-string clue had no apparent recognition or appreciation of it as helping them in their solution of the problem. When specifically asked about the clue, they essentially denied that they had noticed the string being bumped by the experimenter.

In reviewing Maier's string-pendulum experiment, Nisbett and Wilson (1977) emphasized how it demonstrated the inability of people to account for their own behavior, but it also illustrates the ability of people to be guided and informed by clues not explicitly represented in conscious awareness. Let us now turn to an example of a truly important discovery in science that illustrates this basic point. Although I am going to emphasize one particular example, any number of illustrations from the history of science could be invoked to make the same point (e.g., Platt and Baker, 1969). Consider, then, the famous discovery of the benzene ring by Kekulé.

According to Kekulé, he was dozing by the fire, when, in his mind's eye, he saw snakelike structures cavorting before his eyes. And then, suddenly: "But look! What was that? One of the snakes had seized hold of its own tail, and the form whirled mockingly before my eyes. As if by a flash of lightning I awoke" (Hein, 1966, p. 10). What had suddenly occurred to Kekulé was that benzene did not have an open structure as had been supposed previously, but rather a closed, circular structure.

It is useful to consider this famous example of scientific discovery a bit further. First of all, it is in one respect an unusual example, in that most sudden insights leave no residue of their origins. The literature on creativity is replete with anecdotes of how people experienced the occurrence of important insights as if they were some sort of visitation or intervention by an outside agency—God, Mephistopheles, muse, or whatever. This bolt-out-of-the-blue experience is probably misleading, however. There are good reasons to suppose that the sudden insight so fills consciousness with its importance that there is little room for, or interest in, recalling the mental events occurring just prior to the sudden flash of inspiration (Durkin, 1937; Ericsson and Simon, 1980). Recall here Dostoyevsky's description of "contemplating" as distinct from "thinking," and how conscious thoughts and overt action can sometimes be mobilized by dreamlike mental images that are themselves seldom noticed or recalled. In this context, Kekulé's ability to trace his insight about the shape of the benzene ring to a dream about snakes with tails in their mouths is somewhat unusual. At the same time, it is instructive in showing how dreamlike reveries or contemplations that are ordinarily not noticed or recalled can have a profound and sometimes productive impact on our conscious thought and experience.

What yet wants explaining is Kekulé's dream. It seems to me that there are at least four ways of accounting for this extraordinarily prescient vision. The first explanatory model we may refer to as the *deus ex machina* model, whereby God simply generates the dream in Kekulé's sleeping brain, leaving it for the dreamer to recognize its significance for a current scientific preoccupation—namely, the structure of benzene. There is a long religious tradition in which this kind of *deus ex machina* intervention is at least implicit. If it is true, there is nothing that a mere psychologist can hope to fathom, and we must simply resign ourselves to ignorance.

The second model of explanation is more secular—namely, the lottery or roulette model. By this account, Kekulé's dream is a random event, uninfluenced by anything in Kekulé's previous life, yet profoundly altering the subsequent course of his own personal life, and that of the history of science into the bargain. In other words, Kekulé's dream was a bit like a winning number in an intellectual lottery—a strictly random event that nevertheless changed the course of scientific history.

A third account we may call the teleological or omen model. By this, we mean that the dream is not a reflection of Kekulé's past history, but is instead both caused by, and an omen of, future events, namely, Kekulé's imminent discovery of the shape of the benzene molecule. In sum, like Joseph's insight into the dream of seven fat and seven lean kine, Kekulé's dream, by this omen or teleological model, was a portent of things to come.

It will perhaps come as no surprise that I hold no favor for any of the above models as a satisfactory account of Kekulé's dream. Rather, I prefer what we may call, for want of a better term, the intuitive model. By this account, Kekulé's dream was a symbolic condensation or representation of information that he already knew implicitly but had not yet consciously understood. By this model, Kekulé's dream was informed by his thorough immersion in the currently available knowledge of chemistry, and by his continual preoccupation with the problem to be solved. This total immersion of the scientist in his field is a critical condition of genuine creativity. But as important as such immersion is for discovery, it is at the same time a potentially limiting factor on the possibility for a creative breakthrough.

At first blush, it may seem paradoxical that thorough immersion in a scientific subject matter can be both a necessary and a limiting condition on the possibility for inspired insight. But a moment's thought reveals that it is really not so puzzling or paradoxical. The alert and focused mind, informed by explicit knowledge in an area of inquiry, is also a mind that is saddled with conscious expectations of what is likely or probable. Such expectations, of course, are not always correct and can often be seriously misleading (Nisbett and Ross, 1980). Indeed, a genuinely important discovery or insight is considered creative in part because it is highly unusual and novel, which is to say, an unexpected or improbable event (Getzels and Jackson, 1962).

In light of the above considerations, it is perhaps not surprising that, time after time, one can read of original ideas emerging out of states of reverie, or, at the very least, when the investigator was not consciously pursuing the solution to a problem (Platt and Baker, 1969; Shepard, 1978). It is at such times in the life of a mind that relatively unlikely associations of available ideas, information, and images are apt to connect, unhindered by conscious goals, expectations, or strategies of problem solving (Rugg, 1963; Koestler, 1964; Arieti, 1976).

An especially compelling example of the facilitative effect of low arousal on creative thought (Simonton, 1980) was reported by the Nobel Laureate, Otto Loewi (1960). His most famous experiment involved demonstrating the chemical transmission of nerve impulses on effector organs. The experiment occurred to him in the middle of the night, whereupon he awoke and jotted down the gist of it on a slip of paper. Unfortunately, he could not decipher his writing the next morning. Fortunately, he awoke at three o'clock the next night with the same experiment fully formed in his mind. On this occasion, he went directly to the laboratory and performed the experiment successfully. It was clear to Loewi in retrospect that the experiment had been steeping in his mind for a long time: 17 years earlier, the hypothesis of chemical transmission of neural impulses had occurred to him, but without the accompanying notion of how to validate his hunch; two years before he finally performed his nocturnal experiment, he had conducted a very similar investigation for another purpose. It was the nighttime juxtaposition of a 17-year-old hypothesis with a two-year-old experimental procedure that led to his Nobel Prize-winning work.

Loewi's (1960) reflection about this experiment is instructive: "If carefully considered in the daytime, I would undoubtedly have rejected the kind of experiment I performed [as improbable]. . . . It was good fortune that at the moment of the hunch I did not think but acted immediately" (p. 18).

In sum, I am arguing that Kekulé's dream of snakes with tails in their mouths and Loewi's nocturnal insight represented an improbable joining, or juxtaposition, of available information that was permitted symbolic expression in an undirected dream state—a juxtaposition that is less likely to have occurred in an alert and focused mind dominated by conscious expectations rather than by unfettered but informed fantasy (Bowers and Bowers, 1979).

Finally, notice a curious irony in the course of my argument. I earlier emphasized that sophistication about potentially subtle influences often disarms these influences of their power to control thought and action. Recall here that people's awareness of reinforcement as an attempt to influence behavior can render such reinforcement far less potent as a mover and shaper of behavior. On one hand, therefore, conscious knowledge of such potentially undesirable influences limits their impact on thought and action. On the other hand, however, we have now seen that the effect of explicit knowledge and conscious expectation may also work to limit the likelihood of being genuinely informed by tacit features of one's experience. It seems that awareness or consciousness can protect us against subtle attempts to influence thought and behavior; but at the same time, it can prevent tacit information from breaking through the barrier of our conscious thoughts and expectations, thereby reducing the likelihood of achieving a novel insight into the nature of things.

Thus it is that the received wisdom in a domain of inquiry can be both the standard of sophistication and an impediment to inspiration. Mind possesses, and in turn is possessed by, its theories and models of reality in a way that both extends our grasp and limits our vision of nature and our place in it. Perhaps this is one reason that the younger members of a scientific discipline are often the ones most likely to achieve novel and productive breakthroughs: they have enough basic grounding in the topic at hand to define the problem, but not so much as to constrain unduly the search for a solution. In any event, intuition as a source of novel ideas and insights is the beginning of science, and its somewhat shadowy role in disciplined inquiry should not be permitted to eclipse its virtues.

REFERENCES

Arieti, S. (1976), *Creativity: The Magic Synthesis*. New York: Basic Books.
Bandler, R., & Grinder J. (1975), *The Structure of Magic*. Palo Alto, CA: Science and Behavior.

Bennett, H. L. (in press). Perception and memory for events during adequate general anesthesia for surgical operations. In: *Hypnosis and Memory,* ed. Helen Pettinati. New York: Guilford Press.

Bowers, K. S. (1975), The psychology of subtle control: An attributional analysis of behavioral persistence. *Canad. J. Behavioral Science,* 7:78–95.

Bowers, K. S. (1978), Listening with the third ear: On paying inattention effectively. In: *Hypnosis at Its Bicentennial,* ed. F. Frankel & H. S. Zamansky. New York: Plenum Press.

Bowers, K. S. (1981), Knowing more than we can say leads to saying more than we can know: On being implicitly informed. In: *Toward a Psychology of Situations,* ed. D. Magnusson. Hillsdale, NJ: Lawrence Erlbaum Associates.

Bowers, K. S. (1984), On being unconsciously influenced and informed. In: *The Unconscious Reconsidered,* ed. K. S. Bowers & D. Meichenbaum. New York: John Wiley.

Bowers, P. G., & Bowers, K. S. (1979), Hypnosis and creativity: A theoretical and empirical rapprochement. In: *Hypnosis: Development in Research and New Perspectives,* ed. E. Fromm & R. E. Shor, 2nd edition. New York: Aldine.

Bowers, K. S., & Meichenbaum, D. (eds.) (1984), *The Unconscious Reconsidered.* New York: Wiley.

Brehm, J. (1966), *A Theory of Psychological Reactance.* New York: Academic Press.

Breuer, J., & Freud, S. (1895), Studies on hysteria. *Standard Edition,* 2:185–251. London: Hogarth Press, 1955.

Bruner, J. (1961), *The Process of Education.* Cambridge, MA: Harvard University Press.

Dostoyevsky, F. (1950), *The Brothers Karamazov.* New York: Vintage.

Durkin, H. E. (1937), Trial-and-error, gradual analysis, and sudden reorganization: An experimental study of problem solving. *Archives of Psychology,* 210:1–85.

Ericsson, K. A., & Simon, H. A. (1980), Verbal reports as data. *Psycholog. Rev.* 87:215–251.

Evans, F. J. (1979), Hypnosis and sleep: Techniques for exploring cognitive activity during sleep. In: *Hypnosis: Developments in Research and New Perspectives,* ed. E. Fromm & R. E. Shor, 2nd edition. New York: Aldine.

Getzels, J. W., & Jackson, P.W. (1962), *Creativity and Intelligence.* New York: Wiley.

Hazlitt, W. (1821), On genius and common sense. In: *English Romantic Writers,* ed. D. Perkins. New York: Harcourt Brace & World, 1967.

Hein, G. E. (1966), Kekulé and the architecture of molecules. In: *Advances in Chemistry Series: Kekulé Centennial,* ed. R. F. Gould. Washington D.C.: American Chemical Society.

Hilgard, E. R. (1977), *Divided Consciousness: Multiple Controls in Human Thought and Action.* New York: Wiley-Interscience.

Janet, P. (1901), *The Mental State of Hystericals.* New York: Putnam.

Koestler, A. (1964), *The Act of Creation.* New York: Macmillan.

Levinson, B. W. (1967), States of awareness during general anesthesia. In: *Hypnosis and Psychosomatic Medicine,* ed. J. Lassner. New York: Springer Verlag, pp. 200–207.

Loewi, O. (1960), An autobiographic sketch. *Perspectives in Biology and Medicine,* 4:3–25.

Lundh, L-G. (1979), Introspection, consciousness and human information processing. *Scandinavian J. Psychol.* 20:223–238.

MacKay, D. (1973), Aspects of the theory of comprehension, memory and attention. *Quart. J. of Exp. Psychol.* 25:22–40.

Maier, N. R. F. (1931), Reasoning in Humans: II. The solution of a problem and its appearance in consciousness. *J. Compar. Psychol.* 12:181–194.

Nisbett, R., & Ross, L. (1980), *Human Inference: Strategies and Shortcomings of Social Judgment.* Englewood Cliffs, NJ: Prentice-Hall.

Nisbett, R., & Wilson, T. D. (1977), Telling more than we know: Verbal reports on mental processes. *Psychol. Rev.* 84:231–279.

Oswald, I. (1962), *Sleeping and Waking: Physiology and Psychology.* Amsterdam: American Elsevier.

Overton, D. A. (1977), Major theories of state dependent learning. In: *Drug Discrimination and State Dependent Learning,* ed. B. Ho, D. Chute, & D. Richards. New York: Academic Press.

Pearson, R. E. (1961), Response to suggestions given under general anesthesia. *Amer. J. Clinical Hypnosis,* 4:106–114.

Platt, W., & Baker, R. A. (1969), The relation of the scientific "hunch" to research. *J. Chemistry Education,* 8:1969–2002.

Polanyi, M. (1964), *Personal Knowledge: Toward a Postcritical Philosophy.* New York: Harper and Row.

Reedy,G. (1971), Discussion of "Powers of the presidency," *Center Magazine,* 4:7–18.

Ross, L. (1977), The intuitive psychologist and his shortcomings: Distortions in the attribution process. In: *Advances in Experimental Social Psychology,* ed. L. Berkowitz. New York: Academic Press, 173–220.

Rugg, H. (1963), *Imagination.* New York: Harper and Row.

Shepard, R. N. (1978), Externalization of mental images and the act of creation. In: *Visual Learning, Thinking and Communication,* ed. B. J.Randhawa & W. E. Coffman. New York: Academic Press.

Simonton, D. K. (1980), Intuition and analysis: A predictive and explanatory model. *Genetic Psychology Monographs,* 102:3–40.

Smith, E. R., & Miller, F. D. (1978), Limits on perception of cognitive processes: A reply to Nisbett and Wilson. *Psycholog. Rev.* 85:355–362.

Varendonck, J. (1921), *The Psychology of Daydreams.* New York: Macmillan.

Westcott, M. R. (1968), *Toward a Contemporary Psychology of Intuition: A Historical, Theoretical, and Empirical Inquiry.* New York: Holt, Rinehart & Winston.

White, P. (1900), Limitations on verbal reports of internal events: A refutation of Nisbett and Wilson and of Bem. *Psychol. Rev.* 87:105–112.

Zajonc, R. B. (1980), Feeling and thinking: Preferences need no inferences. *Amer. Psychol.,* 35:151–175.

5 Introspection and the Unconscious

Gerald E. Myers

My goal in this essay is to show how the concept of introspection is, and is not, significant for the concept of the unconscious. The many confusions and dead-ends occasioned by this topic mandate a certain amount of distinction-drawing: thus, a large part of the task is conceptual rather than empirical analysis. But my goal includes arriving at conclusions that are also empirically interesting, and towards that end I will propose a special way of thinking about the relation of the concept of introspection to the concept of the unconscious. Before doing so, however, it will be helpful if I place my ideas in a historical perspective by recalling what was said on our topic, for example, by William James and Sigmund Freud.

HISTORICAL CONTEXT

It is virtually unknown that the concept of the unconscious was articulated in America as early as 1871 by Oliver Wendell Holmes, Sr. It figured in an address, "Mechanism in Thought and Morals," delivered by Holmes for Harvard's Phi Beta Kappa Society. Oberndorf (1944), the man who has recovered this event for us, writes:

> Holmes's regular use of the word "unconscious" is of interest. Although William James mentioned the term "unconscious cerebration," he decided that "unconscious" is "better replaced" by the vaguer term "subconscious" or "subliminal." Freud, like Holmes, insisted upon the term unconscious, whereas, in the writings of most of his predecessors and contemporaries,

subconscious had been used to signify mental operations which occurred below the level of consciousness. Other important pillars in psychoanalysis noted by Holmes are the free association of ideas, the role of the censor, and, in the first work of Breuer and Freud, the recognition of the existence of several personalities in the same individual [p. 87].

I have quoted this not because of anything further to be said here about Holmes, but because of the truth contained in this contrast between Holmes and James in their concepts of the unconscious. James was not averse to using such terms as "unconscious," "the unconscious," and "unconsciousness," but, unlike Holmes, he did not attach essentially Freudian meanings to them. It is often noted how thoroughly Freud offended standard philosophical opinion by suggesting that *mental* events might occur detached from consciousness; the standard opinion was that to be mental is by definition to be present to consciousness, so that it sounded like a contradiction in terms to assert that an event might be both mental and altogether outside conscious experience. James was basically on the side of standard philosophical opinion.

In fact, readers of James's *The Principles of Psychology* (1890) understood him as denying altogether the existence of unconscious mental states. In Chapter VI, "The Mind-Stuff Theory," he seemed to mount a sustained and vigorous argument against the hypothesis that states of mind can be unconscious. He wrote that the alleged distinction *"between the unconscious and the conscious being of the mental state"* is really only "the sovereign means for believing what one likes in psychology, and of turning what might become a science into a tumbling-ground for whimsies" (p. 163). Why so? Because, he contended, a mental state, such as suffering a headache, *is* just what it feels like; its *esse est sentiri*. It makes no sense to suppose that a felt headache is different, either at the conscious or unconscious level, from what it definitely feels like. The hypothesis of unconscious mental states, however, implies that at the unconscious level a mental state, such as suffering a headache, might somehow be different from what it consciously feels like. Meaning by "feeling" any mental state whatever, James thought it quite certain that "the essence of feeling is to be felt, and as a psychic existent *feels,* so it must *be*" (p. 163).

Nevertheless, James was prepared to admit that there are at least two ways in which some mental states *can* escape consciousness, but whether or not this admission contradicted his view as just described, the view that the *esse* of mental states lies in their *sentiri,* is a matter of interpretation. Yet we must concede that mental states can occur quite "unconsciously"—for whatever reasons, we fail to notice or heed them; they sometimes happen without our registering them. Since they are ordinarily noticeable if one but makes the proper effort to heed their presence, they fall into what Freud called the "preconscious," or what both he and James called the "subconscious." They lie, so to speak, just below the threshold of consciousness and are rather easily recoverable, while the items in what Freud called "the unconscious" are not. For James (1890) felt experience is a rapidly moving "stream" of feelings, images, thoughts, etc., and consequently we cannot distinctly notice all of it as it flows by. For instance, our "insensibility to habitual noises, etc., whilst awake, proves that we can neglect to attend to that which we nevertheless feel" (p. 201).

To admit this example and a host of others may seem to admit that mental states can occur with their features undetected and thus may seem to violate the principle that it is the essence of mental states to *be* what they feel like, to have their *esse* reside in their *sentiri*. James, I think, was inclined to hedge on the issue. On the one hand, in *The Principles of Psychology,* he saw no way of avoiding the *esse est sentiri* principle; on the other hand, he was committed to the view that introspection is highly fallible, so that mental states, not unlike physical scenes and objects, *can* go ignored by us and remain largely, if not altogether, overlooked even as they are "there" to be witnessed by us. I believe that he was unworried by the threat of a contradiction in his theory on the grounds that even if a mental state is mainly ignored or is faultily introspected, it is still felt just a little bit, is very dimly or faintly apprehended, so that its *esse* is still preserved by a bare minimum of *sentiri.* A mental state, he seems to have held, can occur almost but not entirely outside consciousness. Whether this is satisfactory or not is an interesting question, but it is not among the ones I have set for us to consider in this discussion.

Besides mental states that can be called unconscious to the extent that we overlook them, there is, James thought, another class of states of mind that deserve to be categorized as unconscious. These are discovered in abnormal psychology and were widely reported in the latter part of the nineteenth century, notably in France. Charcot, Binet, and Janet were among the leading investigators in this area. Much attention was given to curious conditions such as "hysterical blindness," which, it seems, is not real blindness at all. James (1890) wrote about it as follows:

The eye of an hysteric which is totally blind when the other or seeing eye is shut, will do its share of vision perfectly well when *both* eyes are open together. But even where both eyes are semi-blind from hysterical disease, the method of automatic writing proves that their perceptions exist, only cut off from communication with the upper consciousness. M. Binet has found the hand of his patients unconsciously writing down words which their eyes were vainly endeavoring to "see," i.e., to bring to the upper consciousness. Their submerged consciousness was of course seeing them, or the hand could not have written as it did. Colors are similarly perceived by the sub-conscious

self, which the hysterically color-blind eyes cannot bring to the normal consciousness. Pricks, burns, and pinches on the anaesthetic skin, all unnoticed
by the upper [conscious] self, are recollected to have been suffered, and   -
complained of, as soon as the under [subconscious] self gets a chance to
express itself by the passage of the subject into hypnotic trance [p. 206].

The point is that abnormal psychology shows conclusively that one can
at a subconscious level somehow see, hear, sense things which one cannot
consciously be aware of. Hypnotism, automatic writing, and other devices
reveal this to be the case. One's conscious, waking self simply may not be
able to apprehend what, in some odd fashion, one is nevertheless seeing,
hearing, sensing, albeit not consciously. Hence, from the vantage point of
the conscious self, mental states do occur in the person, but remain unconscious. How should this be conceptualized and explained?

James (1890) followed Janet in suggesting that such cases are caused by
the fragmentation of the person's ordinary unity of consciousness, the
result being that while the (hysterical) seeing, say, of a pink garment remains outside the consciousness of the conscious (primary or waking) self
or person, it *is* part of the consciousness of a submerged (secondary or
subconscious) self or personality (p. 211). According to this explanation, the
mental state of seeing the pink garment, although unconscious to the primary or waking person, is conscious to a secondary or subconscious self
that is somehow connected with the primary self and its body. In short, the
explanation appeals to the concept of "multiple personalities" (that each of
us is potentially, and sometimes actually, more than a single consciousness
or personality) for explicating how an apparently unconscious mental state
can occur. The idea, again, is that the conscious you may be incapable of
being conscious of the mental state of seeing a pink garment, but, since
there is other evidence (hypnotism, automatic writing, etc.) indicating that
some part or aspect of you nevertheless does see it, the conclusion is that
your secondary, submerged, or subconscious self sees it, so that the occurrence is part of *its* consciousness.

This explanation was attractive to James because it conformed to the
principle of *esse est sentiri* as it applies to mental states: the multiple-person-
ality hypothesis insures a person-subject for every mental state, an experi-
enc*er* for anything seen, felt, heard, etc. A mental state of yours may escape
the conscious you, but, on this hypothesis, there is a secondary (possibly
tertiary) subconscious you which is conscious of that mental state, is aware
of it, is a conscious subject to it as object. So every mental state belongs to a
subject or self of some sort, James continued to hold, and, so far as the
unconscious is concerned, we may say of his view that nothing like an
impersonal unconscious exists. There is no realm of the unconscious that is
simply an impersonal "it." It is precisely here that he and Freud diverged on

the concept of the unconscious, as we will see shortly. And, given James's thesis that all mental states are in the consciousness of *someone* (perhaps a subconscious personality), we can understand how it could be taken to imply that all mental states are by nature *introspectible*.

In comparing Freud's concept of the unconscious with that of James, one comes across the interesting fact, as Wollheim makes us aware, that the concept played a casual, informal role in Freud's writings prior to the famous metapsychological paper "The Unconscious" in 1915 (Wollheim, 1971, p. 176). Accordingly, if one examines the various things said about the unconscious by Freud in his earlier works, one learns that in the 1912–15 period, and finally in his later publications, a single, consistent theory is hard to locate. But for my purposes here a recapitulation of the details of Freud's thinking at different periods in his career is unnecessary and we can proceed to the points in his theory that do concern us. The first point is contained in Freud's (1915) claim that psychoanalytic evidence indicates the existence of "latent (mental) processes as having characteristics and peculiarities which seem alien to us, or even incredible, and which run directly counter to the attributes of consciousness with which we are familiar. Thus we have grounds for modifying our inference about ourselves and saying that what is proved is not the existence of a second [submerged] consciousness in us, but the existence of psychical acts which lack consciousness" (p. 170).[1]

Freud explicitly rejected the view of Janet and James that if a mental state occurs but unconsciously for you, then it must be consciously noticed by a second or subconscious consciousness of yours. What were his reasons for rejecting that view? There were several, including the suspicion that the notion of subconscious subjects or selves being somehow laced into one's psychic constitution might be sheer nonsense, but the main one was that the kind of evidence assembled by psychoanalysis seemed to support the claim that there is a realm of unconscious mental states that, while controlling much of what occurs in both preconsciousness and consciousness, is quite unlike any of the mental states that feature either preconsciousness or consciousness. As Freud (1915) put it:

> The processes of the system *Ucs.* are *timeless;* i.e., they are not ordered temporally, are not altered by the passage of time; they have no reference to time at all. Reference to time is bound up once again with the work of the system *Cs.* [also system Pcs].
>
> The *Ucs.* processes pay just as little regard to *reality.* They are subject to the pleasure principle; their fate depends only on how strong they are and on whether they fulfill the demands of the pleasure-unpleasure regulation.

---

[1]On the issue of whether unconscious states require their own subjects of awareness, see also Freud (1909, pp. 25–26, and 1925, pp. 30–31)

> To sum up: *exemption from mutual contradiction, primary process* (mobility of cathexis), *timelessness,* and *replacement of external by psychic reality*—these are the characteristics which we may expect to find in processes belonging to the system *Ucs.* [p. 187].

It is not our concern to analyze Freud's contentions here, our interest being, rather, to note his grounds for concluding that there is a system of unconscious mental states that differ from conscious ones to such an extent that it is no longer plausible to suppose that the former can be understood or explained exclusively in terms of the latter. Hence, unlike James's, Freud's concept of the unconscious is impersonal, an "it," and its contents are not introspectible. But, even if we accept everything in Freud's view here, a question presents itself—If the states in the system of the unconscious differ so vastly from the mental states in the systems of pre-consciousness and consciousness, why continue to call the former ones "mental"? Well, since the contents of the Freudian unconscious are such items as beliefs, impulses, and especially ideas (with some uncertainty expressed about whether emotions are included), these, despite their special differences from conscious ideas, beliefs, impulses, are still ideas, beliefs, and impulses, and therefore do indeed deserve to be called "mental"; after all, they are among the things that "mental" commonly covers. If an idea or belief is not mental, then what is?

By insisting on the special capacity of psychoanalysis to bring *mental* events out of the unconscious into consciousness, thereby marking a reasonably sharp distinction between mental and nonmental or physiological events, Freud seemed to espouse traditional psychophysical dualism. Given the traditional linkage between mind-body dualism and the respect for introspection as an alleged method for observing mental events, one might assume that his system would maintain a role for introspection. Yet, some have asked, given Freud's view, how can one recognize a mental event that has emerged from the Ucs into consciousness to have theretofore resided in the unconscious? Is there any provision for something like introspective recognition that a mental state has made the transition from a previous latency in the Ucs? Any plausible answer here, I think, will be extremely complex and controversial, involving fine points of Freudian scholarship, and even then the conclusion may be tentative. The reliance by psychoanalysis on putatively scientific inference and diagnosis rather than on a ready acceptance of patient statements about themselves ("free association," note, is *not*, by virtue of its similarity to "reverie-talk," a clear example of what has been called "introspective reporting") appears to weaken respect for introspection.

Freud's own doubts about psychophysical dualism (and therefore about traditional introspectionism) became increasingly evident after Jones's biographical study of Freud in 1957. Theorists outside the inner circles of the psychoanalytic profession came to realize that perhaps Freud, having reiterated his conviction that biology might someday replace psychoanalysis, did not consider the mental-physiological distinction to be all that precious. The door seemed open for adopting a materialistic behavioristic program of conceiving so-called mental states in exclusively physiological and behavioral terms. Theoretically and philosophically, it looked as if we could proceed to redescribe ideas, beliefs, impulses, as bodily occurrences or physiological propensities of sorts. Since we acknowledge as a matter of course that all kinds of things of which we are unaware (unconscious) are constantly occurring in our bodies, we would have no difficulty in acknowledging that mental events, now conceived as being themselves bodily occurrences, also can happen without our being conscious of them. If so, in the Freudian scheme, it may appear that introspection is scarcely relevant to the concept of the unconscious. And this would represent a major difference between Freud's and James's view.[2]

It might even appear that, if a theory such as Freud's were given a materialistic/behavioristic formulation, introspection would then and there be eliminated as wholly irrelevant. It would appear this way to anyone believing that introspection occurs only if mental events in a psychophysical duality are the objects of introspection. But that the elimination of introspection does not follow from the adoption of a materialistic metaphysics is clearly exhibited, if any proof is needed on this score, by the position defended, for instance, by Skinner (1976):

> The position can be stated as follows: what is felt or introspectively observed is not some nonphysical world of consciousness, mind, or mental life but the observer's own body. . . . An organism behaves as it does because of its current structure, but most of that is out of reach of introspection. At the moment we must content ourselves . . . with a person's genetic and environmental histories. What are introspectively observed are certain collateral products of those histories [pp. 18–19].

How useful introspection might be in a materialistic/behavioristic system is certainly questionable, but that it could play a role of some kind is assured, it would seem, if one agrees with Skinner. And that its having a function is not incompatible with materialism, I agree, is indeed the case. There is every reason, including what was mentioned above, for assuming that Freud would also agree. Although some interpretive difficulties might complicate this assertion, I think that James, too, would agree. In asserting

---

[2]For a recent comparison (albeit very brief) of James and Freud, and for a valuable discussion of related issues, including that of introspection, see Bettelheim's (1984, p. 19ff.).

this, of course, we must remember that James's arch-enemy was materialism, so nothing would have made him more discomfited than being forced
into a materialistic metaphysics. Nevertheless in the last decade of his life,
years after *The Principles of Psychology*, he argued vigorously for an alternative to psychophysical dualism, for a system that he called "radical empiri-
cism." In the course of that argument he claimed that the states
distinguished under the labels "mental" and "physical" are really more alike
than different. Furthermore, he always confessed that as far as he was
concerned neither perception nor introspection turned up anything except
physical objects and events. How he was able to reconcile this with his
antimaterialism is an elaborate story that does not require recounting here.
The point to be registered is that like Freud and Skinner, he would have had
no reason for concluding that merely because one espouses material-
ism/behaviorism one must therefore reject introspection. Accordingly, in
seeking next to develop my own contentions about introspection and the
unconscious, I will with clear conscience avoid debates about the merits or
demerits of psychophysical dualism. It will not be at issue in what follows.

CONCEPTS OF INTROSPECTION

If one surveys the ways "introspection" and is cognates are used, one soon
discovers that there are numerous concepts of introspection; not surprisingly, then, the word "introspection" shows up as connoting not one
but many notions. For a sample, consider: it is used to mean attending,
remembering, phantasizing, meditating, intuiting, free-associating, self-reporting, thinking about oneself, being aware of being aware of something,
being set to notice something, immediately retrospecting some occurrence,
and mentally observing something. Philosophical and psychological literature is of course replete with references to introspection, but seldom do the
authors trouble to clarify the idea with the care that they typically devote
to their other technical concepts. Still, what tends to predominate the
literature is the use of "introspection" (and its cognates) to mean what the
modern tradition stemming from Locke has mainly meant by it, namely, a
form of *observation*.

This is what we find in James (1890), again cryptically expressed with
little or no elaboration. *"Introspective Observation is what we have to rely on first
and foremost and always.* The word introspection need hardly be defined—it
means, of course, the looking into our own minds and reporting what we
there discover. *Everyone agrees that we there discover states of consciousness* (p.
185). It is the same with Skinner, introspection being taken by him as a
mode of observation. "To agree that what one feels or introspectively
observes are conditions of one's own body is a step in the right direction. It

is a step toward an analysis both of seeing and of seeing that one sees in purely physical terms" (Skinner, 1976, p. 237). Both Skinner and James follow a lengthy tradition of construing introspection as a kind of "inner perception," a tradition widely criticized in our times, we may mention here, noticeably by such thinkers as Hebb and Ryle. Freud, too, in his occasional references to introspection, seems to have had a form of *observation* in mind; this is shown by the following passage, which I quote sheerly for illustrating that point, leaving the tantalizing question of what more he meant by it for specialists to decipher.

> The complaints made by paranoics also show that at bottom the self-crit-icism of conscience coincides with the self-observation on which it is based. Thus the activity of the mind which has taken over the function of cons-cience has also placed itself at the service of internal research which furnishes philosophy with the material for its intellectual operations. This may have some bearing on the characteristic tendency of paranoics to construct spec-ulative systems.
>
> It will certainly be of importance to us if evidence of the activity of this critically observing agency—which becomes heightened into conscience and philosophic introspection. . . . Silberer has thus demonstrated the part played by observation—in the sense of the paranoic's delusions of being watched—in dream, the formation of dreams. This part is not a constant one. Probably the reason why I overlooked it is because it does not play any great part in my own dreams; in persons who are gifted philosophically and accustomed to introspection it may become very evident. [Freud, 1914, pp. 96–97].

Whatever the relation might be that Freud saw between philosophy and introspection (possibly it was something like that which Wittgenstein saw when he criticized introspectionist tendencies in traditional epistemology and metaphysics) he quite evidently associated "introspection" with "self-*observation*." And, we may add, since the Freudian system of the Ucs lies outside the reach of direct observation of any kind, it is obviously not an introspectible area. On the other hand, since the Ucs, with its special contents, is only arrived at inferentially with the help of psychoanalytic hypotheses, the possibility remains that introspection-as-observation plays a role in the Freudian scheme in supplying important clues or data from which inferences and diagnoses about a person's unconscious may be made.

I want now to develop the thesis that the most important sense of "introspection," the sense in which the concept is most valuable, is *not* its meaning of some form of observation but something else instead, that something else to be discussed shortly. I will argue that, whether the view be Freud's, James's, Skinner's, or anyone else's, whether the main concept before us is that of the unconscious or something else, what will in all likelihood be relevant is a notion of introspection that departs from the traditional one of introspection-as-observation. For this argument, it will be helpful if we set the discussion in the context of the question: Do we have introspective evidence for something called the unconscious?

Some authorities, such as Bruno Bettelheim (1984), have an immediate answer:

> Like the father of American psychology, William James, Freud based his work mainly on introspection—his own and that of his patients. *Introspection is what psychoanalysis is all about.* Although Freud is often quoted today in introductory psychology texts—more often, in fact, than any other writer on psychology—his writings have only superficially influenced the work of the academic psychologists who quote him. Psychological research and teaching in American universities are either behaviorally, cognitively, or physiologically oriented and concentrate almost exclusively on what can be measured or observed from the outside; introspection plays no part. American psychology has become all analysis—to the complete neglect of the psyche, or soul [p. 19].

Bettelheim may or may not be right about the state of American psychology, but two questions can be raised about his claim that introspection is what psychoanalysis is all about—What does he mean by "introspection"? and, In his sense of the word, is his claim correct? Like almost every other author who employs the word, Bettelheim does not pause to clarify it. But perhaps the clue to his meaning lies in his above remark that, unlike Freudian psychoanalysis, contemporary American psychology only observes from the outside, thus implying that Freudian introspection is "observation from the inside." To avoid quibbling, I think Bettelheim is doubtlessly right in claiming that, compared to behavioristic procedures, psychoanalysis relies on what *loosely* can be called "inner observation," *if* this means such things as free-associating, self-reporting, self-diagnoses, deliberate recalling of one's past, and so on. Further, if such things are collected under the label of "introspective evidence," then there is, according to Freud and others, definite introspective evidence for psychoanalytic hypotheses, including that of the system Ucs. It is surely not required that one be able to introspect, in the sense of directly observing the contents of the Ucs, or observing such contents making the transition from the Ucs into the Cs, in order to give the concept of the Ucs scientific credibility. It is the adequacy of the theory that is at stake in debates about the scientific value of the Ucs, not the question of whether or not the Ucs is introspectible. Theories in physics do not falter because protons, say, are not directly observable, but rather because of some inadequacy in their structure of explanation and prediction.

However, if we look more closely at the concept of introspection-as-observation and use terms such as "inner observation" or "inner perception" less loosely, I think that we can begin to share the doubts that have been expressed by Hebb, Ryle, and others about introspection so conceived. Those doubts, if sound, would undermine the claim that the Freudian Ucs is supported by introspection as a special form of observation; they would go to show that the kinds of subjective data (free association, dreams, phantasies, etc.) which are taken as evidence for certain alleged contents of the Ucs do not (at least not typically) involve the subjects or patients in literally observing anything whatever. To make the point, we must first draw a distinction, a distinction between *preintrospective awareness (consciousness)* and introspection-as-observation.

In his picturesque way, James (1890) helps us to see the point of the distinction to be drawn. "If to *have* feelings or thoughts in their immediacy were enough, babies in the cradle would be psychologists, and infallible ones. But the psychologist must not only *have* his mental states in their absolute veritableness, he must report them and write about them, name them, classify and compare them and trace their relations to other things" (p. 189). It is not sufficient for the psychologist, in other words, simply to have a tingling feeling or, we may say, to have a preintrospective awareness, or mere feltness, of the feeling; the psychologist must observe it, study it, classify it, and report it. The whole point of introducing the concept of introspection, if one follows James and traditional psychology, is to get us to recognize a secondary awareness (introspective awareness) that is superimposed upon the preintrospective awareness of the tingling feeling. Initially, one simply has the feeling, and then one can be said to *introspect* it when one subjects the already existent awareness of the feeling to a secondary, studied awareness of the experience. When one adds an "observational" awareness to the already existent preintrospective awareness of the feeling, then one does something more than merely have the feeling, and that something more is what James and other have meant by introspection. Suppose you say you have a tingling feeling, but your assertion is challenged. You are asked how you know or can be certain. The introspective psychologist will reply, "It is by *introspection* that I know that I have a tingling feeling." He claims that he checked his preintrospective awareness of the feeling by a secondary, additional act of awareness or inner observation, and this he calls introspection.

It is this concept of introspection that has dominated psychology and its philosophy. Besides James's, such names as Wundt and Titchener are associated with the conviction that a process of "inner observation" or "internal perception" is the unique method by which psychology obtains its information and by which an individual acquires knowledge about his own mental and inner states. The subsequent demise of introspective psychology and its replacement by animal and behavior-oriented research are in themselves reflections of the fact that all was not well with the traditional claims made for introspection-as-observation. The reports of investigators into the details of mental life often conflicted, and what was offered as introspective information too often seemed unexciting, if not downright dull. Like Bettelheim, I believe that the behavioristic and physiological emphases in psychology's reaction against the earlier period of introspectionism, and their tendency to produce similar emphases in contemporary philosophy of mind, have been excessive. But we obviously cannot ignore the fact that introspective psychology is still mainly out of fashion; and I want to suggest why this will be permanently the case. My suggestion here, I believe, is commonly unnoticed, with the result that the typically unelaborated references to introspection offered by contemporary philosophers and psychologists are even further confounding.

I suggest that the reason behind the decline of introspection-as-observation in professional psychology is simply this: while, admittedly, a form of introspective awareness can occur—conceived as a secondary awareness superimposed or trained upon some preintrospective awareness (e.g., an awareness of an already existent awareness of a tingling feeling)—it normally adds little or nothing to what is already contained in the preintrospective consciousness. For example, suppose that a severe pain suddenly fills my (preintrospective) awareness; suppose also that I can superimpose upon it a secondary, or introspective awareness; that I can, as it were, study or observe my inner state of pain and its built-in preintrospective awareness (the pain, after all, occurs as something I am aware of *before* trying to introspect it); I claim that little more is obtained from the secondary, introspective awareness, than is already included in the preintrospective awareness of the pain. I initially feel the pain, and, deferring to what my own introspective efforts disclose—and what I believe yours will also disclose—I suggest that paying careful attention to, or introspectively studying, that experience—that is, training a secondary awareness on that experience—leads to little more than a heightened or focused consciousness of what the pain feels like. I do not want to deny that some new details *might* be disclosed to such a heightened consciousness, but normally, I claim, they are not. Your introspective efforts will show, according to my experience, that even when you manage the secondary or introspective awareness of the pain of which you are already (preintrospectively) aware, you rarely learn anything new about your experience of the pain; it is less a new cognition of the pain than it is a reexperience of the pain. It is more akin to noticing the very same thing all over again, but without anything new or additional being introduced.

If my suggestion here is correct, then the traditional notion of introspection-as-observation quite obviously appears in trouble. This is the case because the traditional notion assumed that introspection is a form of (inner) perception by means of which discoveries are made, and, if my own introspective efforts are to be trusted, such hoped-for discoveries tend not to occur, whether the setting be a psychology lab, an analyst's couch, or a quiet corner at home. My claim is that introspection, even when it is achieved as a mode of awareness that leads us to call it a form of observation or perception, is not really comparable, as is assumed, to external sense-perception. Careful use of one's eyes and ears does, of course, produce discoveries. Studied observation of objects around us and in the laboratory does, of course, yield new information. But the ability to superimpose a secondary awareness on an experience which is already in place and which has its own primary or preintrospective awareness, rarely (if ever) produces anything over and above what is already present to the primary, or initial, awareness. I am prepared to concede that on rare occasions there may be certain exceptions to my generalization here, but I spare myself the task of speculating further about their character on the grounds that none of the things that I have been able to envisage as likely specimens are crucial for the concept of the unconscious. In short, I have found no reason for supposing that introspection-as-observation succeeds, even on rare occasions, in discovering something or other that goes to establish the existence or the nature of an item in the unconscious.

It follows also that introspection-as-observation is irrelevant for establishing any of the distinctive contentions made by James or Freud about the nature of the unconscious, or for deciding whether James's idea that the unconscious must always be personal is, or is not, preferable to Freud's doctrine that the Ucs constitutes an impersonal system. I may say in addition—although some might challenge me on this in ways that would demand an additional essay on my part—that in *none* of the important senses of "introspection," in senses other than that of "observation," does it seem to me that distinctive theories of the unconscious, be they James's, Freud's, Jung's, or anyone else's, ultimately hinge on what introspection supposedly discloses. I note this now to safeguard against a possible misunderstanding ahead, because I intend next to sketch a concept of introspection, other than that of observation, that does impress me as being indeed relevant to how we sometimes think about the unconscious. If I am right, this concept of introspection must be included in an account of what can *cause* us *in some contexts* to infer the existence of an unconscious of sorts. Yet, even if I am right in this and in what follows, I do not imply thereby that it conclusively affects such questions as whether the Freudian theory of the Ucs is mainly adequate, whether the Jamesian theory of subconscious subjects of consciousness is mainly adequate, and so on. To repeat, such questions are eventually answered by complex theoretical considerations that reduce introspection, in any of its usual senses, to a datum to be explained, instead of being a part of the explanation that incorporates a special concept of the unconscious.

If "introspection" is allowed to cover such diverse phenomena as phantasizing, reports of dreams, self-reports of other kinds of experiences, deliberate recollectings, and so on, then, of course, introspection will certainly be heralded as a supplier of subjective data that theories of the unconscious undertake to explain. Indeed, it will be claimed that it supplies the kinds of data which to an extent constitute "evidence" for such theories. And no one will want to quarrel, for example, with Bettelheim's assertion that Freudian psychology, with its theory of the Ucs, collected self-reports of dreams, phantasies, etc., as being evidence for itself; in this respect, introspection is indubitably relevant to the Freudian Ucs. However, when debates about the adequacy of Freud's or other theories are staged, or when nagging queries in the philosophy of science about the relation between theories of the unconscious and their alleged evidence are raised, then, whatever may have been the initial appeal to so-called introspective evidence, such alleged evidence shrinks into the background as soon as the structure and details of the Freudian Ucs are challenged. All sorts of alternative theories of the Ucs are argued to be consistent with the same set of subjective or introspective data, or, as in the case of behaviorists like Skinner, those same data are argued to be consistent with the denial of the Ucs altogether. Accordingly, on the one hand, introspection-as-self-reporting is clearly relevant to the concept of the unconscious, insofar as theories of the unconscious are founded in part upon it, while, on the other hand, such introspection tends to become increasingly irrelevant once the credentials of those theories are put to the challenge. I think the recent history of philosophical and psychological altercations about theories of the unconscious amply verifies this contention of mine.

If this be so, then trying to assess the merits of a theory about the unconscious will take our eyes off the concept of introspection and into other directions; but I want to keep the focus on introspection, and thus it is not part of our job here to evaluate Jamesian, Freudian, or other notions of the unconscious. Having just agreed that introspection in all its varieties of self-reporting is unquestionably relevant to theories of the unconscious, through being an important part of the data that initially lead theorists to infer the existence of an unconscious of sorts, I now want to isolate a special sense of "introspection," which connects interestingly with the idea of the unconscious. It also connects interestingly with our previous remarks about the tendency of introspection-as-observation to fail in its mission of discovery.

The special concept of introspection to which I wish to call attention is what can be called "self-dialogue." It is sometimes referred to as "internal monologue," "inner conversation," "reflection," "experiment in the imagination," and by other such labels. Once introduced, this notion of introspection invites a virtually endless parade of interpretation, commentary, and elaboration of detail. We could notice its significance for Jung, or its role in psychoanalytic and other forms of therapy, or its function in certain types of fiction, as well as its contribution to the management of our daily lives. My concern with introspection-as-self-dialogue is not as it appears in any or all of its modes, but only when it has the acquisition of improved self-understanding or self-knowledge as its goal and incentive. More particularly, my concern is with the kind of self-dialogue that one executes in the process of trying to reach a certain conclusion about oneself on the basis of what one knows and believes about oneself.

Suppose that John is preoccupied with such questions as "Do I really love Sophie?" "Is my anxiety due to my mother's rejection of me?," and "Was my dream the expression of sexual conflict?" He begins a complex and erratic dialogue with himself (i.e., he becomes introspective) in search of answers; it is a process wherein what he consults for evidence is exclusively what he himself already possesses, namely, his own dreams and reveries, his own memories, his own feelings and impulses, his own beliefs, and his own fund of knowledge about himself. The process is motivated by John's desire to obtain, by means of all this, answers as confident as possible to the questions with which he began. The process remains in motion so long as its stages reinforce that initial desire; a certain kind of dynamics must characterize the process and, as it were, "fuel" the process, else it becomes dull and tedious, causing John to terminate it from boredom or fatigue. Psychology would give its soul to learn the nature of that dynamics, so my own speculations here must be properly modest and restricted.

There is general agreement, I believe, that for the process of introspection-as-self-dialogue to sustain itself in John's case, it must provide him with some sense of direction, of progress or the promise of such, of the indication of some light at the end of the tunnel, or of the sought-for answers being within reach. Perhaps we can also assume a general agreement on the claim that among the many factors responsible for sustaining the process, there will be the states of mind which are continually generated by the succession of questions and answers that John proposes to himself. We have some basis for inferring, that is, that the changes in mental (and other) states, which John produces in himself through pursuing leading questions addressed to himself, will, depending upon their particular properties, tend to either sustain or terminate the introspective process. The way in which the putting of a question to oneself can produce an alteration in one's mental (and other) states—that change then producing still another, so that a dynamic, serial set of changes in one's mental (and other) states is generated—should not be under-appreciated.

Indeed, I think we ought to apply the word "remarkable" to this phenomenon, to the fact that our mental and bodily states are so responsive to the influences of a self-dialogue. It is quite remarkable that our mind/body complexes are so readily modifiable by nothing more than addressing a query to oneself. It is even more remarkable, as I want now to suggest, that the changes in one's mental/bodily states that are successively produced by introspection-as-self-dialogue can function in the service of at least two important achievements. The first such achievement (only on occasion, of course) is to generate, along with other causes, the interest that is required psychologically to "fuel" the process, to keep it going. It is only sensible to suppose that the momentum of the introspective process is due in some measure to the changes in mental/bodily states that the initial questioning sets in motion. I believe that those internal changes must contribute to the sense of direction, of progress, of the promise that the sought-for-answers are within reach, without which John and the rest of us would halt the introspection out of boredom, futility, or fatigue.

The second achievement that the change in mental/bodily states can help to secure is the all-important one of supplying the basis for a confident answer to the question that originally triggered the introspective process. Whatever may be the underlying explanation, we seem to be presented at the descriptive level anyway with the undeniable fact that there are occasions when the process "pays off"; on such occasions, the successive changes in John's mental/bodily states that are generated by the process of self-dialogue converge upon that final change in consciousness which gets expressed by something like "No, I don't really love Sophie," "Yes, my anxiety is due to my mother's rejection of me," "Yes, my dream was the expression of sexual conflict." The point is that the introspective process is (partially) responsible for the delivery of the answer, although whether the answer thus generated is either true or even highly plausible, is, of course, another question. Surely, we must all concur that, even though we should learn (what is clearly dubious) that introspection-as-self-dialogue is surprisingly reliable in generating correct answers, the process is so obviously fallible that no one would be tempted to declare the generated answers to be automatically correct ones. Again, the point is that on many occasions John comes upon the sought-for answer, whether correct or not, to the question that set the introspective process in motion. It is the "sought-for" answer insofar as it tends to satisfy his confidence. Whether correct or not, at the conclusion of the process he has what he did not have at the outset— an answer that he accepts confidently.

There is another component in this introspective process that, I must believe, is inherently connected with the features of the process as just now sketched, another component that is intimately related to the (mostly unknown) dynamics of the process. This is the feature that leads John to say, "No, I don't really love Sophie—and I haven't all along, and I've really known it all along, but I wasn't prepared to admit it to myself." And it is the feature that leads him to say, "I had repressed my lack of love for Sophie into my unconscious," or, "I have at last dredged out of my unconscious into the full glare of consciousness the realization that I do not love Sophie." In other words, this feature causes John to assert, "I have at last *discovered* what has been lurking in my unconscious all this time." I do not pretend to know *how* this feature occurs. I do not understand how this "sense of discovery" arises. I can only suppose that there is something in its relations to the other features of the process, something in the dynamics of such introspective self-dialogue, that is responsible for its occurrence. But what does seem to me quite certain is that it will not do merely to invoke "association" as a mental or cerebral process for explaining it. Neither traditional associationism nor Freudian free association, I believe, can by themselves explain what in the end only the entire dynamics of the introspective process can elucidate.

The preceding is relevant to discussions of Freudian theory of the unconscious. In the Freudian view, a process of "working through" or of sustained self-analysis (with professional assistance ordinarily required) is demanded, and our concept here of introspection-as-self-dialogue corresponds to that. Moreover, Freud stressed "ideas" as being the materials that are repressed into the unconscious, and our example of John enables us to assert that the repressed idea, in his case, is the judgment that he does not really love Sophie. Finally, although this interpretation of the Freudian view may not be wholly uncontroversial, it does seem that the view implies that at some point in the therapeutic process, if a "cure" is to be achieved, the patient must *seem to discover,* and feel the force of the (alleged) discovery, that what has been lodged in the unconscious has now been "brought back again into conscious mental activity" (Freud, 1909, p. 27). The importance, then, that we attached earlier to the conclusion that introspection-as-observation tends to fail as even *seeming* discovery, and that we now attach to the conclusion that introspection-as-self-dialogue does at least produce the sense of discovery or the confident belief that discovery has been achieved, seems to accord with the last feature of the Freudian theory mentioned earlier. A case has been made for the claim that introspection-as-self-dialogue is indeed relevant for the concept of the unconscious in a way that introspection-as-observation is not.

But, again, my effort here has not been directed towards determining whether there is an unconscious, or what, if it exists, it might be like. I reiterate my conviction that to try to determine those matters would take the focus off introspection and place it upon other and more recondite considerations. What I have endeavored to show in this paper is that introspection-as-self-dialogue is relevant to the concept of the unconscious in ways that do not apply to introspection-as-observation, which, recall, is the dominant notion in classical theories of introspection. The introspective process of self-dialogue, by containing the features that we have just recited, can strongly influence a belief in some type of unconscious. Engaging in such a process can lead us to infer the existence of an unconscious realm in which our beliefs and "ideas" have lurked all along, and we can come to believe that we sometimes "discover" ideas and beliefs that we have held for a long time, but somehow outside consciousness. We may describe this sense of discovery as "bringing from the unconscious certain mental items at last into the full light of consciousness." Introspection-as-self-dialogue, I have argued, *is* relevant to this sort of description insofar as it can lead us to adopt such descriptions, whereas introspection as simple self-reporting or as a supposed form of observation is mostly irrelevant in this respect. Yet, while introspection-as-self-dialogue helps to vivify and utilize locutions like "bringing mental contents into consciousness from out of the unconscious," it remains quite helpless before the task of deciding whether such locutions are metaphors to be taken literally.

REFERENCES

Bettelheim, B. (1984), *Freud and Man's Soul*. New York: Vintage.
Binet, A. (1886), *La Psychologie du raisonnement: Recherches expérimentales par l'hypnotisme*. Paris: Alcan.
Charcot, J. M. (1890), *Deuvres complètes de J. M. Charcot*, IX. Paris: Aux bureaux du Progrès Médical.
Freud, S. (1909), Five lectures on psycho-analysis. *Standard Edition*, 11:1–55. London: Hogarth Press, 1957
———— (1914), On Narcissism: An introduction. *Standard Edition*, 14:117–140. London: Hogarth Press, 1959.
———— (1915), The unconscious. *Standard Edition*, 14:166–204. London: Hogarth Press, 1957.
———— (1925), An autobiographical study. *Standard Edition*, 20:7–74. London: Hogarth Press, 1957.
Hebb, D. O. (1949), *The Organization of Behavior*. New York: Wiley.
James, W. (1890), *The Principles of Psychology*. New York: Dover, 1950.
Janet, P. (1889), *L'Automatisme psychologique: Essai de psychologie expérimentale sur les formes inférieures de l'activité humaine*. Paris: Alcan.
Jones, E. (1953–57), *Sigmund Freud; Life and Work*. 3 vols. New York: Basic Books.
Jung, C. G., (1963), *Memories, Dreams, Reflections*. Aniela Jaffe, ed. New York: Pantheon.
Oberndorf, C. (1944), *The Psychiatric Novels of Oliver Wendell Holmes*. New York: Columbia University Press.
Ryle, G. (1949), *The Concept of Mind*. New York: Barnes and Noble.
Skinner, B. F. (1976), *About Behaviorism*. New York: Vintage.
Titchener, E. B. (1909), *Lectures on the Experimental Psychology of the Thought-Processes*. New York: Macmillan.
Wollheim, R. (1971), *Sigmund Freud*. New York: Viking Press.
Wundt, W. (1880), *Grundzüge der Physiologischen Psychologie*. 2 vols. Leipzig: W.Englemann.

6 Emotions and the Self

Raphael Stern

I wish to present in detail a theory of the emotions. This theory, though deriving from many sources, is, on the whole, my own. A set of research groups contributed some of the ideas found in this essay; my essay culminates in a research program. This program is the end product of my work with The Association for Philosophy of Science, Psychotherapy and Ethics (PSPE).

In particular, my initial work on the emotions was done while I was a participant in a seminar on the emotions. (The seminar was sponsored by PSPE). Oddly enough, during this seminar though considerable information and competing theories about the emotions surfaced, very little was said about the self and its ties to the emotions. (I had also worked for a considerable time almost exclusively on the emotions without venturing into theories of the self.) This struck me later as odd, for investigations into one concept, the emotions, would have thrown considerable light on the other concept, the self. It was only later that I began to *see* some of the connections, but there was, almost from the beginning, evidence that the connections were there. How one worked on the concept of the self would be a function of how closely linked one thought the two concepts were: if one did not think them linked one would pursue investigations into the concept of the self quite independently of other concepts. Once I saw that they were linked, I determined that all my research on the emotions would be pursued jointly with research on the self.

While formulating my view of the emotions I began, early in the history of the group, to study interventions and their ties to the emotions. I began from the first to realize that the ties were considerable, but at that stage they remained hazy; for in spite of the fact that interventions are often explained by referring to aims and moods (emotions), it was not clear just what the logic of the relation was between interventions and emotions. It seemed plain to me that if one could find a clue to the logic of this relation, the theory I wished to develop would be very well served.

At about this time, another member of the group—K. D. Irani—began, in conversations and talks to the group, to emphasize notions that promised to help illuminate the logic of the relation between emotions and interventions.

Until then the logical tie between these two concepts had been unclear; Irani's hints suggested a way to define the relevant logic better. Irani suggested the following: When we decide whether an explanation is suitable or the right one for an episode, we do so in a variety of ways, one of the more important being that we ask whether using this explanation for this episode satisfies criteria of rationality.

I can't say I agree entirely with Irani, but he does provide a brilliant analysis of explanation and an important clue that I was quick to use. Emotions are highly cognitive, value-bearing items that are best viewed as fitting and shaping interventions to one another. Since "fitting" and "shaping" are the tasks of rationality, the emotions may be viewed as "agents" of rationality. More technically we shall say that a theory of the emotions and a theory of intervention are each B-subtheories of a theory of rationality. This has a number of implications.

(i)   This is a notion of rationality different from the classical one, which holds that emotions are irrational and what is rational conforms to the principles of logic. In this case, logic as rational is a special case of the sort of rationality I am talking about. There is, however, no suitable account of rationality available now. Such an account remains to be developed.

(ii)   The B-subtheory relation demands the following. If X is B-subtheory of Y, then Y defines the logics needed in X; X is not a subset of Y.

With these three notions—rationality, intervention, and emotion—with these three theories and their relations, and with the sense that one cannot theorize about one concept without implicating the others, we have a much stronger theory than we had before. Our theory, TH, is a theory of rationality with two subtheories. We must now study other ways to advance our theory.

NEUROPHYSIOLOGY AND NEUROPHARMACOLOGY

It is useful at this point to return to the group. After a good deal of discussion of the emotions, the group invited neurophysiologists and neuropharmacologists to speak. It was important to see whether they had any firm theory of the emotions and, if not, what they could contribute to our work. If one begins with a psychological account of the emotions and then entertains a neurophysiological one as well, one faces the difficulty of how to tie one theory to the other. To look at this somewhat differently: when we invite theorists to give a neurophysiological account of the emotions, assuming we already have a psychological account, then we are in effect asking just what a neurophysiological account does or adds vis-à-vis the other account. And how does the first theory, the psychological one, behave with regard to the other? It is plain that our whole enterprise might founder at this juncture on a problem that has beset theorists since Descartes—the logic of the relation between accounts of mind and accounts of body. Ours is a variation on that old problem. In spite of this, it turns out that the scientists made rather substantial contributions—not theories but suggestions—that provided me with a way of coping with a number of theoretical problems. These are: (a) What is the logic of the tie between psychological and neurophysiological accounts of the emotions? (b) What is the formal apparatus that we ought to use in developing the theory TH? Two sets of findings emerged from the scientists:

(i)   From the neurophysiologists we learned that there was no neurophysiological account of the emotions available at this time. However, they were sanguine that accounts would be forthcoming and the members of the group in turn were prepared to include some such account in our respective theories. I, in particular, was prepared to include such an account, when a reputable one surfaced, in my theory. A number of purported resolutions of the logical relation between mind and body have been tried, including identity theories, functionalist theories, dualist theories, and the like. I found, however, that we had a solution at hand. We could turn to the theory TH and look for our solution there: it already contains the right concepts, just those we need. Thus, given that we define a B-subtheory over the theories of TH and given that we have a theory of rationality, we can allow that a physiological account of an episode X will *amplify* a psychological one. Amplification, then, is the relation we seek. The logic of the relation is:

(1)   If X amplifies Y then X adjusts the fits of all subtheories of Y to one another. (2)   Let T be the set of all sentences in Y. Let T' be an extension of T and let T' also contain all of the consequences of sentences of Y. Then if X amplifies Y, X defines a set of functions on subsets of T' to members of Q, with Q a set of questions about the domain of Y. (3)   If X amplifies Y, then X shapes Y so that Y fits the domain better.

(ii)   Neuropharmacologists have accumulated a great deal of clinical evidence but have no theory. Nonetheless, they propose tentative hypotheses that provide the wherewithal for interesting formulations about the emotions. Though the hypotheses are weak, they are suggestive and may guide us to the kind of philosophical and technical contributions we can make to the theory. These contributions enlarge the theory TH.

The following two ideas emerged from the discussions with the neuropharmacologists:

(i) Neuropharmacologists will define an equivalence relation E over two emotions, saying, for example, that Anger E Depression under the following conditions: (a) A patient W is being treated for depression with drug X and X relieves the depression. (b) On occasion, under just those conditions when W should be depressed, we find he is not depressed but angry and when drug X is administered it relieves the anger.

According to the neuropharmacologist, there are a number of cases of this sort, where a drug used to treat one mood acts for another in similar circumstances. From this line of reasoning it follows that a number of moods are equivalent to one another. If this works we can expect to define a number of equivalence classes over the emotions. We could, for example, say that Anger E Depression, and Hostility E Depression, so that anger, depression, and hostility are in the same equivalence class; we could also say that Obsessiveness E Fear, and if neither obsessiveness nor fear is equivalent to anger, depression, or hostility, then fear would be in a different equivalence class from anger. By proceeding in this way we define a number of relations, hence structures, on the emotions. We can imagine devising techniques for introducing even more structure. (This is what a good theory must do.) We might, for example, study the time it takes for a drug to relieve a condition, and then we might find that all of the conditions in one equivalence class are relieved quicker than those in another class. We could then label the classes accordingly, designating the class whose members are relieved fastest by "1" and other classes by "2," "3," and so on. That is, we develop procedures for introducing structure, and we find that the equivalence classes of emotions begin to have the structure of the natural numbers.

(ii) There are still other ways of introducing structure on the emotions. We found, for example, that the neuropharmacologist defines another interesting relation over the emotions—he claims that emotions frequently co-occur. For example, anger is almost always found with depression, and obsessiveness is frequently found with anger.

If we find, as we seem to have done, that research has introduced a set of relations over the emotions—co-occurrence and equivalence relations—then this in a way becomes our data. We are obliged to study the set of relations that neuropharmacologists define over emotions and ask ourselves what this means in terms of the sort of technical apparatus we might feel obliged to adopt for a theory of the emotions. When structure is emphasized to this extent, there may be good reason to study the emotions formally by using topology.

By joining, theoretically, the emotions, rationality, the self, interventions and a formal apparatus, we have assembled a complex theoretical account. There is still more to do before the group's results and my own work lead to the final stages of this program. In what follows we should begin to study in more depth the basic concepts introduced: intervention, emotion, and rationality. We should, as well, attempt to provide an account of the self. In so doing we find ourselves experimenting with a number of different concepts and strategies.

INTERVENTION

We need an account of interventions to facilitate an account of the self and of the emotions. To obtain such an account we need to introduce a few technical terms axiomatically: we will briefly characterize person and self. As our theory grows, the two notions will become clearer and clearer. At this point we intend to lay down a set of axioms to begin the process of clarification.

(i)   A person has a self. (We might have said a person owns a self, but this would be appropriate to a different theory.)

(ii)   A self belongs to a person.

(iii)   There are four major characteristics of the self: the self has bounds; the self is unified; the self has themes by which it lives; the self exhibits self-consciousness. (These four features all need to be better defined; it is the task of the theory to do so; as we enrich the theory our task proves easier.)

(iv)   Persons exhibit cognitive skills such as language use; persons intervene in the lives of other persons; persons are rational (this is not to be understood as being logical or conforming to logical principles; I have a different sense of "rational" in mind); persons have rights; person make claims on other persons.

We shall, in what follows, need to make sense of a good deal of this, and to do so we shall need a very rich theory indeed. We should, for example, suggest how it is that persons have rights.

Given these preliminaries, we should go on to study intervention in more detail.

Central to any account of persons, the self and the emotions is that persons intervene in one another's lives. A condition for understanding interventions and their importance to the self is to understand the relation of the emotions to interventions. When we say that persons intervene in one another's lives, we mean that they restrain one another, arrest miscreants, upbraid those who transgress social norms, instruct one another in the use of language, teach one another new sports activities, sell things to one another, invade corporate territory, exchange stock, attend class quietly, picket, kill one another, strike, jail one another, and go to war with one another. They produce food for others, refuse or give loans, criticize plays, write plays, paint pictures, and so on almost ad infinitum.

Interventions are systematic. They consist of complex acts or sets of complex acts; interventions themselves usually obtain within systems of interventions, and more often than not systems of intervention are sub-systems within still larger intervention systems. Interventions are complex, fraught with difficulty and in need of constant monitoring and adjustment. They may be well-or poorly designed.

Let's see if we can make technical sense of some of the terms just introduced and see where this leads us, theoretically speaking.

A system of interventions is a set of interventions over which we define a set of relations. Systems can be part of larger systems of interventions. In this sense interventions rarely appear alone. Persons and only persons intervene. Each person has the task of managing his or her interventions and this at least means relating one system of interventions to another.

Consider, for example, the case of a father and child. In setting this out, I bracket and label different intervention systems. The first system is in brackets and labelled "A." [The father gives the child breakfast; this consists of juice, cereal and raisins.] = A. The child asks for more raisins. [The father says "No." He gives as his reason that the child is going swimming and should not overeat.] = B. A and B are distinct intervention systems. An intervention system can consist of one or more interventions. A and B can be made to fit together to form intervention system C. In this case, A and B, the parts of C, are called subsystems of C. Fit is an important notion here. Often persons try to fit one intervention system to another. The emotions enable us to fit systems to other systems. In fitting one system to another one attends to moods, aims, community data base, principles of rationality, and the setting.

What sort of relation is fit? What can we say about fit? Suppose we describe the logic of fit by referring to our example. We can then say:

A fits B with regard to the setting C (in the example the setting was the breakfast and then the swimming afterwards) and the community data base D and the theory of rationality E.

Fit here is a five-place relation.

When we introduce a term such as "fit" into a theory we must be careful that the term is not ambiguous. In the case of "fit" and "intervention" the terms are ambiguous and so when we ask for the logic of the term we find that we implicate a number of different relations in describing what we mean by, for example, "fit."

If we were to characterize the logic of intervention we find that there are several distinct relations. One is a four-place relation and can be described as follows—

X intervenes with respect to Y with regard to setting W and the community data base Z.

This is not the only sort of intervention. Thus, when children intervene with regard to one another, when one child grabs another's toys this is mainly from appetite (this is done because the child wants the toy) and with little use of the community data base. In order to characterize intervention in this case, we must use a three-place relation. This can be described as follows:

A intervenes with regard to B with regard to the setting C.

There are several different kinds of intervention. Another, of great interest, obtains in later life when individuals explore different self-images or different lifestyles. I am inclined to call this "the hunting of the self." In essence when someone is searching for a self-image what they do is imaginatively explore new ways to be or to think of the self. They then test these self-images by intervening in the world in ways that are consistent with these new self-constructs. The logic of this sort of intervention is—

X intervenes with respect to Y in setting Z with regard to principles of rationality W and the community data base D and X's new self-construct V.

What of interventions between parent and child or therapist and patient? Do these have the same sort of logic as the other cases of intervention? What characterizes these relations? They have a long history and there are many changes that go on during the course of the relation. In the case of the patient-therapist or parent-child relation there is not just one intervention and one sort of logic, but many different kinds of intervention. The typical relation that holds between parent and child is a n-place one with the value of n greater than 5. Suppose we call this n-place relation "R." Then R stands for a set of relations. Each of the relations in R is a type of intervention with more than five places.

In addition to obtaining in systems, interventions themselves involve systems of beliefs and systems of values. One can intervene to help others or to discomfort and harm others. Whether and how one helps or harms another is a function of proper monitoring and of the sorts of beliefs and values fitted to interventions. Thus how interventions are shaped and fitted to beliefs, meanings, and values, and how interventions are adjusted to one another are of prime importance. For example, suppose I wish to get you to stop repeating yourself. I might first intervene by changing the subject and the mood. Perhaps I notice that this works for a short time, but then, obsessed with old themes, you return to them. How shall I intervene a second time around? How shall I fit the second intervention to the first one and to your needs? Shall I again introduce another topic? My behavior may be a function of a class of theories or a class of stories (sets of beliefs) to be "found" in the community's data base, stories about how to remedy situations of this sort; or it may be a function of my aims, values, and so forth. Clearly, intervening is complex and needs "fitting and shaping."

Emotions are among the main instruments for fitting and shaping interventions. They are perfect for the role, for they are repositories of belief and value—as we have suggested, it is in large part by virtue of our beliefs and values that the emotions have the task of shaping our interventions. Throughout this study we shall work back and forth among studies of emotions, interventions, and the self.

EMOTION

Our inquiry has had from the start the aim of understanding the emotions. Since emotions fit and shape interventions to one another, we should begin to get some idea of what emotions are. But understanding the emotions also entails understanding interventions, and so we set out to describe each concept in the hope that as we did so we would catch glimpses of the other concept. We began with interventions, and now we turn to emotions. How do emotions accomplish the task of fitting and shaping interventions?

1.   Fitting and shaping interventions is one of the human beings' great achievements.

2.   In order to facilitate fitting and shaping, emotions must be value-bearing

3.   Emotions must also be highly cognitive, with the capacity for problem solving.

4.   On the theory I am presenting, I admit appetites with a set of relations over these appetites. In part, emotions satisfy appetites. Appetites are not part of emotions. (People think of the relation as follows: emotions = appetites + beliefs + ...) Emotions frequently obtain in systems of emotions. (A system is a set of emotions with relations over the set.) Not every emotion or system of emotions satisfies an appetite, but very many do satisfy appetites. There is a *set* of relations, not just one relation between appetite and emotion. (Other theorists from time immemorial have treated the problem as a very simple one and looked for just one relation.) Thus if X = appetite and Y = emotion or system of emotions, then X is related to Y as follows:

1.   Y satisfies X by contributing to plans for achieving the want
2.   Y shapes X

3. in some cases (Y amplifies X)
4. in some cases (Y links X to a right)
5. in some cases (Y elaborates X into a disposition)
6. in some cases (Y elaborates a character trait around X)

Let me illustrate some of this. If what I want is to make money, then a host of emotions and other cognitive skills may begin to shape a character trait—a talent for making money. If what I want is to make things, then the emotions may shape this into a disposition to build.

That these things go on in some such form is obvious from our daily lives. Where a want is inappropriate, a set of emotions may reshape it so that it is more appropriate. The question is how to develop these notions theoretically. I think one clue is that there is a forward dynamic in the set of relations described above (1–6). We tend to go from simple wants to more complex things like rights. We might also think of 1–6 as illustrating a kind of movement, or dynamic or way of changing structures. Suppose we adopt a model. Suppose we think of a want as asking a question—Can I be satisfied? Suppose we assume a list of available talents of the organism: it can read, it can talk, and think, and it has a lot of information available. Then in conjunction with these talents and in response to the question, we might think of a system of emotions as providing an answer by appropriating one or more of the relations of 1–6. So overall the relation between appetite and emotion is like a logical one: emotions "answer" questions. And 1–6 behave similarly to rules of logic, for they take us from one string, a question, to another, an answer. Since the development of aims and character from wants provides the themes of the self, a characterization of the logic of emotion-want relations enables us to work out how we get the themes of the self—we do so when emotions modify wants under the logic provided by a schema like 1–6. As we develop the themes of the self, we begin to develop complex personal values. Interpersonal and personal values can be seen to be linked to the complex development of emotions, the self and interventions, and in particular to the interrelations of the three.

Emotions obviously shape appetites and interventions. Emotions also fit them into hierarchies: a hierarchy over interventions indicates which is preferable. A hierarchy over wants indicates which is to be satisfied first. These orderings are not value free. The emotions are value-bearing in a specific sense—they contain the valuational wherewithal to assess interventions and wants. And neither interventions nor wants are assessed singly but rather as parts of systems of intervention and systems of wants.

6. We shall also say that emotions have a semantic dimension. This is revealed in part by our use of prepositions to describe emotions. Thus an emotion such as anger is *about* something, surprise is *at* something. Suppose Bill was surprised at John's hostile expression. The semantic aspect is the

preposition plus the expression following it, namely, John's hostile expression. Suppose we ask for a reason for Bill's being surprised.Reason-giving is often thought to be very different from the semantics of emotions and actions. However, the semantic dimension is quite important to reason-giving. Thus if we do seek a reason, the reason we can give is provided by the expression following "at," namely, the reason he was surprised was that John had a hostile expression. The reason we often will give, subject to grammatical transformations, is identical with the expression that, along with "at," constitutes the semantic dimension of the emotion.

Now that this side of things, about the emotions, is a bit clearer, we can ask again just how the enmotions shape interventions and just what intervention systems are like.

SHAPING INTERVENTIONS AND INTERVENTION SYSTEMS

Philosophers relied for a very long while on models based on logic and thinking. These were, as it turned out, rather poor models. Philosophers attempted to account for a number of things using these models. If one attempted to use these models to account for interventions and shaping interventions, one would probably be inclined to say that to control or shape intervention X, a person would need to sit and think about X. Only as a result of prolonged thinking about X could one devise the appropriate strategies for shaping X.

This is not, on the whole, the way things are done. Let me give an example:

A)   Suppose X is vain and under the circumstances only the following interventions are available: going into John's house and boasting = a; going into John's house and complimenting John = b. X being vain, it is likely that X would put the following preference structure on the two possiblities: Prefer (a, b). With this reading, a is preferred to b. In shaping interventions emotions such as vanity regularly play a role. Other people who, under the influence of still other emotions, may react in shock to what X did and can force a reshaping of the preference structure so that we might later get: Prefer (b, a)

B)   Suppose X does in fact intervene by going into John's house and boasting. Suppose Y intervenes and tells X that he is appalled at the way X behaved and that John is very distressed by X's behavior. Suppose as a result X now goes into John's house and tells John how nice the house is and how lucky John is and only then proceeds to boast a bit (but far less than before).

C)   If this obtains, then we can say that X's preference structure changed and that Y's intervention compelled X to modify X's intervention and also to modify the structure X placed on a set of interventions. This is what I mean by a complex reshaping of interventions by the emotions.

This way of viewing emotions as shaping interventions does not derive from the logical model (where thinking is what is important and one sits down and thinks out a problem) but rather from a new model of emotions as cognitive and as value-bearing.

AN ASSESSMENT: OTHER PROBLEMS

At just about the time I had decided to develop a theory in which I explored the concept of the self, the emotions, and interventions simultaneously and also began to see how the emotions shape interventions, the work of the group was winding down. We were still saddled with a host of problems. I have indicated how the work of members of the group influenced my own. With the group coming to an end, a very fertile source of inspiration was gone. Furthermore, the group left me with a number of unresolved issues: the group did little to encourage new models; it did not encourage work on the emotions as value-bearing, though clearly this was quite important; there was virtually nothing done on the "hunting of the self"; we had no account of the imagination, and accounts of the imagination and of fitting and shaping and of the hunting of self all require aesthetic notions but nothing had been done to explore the ties between aesthetic notions and the self, and aesthetic notions and the emotions. Ties between the emotions and the unconscious and between the emotions and developmental theories were left unexplored as well.

At this point PSPE developed a series of conferences and seminars that would provide the wherewithal to solve some of these problems. I benefited from some of the suggestions of those at the conferences and incorporated these ideas into this paper. I aimed at the following additional solutions:

(i)   to provide a model of intervening that would shed light on the role of the emotions and of ethical notions and on ties between intervening and the self;

(ii)   to provide a suitable account of the imagination.

SOME SOLUTIONS: HIERARCHIES OF EMOTIONS: THE UNITY OF THE SELF

At this point, given what had already been done, I began to solve certain problems. (We don't resolve the problem of the hunting of the self until later when we enrich our theory still more.) We know emotions are value-bearing and that they are also shaped and fitted to one another. What is also characteristic of emotions is that they obtain in structures called "hierarchies." There is a topmost node to a hierarchy at which we have an emotion "sitting," and then there are branches from the top node ending in still other nodes at which still other emotions "sit," and so on. The hierarchy of emotions is a tree structure with emotions at the nodes. One such hierarchy has the emotion love at the topmost node and other emotions, for example vanity and anger, sitting lower down at other nodes. In the case of this hierarchy, call it "X," with love at the topmost node, the emotions at the highest node is preferred to those at lower nodes, and the topmost emotion regulates lower level emotions. The tree of emotions represents a preference ordering on the emotions sitting at the nodes of the tree. Thus, if love is the preferred emotion and if the hierarchy is as described, then anger, which is lower down, would be modified or operated on by love. Love provides a set of values that we can use to assess the other emotions in X; X "tells" us that we can use love to assess other emotions because love is at the topmost node; we assess the other emotions using the values that are part of the emotion love to see whether the other emotions meet the standards of love. If they do not, then we may alter them. For example, suppose I am a Christian and prefer love to anger (hence love would be higher on the tree than anger). Then in situations where I am sorely provoked and where my first impulse is a violent one, my belief in the virtue of love will check my other emotions.

Our theory of emotions is now powerful enough and rich enough to resolve one of the problems associated with discourse about the self—how to define the self and, in particular, how to begin to say what we mean by "self-consciousness." Thus, if we predicate, as we do, the emotions just discussed of the self (if we say "I love . . . .," "I am angry . . . .," etc.), then the self is scrutinizing itself by having these emotions. That is, the self scrutinizes itself by way of emotions predicated of the self, such as love and anger. But this is nothing more than the property of self-consciousness, and we can begin to clarify this problem once we have a rich enough theory of the emotions.

Thus a rich theory of the emotions will provide the concepts we need to define the properties of the self but a weak one will not. A rich theory is one that includes intervention, the self, and the imagination.

I think we can go on to resolve still another difficulty. We would like, if we can, to specify what we mean by the unity of the self. I think we can do this as follows:

(i) Emotions are value-bearing.

(ii) Emotions become more and more unified in the sense that they operate more and more in hierarchies; the hierarchies themselves become more and more tightly bound to one another and function as a whole.

(iii)   If this is so, then the values that the emotions embrace will also operate as unified wholes. To some degree how we see ourselves is a function of our values.

(iv)   Selves are unified in two ways: when, for the sake of some theory, we postulate "parts" of the self, a set of structures, and we show how these are unified; and when the self perceives itself as a whole.

(v)   If values are more and more unified by virtue of emotions becoming more and more unified into hierarchies, and if values determine in large part how we see ourselves and the world, then we shall gain a more and more unified perception of ourselves and the world. This is the second sense of unities in (iv).

(vi)   A unified self is one whose emotions are unified in hierarchies of emotions, and it is also one that perceives the world in a coherent and unified way. It functions in such a way that it deals with the world as a whole by virtue of its "parts," the emotions, functioning in a balanced way. It is also unified by virtue of seeing itself as a whole given the unification of values.

Theories are never complete; there are always problems to solve. If during the work of the group the self was largely ignored, it became clear that during the work of the conferences the self and its relations to objects and the structuring of the self became quite important. I was never convinced that the conferences had come to grips with all the issues surrounding the self. I think we begin to in this paper. I wish to consider another problem—the boundaries of the self—by once again enlarging our theory. I will, below, present a model of intervention.

INTERVENTION: A MODEL

To understand better what is involved in intervening, let us consider as the model of intervening—the parent-child situation. When the infant is born, the parent is faced with a helpless organism for whom he or she must provide. Provisions are made for feeding; interventions are designed for safety. As the infant becomes a toddler, interventions are designed to show the child how to walk, talk, and eat. Intervening on the model of the helpless infant is for a long while almost total and almost entirely at the discretion of the parents. In terms the logician would use, intervening is asymmetric, irreflexive, and nontransitive.

It is the asymmetry of an intervention that lends it its tyrannical air. To be more specific—

An act X is tyrannical if a/ a person W performs X with respect to a
person W'
b/ W $\neq$ W'

c/ X is an intervention

d/ in deciding to to X, W does not take account of the wishes and desires of W' and W shows no indication of taking the wishes of W' into account when performing X.

Given this, we can say that most acts of the parent with regard to the child have a tyrannical air to them: they are one-sided and do not take the wishes of the child into account.

Meanwhile the fledgling organism has its own propensities. Almost from the beginning the infant avails itself of refusal mechanisms when interventions are overwhelming. When there is too much stimulation, the infant will turn away or cry. That is, even though intervening is virtually tyranical and at the discretion of the parent, the child has from a very early age mechanisms for moderating or, if you will, refusing interventions. These mechanisms are not as systematic as those the adult develops, but nonetheless they are present and operative at a very early age (Robison, 1979, 1984).

Still, in spite of monitoring interventions from an early age, the infant and then the toddler, is fairly helpless and at the mercy of the parents. But as the child grows, things change: the infant, then the toddler, then the young child, then the young adult develops more and more sophisticated methods for refusing interventions. Turning away, breaking eye contact, and crying no longer suffice if the child is to develop in suitable ways. The tyranny must be moderated and reversed. Here is the place for the concept of "freedom" in child development: tyranny is the first and most natural state one experiences as an infant, in developmental terms freedom means the development, in stages, of a variety of more and more systematic refusal patterns. We begin by crying and turning away; we progress to arguing with and yelling at our parents; but later on, with increasing mastery of our cognitive house, we begin to alter our style and start to renegotiate interventions. In so doing we begin to learn the interpersonal vocabulary of "rights" and "duties," and we begin to insist on our "rights" while others insist on our "duties." We begin more and more to systematize our wants, to assess them in comparison with the refusal patterns of others. We learn how much intervention others can bear, and we begin to decide to what extent we shall refuse the interventions of others. We refuse to tolerate some interventions; we acknowledge those interventions we wish to undergo. We renegotiate interventions, and in the process we change what we are willing to countenance and endure. But, clearly, what we will endure and what we refuse to endure are part and parcel of what we mean when we talk about the boundaries of the self; we can, then, formulate at least in part, the notion of "boundary" in terms of what we will and will not endure, in terms of an "outside" world that the "inside" world disavows or refuses to admit. Thus "boundaries" can be formulated in terms of interventions, renegotiations, and rights.

Defining the boundaries of the self entails developing a family of systems of interventions and patterns of refusal that enable us to spell out in a variety of ways just how the organism is learning to be free. One of these ways involves the organism's getting a sense of self and of another entity by refusing the interventions of that entity: having a sense of boundaries is tantamount to having a sense of *another*, and this involves learning to refuse the interventions of the other person. At the same time, the vocabulary of rights and duties provides another way of developing the bounds of the self. It provides a way of discovering one's own interventions, those one wishes to do and feels one has a right to do. There are two sides to this: learning to refuse the interventions of another provides a sense of self, and learning what one wishes to do provides one with a sense of self and others. In talking about the self from the point of view of an organism's developing bounds through shaping intervention systems, we are providing a natural history of rights and duties.

Thus, ethical notions are central to developing a sense of the bounds of the self. Since emotions are value bearing, they contribute the ethical notions we need to get a sense of self. Hence, the emotions help define the bounds of the self.

Our theory is now rich enough to solve three of the four problems about the self. A solution to the fourth problem requires a further enrichment of the theory. The third problem was resolved by introducing an intervention model; to solve the fourth problem we need to introduce an analysis of the imagination and its ties to the emotions, and then exhibit the relation of aesthetic notions to the imagination and to the emotions. Before going on to this, I should like to consider two points, one about information theory and the other about the logic of emotion-intervention ties. Both points are important to our theory.

INFORMATION

There are a number of things one can do with information: one can store it, access it, alter it, make it evident, and so on. There are generally two ways of dealing with the relation of information to something such as the emotions: one can either admit that information is stored elsewhere but that it is made accessible to the emotions, or that all of the operations on the information go on in emotions (the emotions store, access, etc.). I admit a modified view: information is stored in the memory as functions; but after it is accessed the emotions can temporarily store the information in the form of a space of functions and can alter the space of functions.

There is another aspect to this information-theoretic view of the emotions. We have seen, given our technique of considering side by side a number of related concepts that have never been viewed as mutually interdependent, that emotions are tied to interventions. Intervening is fundamental to human beings. Viewed from the perspective of a theory of interventions, emotions are feedback devices enabling us to assess and reassess intervention subsystems and then fit intervention subsystems to our aims, moods, and needs and fit one intervention subsystem to another. Systems of emotion develop into more and more refined feedback devices.

Assessing old fits and creating new ones, testing new ones, and restructuring them is one of humanity's great needs and most fundamental achievements. Abstract thinking does this for us once in a while when we have the leisure to sit and think, but the emotions achieve this sort of thing for us from moment to moment. They assess and fit quickly and naturally, and by so doing they enable us to fine tune our behavior to that of others. It is precisely this quickness that requires an explanation within our theory; we appeal to Bowers' notion of intuition to work this out.

Also, as Sartre reminds us, the emotions process quickly, without our being conscious of what is going on and we wish to account for this. Bowers' account enables us to do just this, for he suggests that by intuition we mean some method of processing that "leaves out" a process or two that we find in an analogous, highly cognitive style of processing information. And he ties intuition to the imagination. But we have already tied imagination to the emotions, and in our account we can allow that imagining in a number of forms is part of an emotion. It follows that we can through our account and Bowers' account tie intuition through the imagination to the emotions and so give an account of how emotions process: they process through intuitions which are part and parcel of what we mean by having an emotion (for some emotions at least).

INTERVENTION TIES: A LOGICAL MODEL

A study of these ties is important in itself: the *bete noire* of action theory and philosophy of mind has, for some time, been the logic of this tie. There are, however, still other reasons for studying this tie: for one, it enables us to establish once and for all just how central aesthetic notions are to the study of the mind.

Interventions are essential to emotions. For example, when angry we often have a very strong need to do something in the world. When in love, we have a strong desire to aid, abet, and alter the life of the loved one.

Once it is clear that emotions and interventions are closely related, it behooves us to spell out just what these relations are. As a start, I would say that many emotions are related to their interventions in the following way: An intervention X is emotion Y's way of *laying claim* to some part of the world.

The relation is as follows: An intervention X is emotion Y's way of laying claim to Z. At the same time one might think of an emotion as "having a need" to stand forth in the world through the action and be "noted". The relation here would be: Emotion X stands forth in the world through action Y for Z.

Now how would we analyze these relations? The relations irrestibly suggest theatre. They call to mind what characters on a stage do: characters in a theater shout, rant, emote, in a very bold display. If then, one is to characterize the logic of emotion-intervention relations, one must turn to the first-level language used by critics to study and analyze theater and related domains, and then also to the second-level language used to analyze assertions in the first-level language, where the second-level language is aesthetics.

Aesthetic notions prove essential to our theory. We shall explore this further when we study the imagination and the hunting of the self. That is, we are obliged to define and explore this fourth feature of the self. To do so, we need to develop an account of the imagination and its ties to the emotions and then suggest the role aesthetic notions play. All this will enable us to see how the emotions provide a solution to the hunting of the self.

IMAGINATION

Our position here is that in order to develop an account of the self we need a view of the emotions and imagination. I shall pursue this now by making the following points:

(i) Theories of the imagination frequently suffer from the theorist's inability to distinguish enough uses of the term "imagine," or, to put it another way, perhaps better, from theorists' disinclination to see just how intrinsic the imagination is to such other, apparently disparate, mental phenomena as the emotions.

On the whole, theorists recognize at least two kinds of imagination—fantasy and supposing. Distinctions are usually drawn on semantic grounds and by virtue of the role each type of imagining plays in our mental life. Theories of the imagination suffer from inattention in philosophical circles. Our task is to broaden our view of the imagination, tie it to the emotions, and then explore different models for illuminating both the emotions and the imagination.

(2) Suppose I am trying to solve a problem involving factual data. I have heretofore been assembling data and then incorporating it into hypotheses, but with little success. If I experiment, try new ways of assembling and using the data, one can then say that I have used the data imaginatively. My imagination is at work in the process of thinking out the problem. Imagining constitutes, in part, what we mean by "thinking out a problem," at least in cases of this sort. If we analyze what may be involved here, we find that we credit people with imagination when they look for *alternatives* and attempt a proper *assessment* and *utilization* of the alternatives. This obtains when they attempt new fits of the new data with other data they have already assembled, or when they attempt new ways of shaping existing data. Since this sort of behavior—proper ways of fitting and shaping—is what I call "rational behavior," imagination, rather than being antirational, is here a species of rational behavior.

(3) When I ask you to *suppose* something to be the case that is not the case, I am doing what one thinks of as "semantic bracketing"—I am suggesting that *what is supposed* is neither true nor false, also that it is not to be confirmed now, that interventions based on assumptions that it is true or that it is false are inappropriate at this time. I am asking you to *suppose* it is so, though, and then draw conclusions.

However, when I mentally *rehearse* new behaior, I am not suggesting that what is rehearsed is neither true nor false. In most cases, I am suggesting that it is *likely* to be true and that I am willing not to take it all *that* seriously—not to believe it is true or false, just yet. The semantics of *rehearsing* is different from that of *supposing*. Rehearsing is a different form of imagining. It is bracketed semantically, and there is also an attendant sort of intervention bracketing (I know enough not to act on my rehearsings just yet).

I suggest that imagination as rational activity and imagination as rehearsing are two other forms of imagining—and there are still others equally neglected—that are important for understanding the emotions and the points we wish to make here.

I may also mentally rehearse other things—new ways to think, new ways to talk to people, how to modify my character. To a large degree, rehearsing is learned. How do we learn it, and where do we find just what subjects are appropriate for rehearsings? One important model is the theater and film.

(3) There are still other kinds of imagining. There may be life situations that call for some "study." All of us behave in untoward ways, ways we regret, and we may wish to assess what went on. We may wish to *review* a situation in a very special way, not exactly as it took place. Rather, keeping in mind what did happen, we may, as we review it, make changes in how we think of it so that what is reviewed is sufficiently different to contrast with what we actually did, and so it helps us highlight what we did that

was wrong. In this case we *re*-present what we did do in somewhat different terms—we behave symbolically. It strikes me that this is a very significant assessment tool available to us. But the nature of this activity, the way we do it and talk about it, affords us considerable insight into the ties between imagination, the emotions, aesthetic notions, and ethical concepts. Both ethical conceprts and aesthetic notions are intrinsic to doing this sort of thing well.

(4)   There are other imaginative activities that we engage in— we *relive* situations, we *rebuild* our self-image, and we *reconsider* things by imagining them differently. At this point it becomes evident just from our terminology that in characterizing different kinds of imagination we have more and more recourse to aesthetic terms and terms used to talk about art domains, as, for example, "rehearse" used with reference to the theater. Thus, aesthetic notions and terms used to characterize art domains are intrinsic to talking about the imagination. It is also fairly clear that many emotions entail imagination. For example, in the case of the empathic emotions such as love and kindness, we tend to put ourselves in another's place, we tend to try to "become" another, to rehearse our past as if it were the past of another to see just how damaging that past was to him. Thus we cannot understand and define emotions without recourse to ethical notions, to the imagination, and to aesthetic notions.

We can now, I think, solve the problem of the hunting of the self. We shall find that the emotions, imagination, and aesthetic notions are all important. What obtains when someone hunts for self? He or she seeks an alternative self or a new self-image. And how is this managed? Well, we rehearse new self-images in the imagination; and if the imagination is part of some emotion or system of emotions, then we might view the emotion by virtue of the workings of the imagination (which is part of the emotion) as helping one to define the self.

There is no doubt that the emotions fit and shape interventions and fit new self images to old ones. The theoretical reconstruction of the imagination is a very powerful tool. It will allow us now to tie the emotions to the unconscious (to any form of the unconscious to which imagination is related). Myers contends that introspection is a form of unconscious processing and that it is a form of imagination as well. We, for our part, contend that most forms of imagination can be part of the emotions. With slight adjustments, it turns out that Myers' sort of imagination cum introspection is easily assimilatable to our account and hence easily assimilatable to the emotions as well.

SUMMARY

We have a theory of the emotions that grows more distinctive and powerful as we add various concepts and subtheories that can be of use in solving central problems set for the theory. After solving the problem of the boundaries of the self and finding that aesthetic and ethical concepts were needed to define what we meant by the boundary of the self, we had one problem left. This was the hunting of the self. Since this involved the individual's having the ability to conceive of alternative self images, we assumed that we would need to add an account of the imagination to our theory. We found that the imagination works to produce theater—to generate alternative images of the self. To conceive of all this theoretically we distinguished different senses of "imagine" and found that the imagination, working as part of the systems of emotion, could develop these alternative self images.

At this point we should ask still another question. The individual would want to test these self images before adopting one. How are they tested? To do so at all, we need to bring to bear values on the self-image. We need, then, someting that is a repository of value. The emotions fit the bill. The emotions, which are value bearing entities, can measure the self-images to test them.

We now have very good reason for suspecting that any theory of the emotions entails bringing in a complex set of terms about art domains and also bringing in aesthetic terms.

At this point it is interesting to note that we would like to introduce aesthetic notions into our theory more systematically, and we would like to see what other functions they serve. For example, can they help us define a whole new class of emotions, or can they help us clarify even more emotions that we have already considered. It became evident as we proceeded with the conferences that we could indeed turn the aesthetic notions into a very powerful tool.

Perversions, Aesthetic Notions, and the Emotions

We wanted to see whether there was any way of confirming our assumption that we would benefit theoretically by adding aesthetic notions to our theory. Was anyone else doing anything like this? Could he provide clinical or experimental backing? In addition, could we use these insights—our own and his—to add to the theory.

A complete theory of the self and of the emotions seems impossible without bringing in aesthetic notions. But how can we test this assumption? To this end, we invited Robert Stoller to the conference to talk about his ideas and clinical experience. His clinical experiences lead to the idea that he could best characterize the perversions by using, in part, aesthetic notions. His clinical experience would provide some weak confirmation of our ideas, in particular if his notions could somehow be added to our own.

For Stoller perversions are systems of acts and emotions that involve humiliating another person and that involve theater on the part of the person acting out the perversion. This is to say, the person acts out the perversion in a dramatic way. Thus, in order to construct a theory of perversion, Stoller feels we must introduce aesthetic notions.

The usual domain for a theory of emotions is emotions and certain systems of action. I decided to enlarge this domain by including the emotion-action systems that we call "perversions." The perversions would then benefit from the theory of emotion already elaborated, and the theory of emotions would benefit from the account of perversions that Stoller introduced (or some suitable modification).

Aesthetic notions are by now a permanent feature of our theoretical landscape. Our rationale for building aesthetic notions into our theory of emotion derives in part from Stoller's clinical experience.

To get some idea of the range of the amended theory, I took it upon myself to see just how many emotions involve aesthetic notions. Clearly love, hate, kindness, anger, vanity, and many others do. To build these aesthetic notions systematically into our theory, we would need to describe the role they play and the semantics of emotion words that entail aesthetic notions. Thus, anger is often theatrical, and this entails a certain dynamics of anger. That is, the theatrical side of anger keeps it alive, enables the one who is angry to play with various images of himself, thereby enlarging the scope of the anger; from a semantical point of view that someone who is angry is theatrical in anger indicates that we probably ought not take the anger as seriously as we would have were the person not being theatrical. To claim that something X is theatrical is to set up a kind of semantic bracketing around X, often precluding the possibility of taking X seriously. The dynamic side can occasionally be decisive—can operate in such a way that it elaborates and prolongs and heightens the anger so that we must take it seriously. But in the absence of this, or where the dynamic side is downplayed, we often do have grounds for not taking the anger quite as seriously as we would have had the theatrical element been missing.

There are still a number of things to be done to make our theory complete. We already have a Kantian or structural account, in large part through our account of rationality. In this view, the emotions are seen as structure-giving and structure-adjusting. We now need to supplement this with an historical account of the emotions. Once we introduce the concept of "history" into our theory by making sense of the concept "the history of an emotion" (and to the extent that selves and persons depend on emotions, our account can begin to show us how to make sense of the "history of the self" and "the history of a person"), we can then turn to developmental theories that also rely on the notion "history" and try to fit some developmental theory to our account.

With these aims in mind, I suggest we develop a theory competent to talk about the "history" of an emotion by introducing the theoretical vocabulary that will enable us to talk about the birth and death of an emotion.

HISTORY: LOVE AND THE DEATH OF AN EMOTION

One characteristic frequently attributed to the emotion of love is that it is not simply a set of belief systems, feelings, values and aims, like other emotions, but that it has for some time sat at the pinnacle of our hierarchies of emotions. As a result it is an operator emotion and a semantic operator as well. What does this mean? We have discussed hierarchies of emotions—we order emotions according to which is best or more important to us, and for a long while our society sanctioned love as an emotion that is most worthy and most worth encouraging. We were enjoined to try to love others and to prefer love over other emotions. This, in turn, cast love in the role of an operator emotion—it operated on other emotions, altering them or mapping them to new emotions. Thus, if I felt anger and would have expressed it were it not for love, an emotion that is lauded, I might, in light of feelings of love I was encouraged to have, had modified the anger and the expression of my angry feelings.

How is love a semantic operator? Suppose I love someone and it comes to light that she has embezzled money and, I feel, behaved very badly. I can simply confront her with the facts. However, if I confront her with these facts in a spirit of love, I not only perform a truth-telling act, I may also provide truths of another order—I may open my loved one up to the world in the sense of showing the suffering she has caused, but showing it in the light of my love and forgiveness for her. I may, out of love, use my utterances and fact-telling in a symbolic way—showing her how this behavior can be universalized to give her some understanding of how humanity suffers from acts of this sort. Love, in a formal sense, maps a truth-telling utterance to a set of virtues definable by new, different concepts of truth. Love casts utterances in a new semantic light.

But to do this requires skill. How can we associate skill and learning with an emotion—presumably emotions are quick, unhesitating, fierce—on the model of Freud's cauldron thesis. To do so we must acknowledge various kinds of emotions. Emotions like love are ceremonial emotions—they involve ritual-like behavior, social models, learning, changing, trying. They also involve "actors," the couple in love, who are at center stage, and other "actors" who ar peripheral to the drama being played out. These emotions involve learning skills, just as one would learn skills to engage in and perform any ceremony. When love operates semantically to cast a new light on things, we learn these new semantic attitudes by learning how, in the light of love, to paint the world differently for ourselves and for other people. The people, both central and peripheral, in the drama played out are most affected and learn the new semantic skills. We use love, to take a leaf from Eagle, to introduce conditions of safety. We use it to create a stage on which we may project a review of our actions in the light of our love so that we can view with a degree of safety what it is we do. We create a kind of shelter within which we can reassess our acts. But implicit in all this is that we acknowledge that the imagination is central to emotions, at least to some emotions, and to systems of emotions, and that at least some of the appropriate models for understanding the imagination and the emotions come from aesthetics and the theater.

Emotions exhibit a complex dynamics; so do imaginings. Imaginative rehearsals are frequently part of what goes on when we undergo emotions and, in particular, when we attempt to find new ways of working out our relations to others through the emotions. This is true of love; it is also a condition for understanding how an emotion such as love can die.

HISTORY: THE DEATH OF LOVE

We are now ready to discuss the death of love. I wish to remind the reader, however, that I have studied emotions and their characteristics in such a way that we are forced to become competent to talk of the death of love. I have forced us to consider certain ways of talking about the emotions because it is only if we do look at the emotions in these new ways that we become competent to tie the emotions to history: It is by being forced to use aesthetic and ethical models to understand love and the imagination and to see how the one is related to the other that we can make sense of the death of love. To make sense of the death of love, I suggest the following:

For some time, society has sanctioned the use of the emotion of love to work out our individual characters by exploring the virtues of our own class vis-à-vis the needs and virtues of other classes. Thus, suppose you are a banker in a small farm community. You go to church every weekend and, like other members of your class, you squeeze the farmer during the week. But when you go to church you learn the Christian virtues which, in particular the virtue of love, have forced you recently to question the virtues of your own class (bankers) with regard to the needs of other classes (farmers).

As a result, you rethink the typical interventions of bankers vis-à-vis farmers, and you find these wanting. You then ask whether there are not other aims and interventions that you might espouse to replace those which make you uncomfortable. Since these interventions—the new ones—are not those of the typical banker, you have begun to redefine your relations to your own class.

To provide another example, love played a central role in the charac-terological working out of the relations between whites and blacks in the 1960s. This was possible partly because of the imaginative components of love, explicable in aesthetic terms, and partly because we could imaginatively reconstruct what "not to be free" means. In this sense, love was a "socially significant" emotion because it could enable one to redefine one's relation to one's own class and to redefine the way that class could intervene in behalf of others.

But recently love has lost its social significance, for one of its main historical tasks is now over, *and it is in this sense that it has died.* Society is now far more cynical than it was; it no longer rewards or sanctions love in the way it once did. With the current "explosion of rights," where everyone feels a narcissistic right to anything and one gains one's rights simply by asserting them, we no longer need to use emotions like love for the very fine, subtle working-out of our rights in relation to others. Love no longer has the place it once did in our social lives, a phenomenon that can be understood by an explanation of the changes in society's attitudes towards rights. Before getting on to the birth of an emotion, suppose we take stock.

HISTORY: IMPLICATIONS FOR THE 19TH AND 20TH CENTURY MODELS

What does all of this mean? To explain "the death of love," it was necessary to bring in notions like "rights" and "imagination" and to investigate new models, from aesthetics for example, for talking about the imagination. This new vocabulary could not be developed in a helter-skelter fasion; it required systematic theorizing. Our theorizing involved the following: We have introduced a Hegelian touch to add to our post-Kantian musings. We are trying to reconcile 19th century thinking about history with 20th century thinking about structure. We must now acknowledge the timidity of the philosopher and note that the psychoanalyst seems to be functioning as the 20th century philosopher of mind. But we also acknowledge that, for a number of reasons, the psychoanalyst philosophizes in a different way, is less rigorous, and needs to find his conceptual place—needs to understand the conceptual underpinnings of his metapsychological excursions.

Before continuing I should like to make just two further points: If there is a balance between the cognitive, rationality-seeking aspect of the emotions and the appetites in a society, all good and well. Today, however, we find an extraordinary degree of narcissism—an explosion of attention to the appetites with "rights" all too often reinterpreted to serve these appetitive needs and a corresponding lack of attention to the cognitive side of the emotions. The result is that we are no longer able to mobilize emotions such as love and "use" them to test the virtues of our class. No one is really interested in this sort of thing any more.

To talk of the death of love does not mean that no one loves any more; rather it suggests that some significant aspect of love is lost, the socially significant side. (In the same way to raise the Hegelian prospect of the death of art is to say, not that no one will ever produce works of art any more, but that hereafter they will have in some sense lost their significance.) The trick is to underwrite an account of love, art, and history with some theory that makes sense of the death of art, love, whatever. In my case I underwrote the account of history with an account of the emotions rich enough to make sense of this.

The structure of the emotions and of the imagination is extraordinarily complex. For example, when we imaginatively rehearse new possibilities, we do so for certain purposes and with certain attitudes (attitudes are emotions). Hence, when we speak of imagining something, we are talking about a family of relations, including a five-place one as below, namely, X rehearses (imaginatively) Y by doing W for (purpose) Z and with attitude Z'. Some emotions are important to defining imagination.

We need new models and a new vocabulary, as Kuhns suggests. One way of getting these new models is to enjoin a kind of 19th century task upon ourself—to look at the emotions from an historical point of view. In so doing, we are compelled to investigate new tools, which may possibly turn out to be just what we need. To implement our study of those new tools and concepts, we asked ourselves in what sense emotions can die, a study that involved appealing to concepts like "rights" and "freedom." We shall now add new tools by asking ourselves in what sense an emotion can be born. This exploration, I warrant, will yield new models as well.

THE BIRTH OF AN EMOTION

Emotions are of great interest in theories of motivation and theories of development. It behooves us, then, to develop a way of treating them historically to see just how it is that an emotion comes into being. In account of this sort, one of our areas of study is how emotions become tied to actions so that they are said to explain the actions and can be said to inform the actions with "color," meaning, and information content. This is part of what we mean by the birth of an emotion. This is, by and large, a problem of explanation. I should like to focus here on this aspect of the birth of an emotion. To make a start in understanding this problem, I should like to discuss it in terms of already familiar acts and emotions and study how we come to accept new, unfamiliar ties between them.

I take as evident that social smiling in babies begins at about six months and that most of us assume that a tie between snmiling and some emotion, such as contentment, is natural, perhaps even wired-in. Suppose we assume that this is wired-in. Ties that are wired-in are one sort of tie. For purposes of our theory, we introduce another sort of tie between emotions and behavior that are seemingly natural ties but not strong enough or clearcut enough to warrant assuming they are wired-in. I propose that we do admit that this second sort of less natural-seeming tie, and then I wish to explore theoretically what we need to add to our theory to account for the second sort of tie. Understanding what it means to talk of the birth of an emotion is, in part, tantamount to understanding this second sort of tie.

It may very well be that to understand how smiling comes to be tied to being happy we need only appropriate models from neurophysiology and studies of the family. But I wish now to explore ties that occur *later on* in life and seem more problematic. In such cases, the models appropriate to earlier stages might not work out very well, and it is for these ties that problems of explanation crop up. I am thinking of such instances as someone smiling out of exasperation, or anger, or irony. How are these connections developed? To understand this, let us create a fictitious scenario about how these ties might be produced and then ask ourselves what this means.

Suppose no one had ever heard of the tie between smiling and exasperation. Suppose the very first time anyone comes across it is in the writings of Samuel Beckett—perhaps Malone smiles from exasperation. Initially, while reading this you might become a bit uncomfortable. You reread the passage and try out the new connection in your mind's eye. Perhaps you admit the connection, first rather tentatively, because it illuminates a passage in the book and because of coherence criteria as well. Perhaps other readers who read the book do this too. This is still a very tentative acknowledgment of the tie. How might the connection become current? One might the next day notice what seems to be an odd smile on someone's face and wonder whether the person is smiling from exasperation. One might try this explanation on to see how well it does the job. But even if it begins to seem more acceptable, we are still a long way away from fully acknowledging it.

Then how do we fit explanations (meanings) to acts? I suggest that the appropriate model for understanding this is the artist. Extending the concept of "landscape," I recommend that just as there are landscapes in painting and film and sculpture, so also can we regard scenes in mind-plays as landscapes. The mental landscape is achieved through imaginary mind-play, where we rehearse various scenes in which people smile from exasperation and we attempt to see how this fits into a whole, very much as Monet tried to see how to fit figures into countryside scenes. There is a good deal of experimenting, change, pushing and pulling before a decision is made. One might engage in mind-play to see just how a figure smiling from exasperation sits in the general scene, how he plays off against the other characters. One might observe how this interpretation adds meaning to the situation, how it enhances one's view of the situation, whether and how it illuminates what goes on, how it feels, whether it is right, and what one learns. One might conclude that a person need not grunt from exasperation, that one can be far more subtle—that if the other characters in the scene call for it, then claiming that someone smiles from exasperation can enhance the meaning structures implicit in the scene. This way of working with new possibilities—this way of fitting, experimenting, shaping in the imagination—smacks of the way an artist works. The connection between exploring new ways of putting fitures into paintings and generating new meanings is not only similar to what is entailed in efforts to tie behavior to an emotion, but also is one of the ways such ties are effected. I do not think such connections are analytic at all. What fosters at least some assurance is the way an explanation illuminates a scene, opens us up to new interpretations, new connections, and what the connection suggests—that by juxtaposing this explanation to the smiling/contentment connection, we introduce a new and subtle play of meanings; It feels right.

I am, of course, suggesting that new emotions are born, not solely from what is wired in, but from an astonishing array of interpersonal and cultural needs, and that action-emotion ties are facilitated by, for example, imaginary exercises in which the criteria for what fits are very much like those used by a painter doing a landscape. These are not the only criteria, but understanding what goes on when we explain actions by alluding to emotions takes us far beyond simple neurophysiological models.

To sum up and amplify a bit:

1.   Our theme—the birth and death of an emotion—recommends a Hegelian approach to generating models for understanding how we give meaning to actions, intervention and emotions, and also firmly commits to models deriving from both Kantian and Hegelian concerns. It is a firm wedding of 19th century and 20th century ideologies and styles.

2.   I have suggested what some new models are likely to be, including models from our discourse about ethics and art.

3.   The metatheoretical work of, for example, Rubinstein and Eagle, and to some extent Stolorow and Kernberg, constitutes a 20th century philosophy of mind, but one that is to some degree uninformed by the rigor and sense of how problems are generated that informs 20th century philosophical discourse. I have suggested also that these new philosophers of mind would benefit from some of the work of philosophers of the past.

4.   This account of the history of the emotions goes a very long way to completing our theory. The current theory has the following features:

(i)   We provide a full account of the emotions.
(ii)   We define the self and examine all of the defining features.
(iii) We treat the defining features of the self as problems generated internally to the theory, which force us to enlarge the theory.

(iv)   There is an account of intervention.
(v)   The role of ethical and aesthetic notions is examined, in particular with efforts to give accounts of the self and of the emotions.
(vi)   We work out some of the subtheory relations—thus the theory of emotions is a subtheory of a theory of art and is also a subtheory of a theory of rationality.

REFERENCES

Robison, E., & Fontana V. (1984), Observing child abuse. *Journal of Pediatrics.* 655–660.
_____ & Solomon, F. (1979), Some further findings on the treatment of the mother-child dyad in child abuse. *Child Abuse and Neglect,* 3:247–251.

III NEW APPROACHES TO THE UNCONSCIOUS, METATHEORY, AND THE SELF

7 Psychoanalytic Hypotheses and the Problem of Their Confirmation*

Benjamin B. Rubinstein

Among the functions of scientific hypotheses the most often mentioned are explanation and prediction. A third function of at least some sets of scientific hypotheses is to give a picture of the segment of the world, or of one part or aspect of this segment, with which the science in question is concerned. Psychoanalytic hypotheses appear to have these three functions, although manifested in unequal measure. Only explanation is closely enough related to the corresponding function of scientific hypotheses generally to warrant description in at least roughly similar terms.

I should mention that, when I speak about explanation, I have in mind one particular view of it, namely, the view developed mainly by Hempel (Hempel and Oppenheim, 1948; Hempel, 1965). Although it recently has come in for criticism (see Suppe, 1974), in its main features it still remains a useful model for the analysis of psychoanalytic explanation.

My primary focus will be on a particular aspect of the clinical theory of psychoanalysis, namely, the aspect we may refer to as its cognitive aspect. To avoid premature introduction of metapsychological modes of thought, I will have to use a somewhat different terminology. What I hope to achieve is (1) to delineate the way various hypotheses enter into the process of clinical explanation, (2) to identify the function of metapsychology in the overall process, and (3) to indicate the principal shortcomings of current metapsychological formulations. In a brief paper these points can ob-

*This chapter previously appeared in *Pathology and Consciousness,* ed. K. D. Irani and G. Meyers (1978). New York: Haven. © Association for Philosophy of Science, Psychotherapy, and Ethics. Reprinted by permission.

viously be dealt with only in a quite cursory manner. I will consider the last two even more cursorily than the first.

Clinical psychoanalytic hypotheses are of several types.[1] I will refer to the simplest of them as *particular clinical hypotheses.* When presented to a patient in psychoanalysis they are called "interpretations." They are designed to explain why, in certain situations, people sometimes behave in unexpected, and hence puzzling, ways. As Hanson (1958, p. 86) and Toulmin (1961, pp. 44ff.) have pointed out, this is how hypotheses are often generated in science: we come up against an unexpected, and hence puzzling, event and thus feel the need for an explanation. In the psychoanalytic case, obviously, to ask for an explanation of the behavior of a particular person we must first have established that the behavior of the person in question differs from what we would have expected, our expectations being based either on how most people behave in similar situations or on how this person has behaved in such situations in the past. I will not discuss how we know how most people behave in certain situations except to say that this knowledge is part of our everyday commonsense psychology.

Let me take a simple example. A woman in her mid-thirties, let us call her "P," is excessively concerned about her mother who is in perfect health and lives in comfortable circumstances. Ordinarily P telephones her at least twice a day to inquire how things are. She gets quite anxious if she has not talked to the mother for over a day. Although attractive and not a homosexual, P is not married. She explains that between her job and having to be constantly prepared to help her mother out in an emergency she simply has neither time nor energy for marriage. There is no doubt but that this is unexpected, and hence puzzling, behavior. Accordingly, we feel the need for an explanation.

Direct questioning of P does not lead very far. Of course she is concerned about her mother, she says. Her mother is an older person and anything can happen to older people. P is reminded of the fact that her mother is in perfect health, not all that old and that, besides, P, for years, (since the mother was quite a bit younger than she is now) has been overly concerned about her. In response P merely shrugs her shoulders saying impatiently "Well, I guess, that's just the way I am."

Having pursued this lead for a while and found that it is not likely to yield additional relevant information, we now, without clear awareness that that is what we are doing, follow the Hempelian schema and adduce a

---

[1]In a previous paper (Rubinstein, 1975) I have discussed these hypotheses in much greater detail than is possible here. On the other hand, I will try to take the general idea underlying both papers a step further than I did in the earlier paper.

set of higher level (at least fairly general &/or abstract) hypotheses in accordance with which the main features of the description of P's behavior just given are deducible. The most general of these hypotheses is derived from Freud's view (1901) of the ubiquitousness of motives as psychological determiners. I will refer to it as the *hypothesis of motivational determination*. In psychoanalytic practice it is usually regarded as applying to any situation to which it conceivably may apply. We may, however, more modestly also regard it as merely applying *in all probability* to such situations. As is customarily done, I will use the term "motive" as a generic term including (mainly) wishes and certain feelings, such as love, hate, curiosity, fear, and anger.

The hypothesis of motivational determination allows us to infer merely that P's excessive concern about her mother is most likely prompted by a motive. Since P is unable to identify a believable conscious motive we further infer that her motive may be unconscious. This inference is made possible by our adducing, in addition to the hypothesis of motivational determination, another higher level hypothesis, namely a hypothesis we may refer to simply as the *hypothesis of unconscious motives*.

Clearly we can accept this hypothesis only if we are able, at least in a general way, to account for how motives may be rendered unconscious. One possibility, and that is the possibility Freud turned into a cornerstone of his theory, is that in certain cases a motive is in some way rendered unconscious if the person entertaining the motive, for one reason or another, cannot bring himself to acknowledge it. Freud spoke here about defense. Because the concept of defense has acquired part of its meaning from metapsychological considerations, I prefer to refer to the hypothesis derived from the possibility just mentioned as the *hypothesis of elimination of overt inner conflict*.

The two last considered hypotheses are clearly ancillary to the hypothesus of motivational determination. I will refer to all three hypotheses as *general clinical hypotheses*. It is obvious that, adducing them, only gives us a general framework for an explanation of P's behavior. What we can deduce is that there may be a motive operating in P and that, because of her reluctance to acknowledge this motive, it has been rendered unconscious through the operation of a special form of elimination of overt inner conflict.

To give this framework concrete meaning we obviously must identify events that fit both it and the behavior to be explained. The events, of course, must be at least imaginable. The following construction—one of a number of possible ones—meets these conditions reasonably well. I will posit (1) that P hates her mother, (2) that she cannot bring herself to acknowledge her hatred, (3) that to avoid having to acknowledge it she repeatedly resorts to behavior, namely, excessive concern, that is far removed in kind from any behavior that would directly express her hatred, and (4) that the hatred is thus rendered unconscious.

The four points just listed constitute a *particular clinical hypothesis* fitting P's case. In arriving at this hypothesis, in addition to the indicated general clinical hypotheses, I have (1) adduced the quasi-generalization that people who hate a parent usually somehow know they must not do that, (2) made the observation that hating and somehow knowing one must not do that constitute an overt inner conflict, (3) adduced the quasi-generalization that people as a rule will try to eliminate their overt inner conflicts, (4) surmised that one way to eliminate an overt inner onflict is not to acknowledge the feeling giving rise to the conflict, (5) surmised that perhaps the most effective way of not acknowledging the feeling is to somehow render it unconscious, and (6) surmised further that, maybe in conjunction with repression, a feeling may be rendered unconscious by the person's engaging in behavior that in some sense is contrary to the behavior the feeling in question, if allowed free expression, might lead to. I will add, parenthetically, that when I, as we commonly do clinically, speak about an unconscious feeling I, of course, use ordinary language and that in a theoretical language, since in its literal sense the term "unconscious feeling" is self-contradictory, a description of a different type must be used. On this point, Freud (1915, pp. 177f.) has taken a similar stand.

I will refer to hypotheses illustrated by each of the two quasi-generalizations (points 1 and 3 in the preceding paragraph) and the three surmises taken together (points 4, 5 ,and 6 in the same paragraph) as *special clinical hypotheses.* Referring not to a particular individual but *to people more or less generally,* these hypotheses clearly are more general than the particular clinical hypotheses. But, since as in the case under consideration, they refer to *specific* motives and *specific* modes of elimination of overt inner conflict, they are less general than the general clinical hypotheses. The specific mode of elimination of overt inner conflict described in the third of the special clinical hypotheses I have adduced, Freud referred to as reaction formation. Since it is largely based on metapsychological presuppositions, I have not in the preceding discussion considered Freud's concept of signal anxiety and the role he assigned this in the elimination of overt inner conflict.

The particular clinical hypothesis mentioned provides an explanation for P's behavior. It is not enough, however, that the hypothesis explains the behavior, that to an outside observer this behavior now has a meaning, albeit a rather twisted one. As I have indicated, the explanation we are considering is only one of a number of possible explanations. Furthermore, the suggested explanation is hypothetical also in the sense that it, or rather the sentence expressing it, includes theoretical terms, mainly the terms

"unconscious motive" (and related terms) and, implicitly, "reaction formation." Accordingly, this explanation, our particular clinical hypothesis, must
be confirmed.

There are two principal ways of confirming the explanation provided by
a particular clinical hypothesis of the type I have considered. One is to
derive a prediction from the hypothesis[2], the second to deduce postdictions
in accordance with it and then proceed to test the prediction and the
postdictions in turn. For reasons that will become clear later, we need only
consider the confirmation of the posited unconscious motive. We should
note that in the case of most sciences, explanation and prediction are in a
sense mirror images of one another. Thus, scientific explanation has
(roughly) the form of the sentence "$\underline{B}$ because of $\underline{A}$" and the corresponding
prediction the form "If $\underline{A}$ then $\underline{B}$." As a rule both $\underline{A}$ and $\underline{B}$ refer to observable
events. Psychoanalytic explanation also has the form "$\underline{B}$ because of $\underline{A}$." In
this case, however, whereas $\underline{B}$ refers to an observable event, the term $\underline{A}$
includes in its reference an unconscious motive which obviously is not
observable. Since $\underline{A}$ has the same referent in explanation and prediction,
that clearly is true of psychoanalytic prediction also.

This situation is not unique. In the prediction on which Michelson-
Morley's experiment was based $\underline{A}$ stands for the movement of the earth
through a hypothetical ether and $\overline{B}$ for the predicted different effect of this
hypothetical event on two light beams, the one travelling in the direction
of the earth's movement in space, the other in the opposite direction. Here
$\underline{A}$ obviously has one thing in common with an unconscious motive, namely that what it refers to is not observable. The referent of $\underline{B}$, on the other
hand, as in the case of every scientific prediction is not only observable but
also an exactly specifiable individual event or set of events.[3]

I intimated in the beginning of this paper that psychoanalytic prediction
differs from prediction in other sciences. I have noted that the term $\underline{A}$ in
psychoanalytic prediction refers to an unobservable event. In this respect
psychoanalytic prediction differes from many, although, as we have just
seen, not from all predictions in other sciences. There are, nevertheless, real
differences. One is that usually psychoanalytic prediction of the type with
which we are concerned is merely implicit, another that, even when a
prediction is made explicit, conditions for the occurrence of the predicted
event can only vaguely, if at all, be specified. The most striking difference,

---

[2]For the sake of simplicity I speak about deriving a prediction from a particular clinical
hypothesis even though we usually derive a set of predictions from such a hypothesis.

[3]It is irrelevant in the present connection that the prediction on which the Michelson-
Morley experiment was based is not derived from a simple explanation-prediction relationship of the type I am considering but from a set of presuppositions that are expressed—highly
simplified— in the formula "(E implies A) implies (A implies B)" where E stands for the ether
theory of light.

however, is that in the formula representing psychoanalytic prediction the term $\underline{B}$ does not appear. From the psychoanalytic explanation "$\underline{B}$ because of $\underline{A}$" we cannot, in other words, derive a prediction of the form "If $\underline{A}$ then $\underline{B}$." The prediction we do derive has the form "If $\underline{A}$ then $\underline{X}$," where $\underline{X}$ is related in a special way to $\underline{B}$.

It is important to note that the event $\underline{X}$ referred to is not an exactly specifiable individual event but any one of a specifiable *class* of individual events. The event the term $\underline{B}$, as it occurs in the formula, has reference to (our original observation), is itself a member of this class. The next question is obvious. How is the class defined? To arrive at a definition we must take a somewhat circuitous route. To begin with we have to consider that *by itself* the hypothesis of motivational determination allows us to infer only that (1) if an observed event by its attributes qualifies as the fulfillment of a motive, it may in fact be the fulfillment of this motive and the motive may accordingly be present, and (2) if an observed event by its attributes qualifies as a means to the fulfillment of a motive, it may in fact be a means to this fulfillment and the motive may accordingly be present. Without involving us in a full-dress discussion of the matter I will simply state that these inferences are made possible by two *rules of inference*, the motive-fulfillment and the means-end rules, that are entailed in the hypothesis of motivational determination.

These considerations apply mainly to conscious motives. In the case of an unconscious motive, events qualifying as the fulfillment of the motive cannot occur by definition. Events qualifying as the means to the fulfillment of the motive may occur but without being recognized as such by the agent. In this situation we may, *in compliance with common psychoanalytic practice,* introduce a general motivational hypothesis stating that an unconscious motive, if at all related to observable events, is most likely related (among others) to events that represent parts or aspects of the fulfillment of the motive, or to events that are in some sense analogous to or otherwise resemble this fulfillment or parts or aspects of it, or to events that are parts of the context in which the corresponding conscious motive would be likely to occur. I will refer to this hypothesis as the *hypothesis of partial functional equivalence.* We should note that *by itself* this hypothesis does not state that prediction is possible. What it does is merely to specify the kinds of event that can be predicted in case prediction is indeed possible. I may mention that, in conjunction with a hypothesis to be considered presently, the hypothesis of partial functional equivalence operates not only in the confirmation but also in the generation of particular clinical hypotheses.

Except for the last, the points just made amount to a definition of the class of events that in the indicated way is involved in psychoanalytic prediction. It is the class of those events that can be related to the posited unconscious motive from which the prediction was derived primarily by the rules of inference entailed in the hypothesis of partial functional equivalence. Some events relatable to the posited unconscious motive by the means-end rule, or I should add, by rules entailed in various special clinical hypotheses of elimination of overt inner conflict also qualify for membership in the class.

As I intimated in introducing the hypothesis of partial functional equivalence, I find it useful, at least in the present context, to regard this and similarly functioning hypotheses as merely *defining* the class of events analysts, led by the formula "If $\underline{A}$ then $\underline{X}$," implicitly predict. The claim that events of this class are likely to occur *in fact* must accordingly be expressed by adducing yet another hypothesis. I will refer to this hypothesis, merely descriptively, as *the hypothesis of the persistent manifestation potential of unconscious motives*. Clearly, only if we assume its validity are we at all able to speak about psychoanalytic prediction of the type we are considering and to recognize its role in clinical confirmation.

We can say, in summary, that the inference rule entailed in the hypothesis of the persistent manifestation potential of unconscious motives allows us to infer that, if unconscious motives can be assumed to be present, they are likely to have observable effects. The rules of inference, on the other hand, entailed in the hypothesis of partial functional equivalence and in hypotheses functioning together with it allow us to infer the kinds of effects unconscious motives, if present and having effects, are likely to have.

Let me briefly return to P. In her case, two observed events clearly qualify as members of the class of events predicted, if present, by her unconscious hatred of her mother. One of these is that P at work (almost infallibly) sooner or later becomes resentful of and gets into difficulties with older female superiors. The second qualifying event is a dream in which P in some way officiates at the funeral of a woman, possibly the mother, who in reality is very much alive, of a friend of hers.

Clearly, one or two events belonging to the class of events predicted by a posited unconscious motive may occur by chance. It would seem that chance occurrence becomes increasingly less likely, and, accordingly, confirmation of the corresponding hypothesis increasingly acceptable, the greater the number of events belonging to the indicated class are observed. We should note, however, that, in gauging the degree of confirmation of a particular clinical hypothesis, what counts is not only the *number* of events but also the *way* these events qualify for class inclusion. This is a complicated question and too technical to be broached here. One thing is clear, however: Even the high degree of flexibility permitted by our rules of inference does not enable us to fit any observed event into the class of predicted events. In fact, in the course of an analysis we generally formulate a number of hypotheses about unconscious motives which are quietly dropped because of lack of evidence. Popper's claim (1962, p. 36) that in psychoanalysis we can find confirmation for practically any hypothesis we care to formulate is thus without foundation.

It is worth noting in this connection that Popper's *refutability criterion* for scientific hypotheses does not work at least for a number of particular clinical hypotheses. Even though the point can be demonstrated by reference to P's unconscious hatred of her mother, it can be more clearly demonstrated if we speak instead of an unconscious wish on P's part for her mother to die. Take the sentence

1. P has an unconscious wish for her mother to die. This sentence, clearly, is not contradicted by the sentence

2. P has an unconscious wish for her mother not to die. Like love and hate the two contrary wishes may well coexist. The first sentence, however, is obviously contradicted by the sentence

3. P does not have an unconscious wish for her mother to die, and also by the sentence

4. P has a conscious wish for her mother to die.

To refute the first sentence, according to which P has an unconscious wish for her mother to die, we thus must confirm the third, according to which P does not have such an unconscious wish, and also the fourth, according to which P has a conscious, not an unconscious, wish for her mother to die. Everything P has said and done adds up to a refutation, not a confirmation, of the latter sentence. To refute the first sentence it then remains for us to confirm the third, the sentence that P does not have an unconscious wish for her mother to die. This sentence, however, can be confirmed only by a *lack of confirmation* of the first sentence, the reformulation, in terms of a death wish, of our original hypothesis. In the case of a hypothesis like the one we are considering, refutation is thus in part equivalent to lack of confirmation. Accordingly, whatever confirmation we gather must be given due weight.

I mentioned that, apart from prediction, *postdiction* may play a role in the confirmation of particular clinical hypotheses. The general and special clinical hypotheses I have adduced so far are all *motivational* hypotheses. In addition to these we operate in psychoanalysis with two other kinds of general and special clinical hypotheses, namely, hypotheses I refer to as *situational* and *genetic,* respectively. According to one special situational hypothesis, if a person feels rejected by another he will usually resent this other person. When applied to what can be seen as possible, more or less persistent effects of childhood experiences, this hypothesis is turned into a special genetic hypothesis. In P's case, we can derive from it the particular clinical hypothesis that as a child P felt rejected by her mother. P does not remember that she did. On the other hand, however, piecing together little anecdotes and scraps of memory we can see P's mother emerge as a vain, self-centered woman who was, and sill is, involved for the most part, with her own rather frivolous interests. It is, therefore, at least somewhat likely that, although she does not remember it, P did in fact as a child feel that her mother rejected her. The hypothesis of P's hatred of her mother thus receives this additional, albeit inconclusive, confirmation. I should add that to assign greater weight than that to the confirmation would be to take more seriously than is warranted (by the scant data we have available) the implicit assumption that P's feeling rejected by her mother has been repressed. At the end of the paper I will briefly return to this question.

So-called transference reactions are inferred in accordance with a general situational hypothesis we may refer to as the *hypothesis of partial functional equivalence of past and present situations*. This hypothesis allows us to postdict past situations on the basis of certain present ones, including a patient's reactions in the psychoanalytic situation. Inference by analogy is even more predominant here than in the case of the motivational hypothesis of partial functional equivalence. The confirmation of a hypothesis of this kind does not differ from the confirmation of other postdictions, such as the one just alluded to in the case of P. A transference reaction, however, may be used, not only to postdict a past situation, but also as evidence in favor of a similar postdiction arrived at in other ways. If P were to feel that the analyst is not really interested in her, then her expressing this feeling, if judged without substance by the analyst, would be regarded as at least in some measure corroborating the hypothesis that as a child she felt rejected by her mother.

I mentioned that deriving predictions and postdictions from a particular clinical hypothesis represents the two principal ways of confirming this hypothesis. One might think that the most unequivocal confirmation of the presence of an unconscious motive is the patient's becoming aware of this motive, either spontaneously or after a series of appropriate interpretations. Although undoubtedly of some value, I agree with Eagle (1973) that we often cannot put much weight on confirmation of this type. For example, having become conversant in a lengthy analysis with the psychoanalytic mode of thinking, the patient, on the basis of the same observations as the analyst, may well have arrived at the same conclusion. For this reason among others, as Freud (1938) has noted, analysts rely heavily on indirect evidence of the types considered. In regard specifically to particular responses to interpretations, I will only mention that by and large the more affectively charged a patient's corroborative response to an interpretation, the more this response will count as confirmation of the interpretation. The absence of such a response, on the other hand, is difficult to evaluate, mainly because of the ready adducibiliy of an appropriate special hypothesis of elimination of overt inner conflict.

It seems that clinical confirmation of particular clinical hypotheses is characterized by more uncertainties than confirmation in most other sciences. Clinical confirmation may be problematic to an even higher degree than in the above instances when, in accordance with one or another special genetic hypothesis of partial equivalence, we try to explain adult behavior on the basis of (at times) quite slender analogies with partly observed, partly inferred, behavior at some early developmental stage.[4] That does not mean, of course that there are no instances of particular clinical hypotheses that are reasonably well confirmed clinically. There undoubtedly are a number—presumably in most analyses. To demonstrate that, however, does not get to the heart of the matter. The question is on what basis we assign any validity at all to our clinical methods of confirmation—at least to those that seem far removed from accepted scientific practice &/or from our habitual common-sense modes of thinking. To answer this question we must approach our problem from an angle that I have not so far considered.

It can be readily appreciated that *all* general and special clinical hypotheses entail specific rules of inference. The following considerations apply mainly to the general motivational, but also to some of the less obvious general situational and genetic hypotheses. It can be maintained that these hypotheses have no meaning beyond the rules of inference they entail. This is reminiscent of a claim made by Toulmin (1953) years ago, partly following Ryle and Schlick (e.g., pp. 79, 91f., 93f., 103), about higher-level scientific hypotheses. It is, however, possible to give the hypotheses we are considering existential meaning (i.e., to take the theoretical terms they include seriously, not just as dressed-up pure disposition terms). Contrary to views expressed (in different words), among others, by Klein (1976) and Schafer (1976), it seems to me desirable to do so. Softening his original radical position, Toulmin later (1961), in effect, did it for science generally. In the case of psychoanalysis, the alternative is conventionalism, the turning of psychoanalytic theory into a more or less arbitrary interpretative system. That, clearly, would reflect on the particular clinical hypothesis since, no matter how well we regard them as confirmed clinically, the claim can always be made that their formulation as well as their confirmation is contingent on a choice of rules of inference that is quite idiosyncratic. The claim may be unfair. But we have no way of countering it effectively.

In this connection it is important to consider that, whereas, for example, in physics there is no ultimate, independently verifiable reality beyond the events physicists observe and infer, in psychology there is such an ultimate reality, namely, the reality of the nervous system. If clinical confirmation of psychoanalytic hypotheses were as reasonably well established as confirmation in physics, this consideration need not concern us. But it is not. Ac-

---

[4] As reported by Escoli (1977), Clower (pp. 219f.) and Weinshel (pp. 225f.), without specifically focussing on the problem of confirmation, have in a general way commented on the difficulties involved in applying developmental concepts to adult analysis.

cordingly, we cannot lightly, in the name, say, of scienctific purity, dismiss the happy circumstance that each of us possesses a brain. Even though he may not have clearly realized that himself, the most profound import of Freud's metapsychology is that he gave the general motivational hypotheses an existential meaning, *in principle* of the kind I have in mind. Freud, of course, did not identify the general motivational hypotheses as such but conflated them with his metapsychological hypotheses. If we keep the two sets of hypotheses apart, we will realize that the metapsychological hypotheses, if substantiated, would lend theoretical support to the general clinical hypotheses.

The hypothesis of moitvational determination can thus be derived in accordance with Freud's drive theory and the hypothesis of elimnination of overt inner conflict in accordance with the theory of a censorship at the border between the systems *Ucs* and *Pcs* and with theories of ego-id-superego relationships which superseded the latter theory. The hypothesis of the persistent manifestation potential of unconscious motives and in part the hypothesis of partial functional equivalence are clearly derivable in accordance with the theory of psychic energy (more specifically, in accordance with the hypothesis of constant pressure for discharge of the energy and of its specific modes of discharge in its freely mobile condition).

Unless we adopt some form of mind-body dualism, we cannot disregard the fact that Freud's metapsychological theories and hypotheses in their literal (physiological) meanings have been convincingly refuted. The remedy in this situation is not, as Klein and Schafer propose, to discard all metapsychology but to construct a new metapsychological or, as I prefer to say, extraclinical theory that is compatible with whatever we know today about neurophysiology. The gap between the two theories, psychoanalytic extraclinical and neurophysiological theory, is of course enormous. With some effort on the part of both analysts and neurophysiologists there is, however, some hope that this gap will gradually narrow. Obviously,such an extraclinical theory would not only put the general motivational (and hence the corresponding particular clinical) hypotheses on a firmer footing than they are at present, but it would also give a picture of the segment of the world, namely, the so-called inner world, the mind-brain concatenation, with which psychoanalysis in large measure is concerned. Left to themselves neurophysiologists would not be able to construct such a picture. They simply would not know what questions to ask.

To engage in an enterprise of this kind we need to begin with an appropriate language (a language that, although primarily psychological, lends itself to being gradually transformed so that it eventually will more or less closely approximate the language of neurophysiology). A first step is a *depersonification* of ordinary language. An example is when we refer to motives as, together with other factors, *causing* certain actions to occur instead of speaking about a person's desires, etc., as the *reasons* for his engaging in these ations. A depersonified language of this kind is of course readily transformed back to ordinary language. On the other hand, being itself a primitive process language, it is more closely related to the language of neurophysiology than is ordinary language.

We must briefly consider *six* additional points. Most of them I have already alluded to above. The *first*, which I have so far not mentioned, is that special situational and at least some special genetic hypotheses may be tested by *extraclinical psychological* (in a broad sense experimental) methods.[5] As far as I can see, however, extraclinical psychological methods can only within fairly narrow limits be applied to the general motivational hypotheses. Accordingly, the use of such methods presumably cannot—at any rate at the present stage of psychological experimental sophistication—conribute much to the validation of these hypotheses, that is, to the justification for our applying to clinical material the inference rules they entail. That is an additional reason why a neurophysiologically informed extraclinical theory is called for.[6]

The *second* point ties in with the claim I referred to above that the formulation as well as the confirmation of particular clinical hypotheses is contingent on a choice of rules of inference that is quite idiosyncratic. One might argue against this claim that our clinical inferences make sense, that they impart meaning to what, taken at face value, seems like a jumble of symptoms and other phenomena and that that must be indicative of the validity of the inference rules we employ. Although in one form or another often used by analysts, this argument is seriously flawed. The effect just mentioned of applying the rules is indicative only of their effectiveness as principles for ordering our clinical material in a reasonably coherent fashion. And that, at best, allows us to formulate a *hypothesis* to the effect that the rules may indeed be valid, not to assert that they are likely to be in fact.

The *third* point takes us back to my insistence on the necessity of a neurophysiological model and repeats in a slightly different wording my original rejoinder to the claim just considered. Looked at in the light of a prospective model of the indicated kind we can interpret the rules of in-

---

[5]As an example of a partly negative finding I may mention that, even though the existence of an "anal personality" (Freud, 1908) can be demonstrated with extraclinical correlational methods, methods of this type fail to show that there is a functional relationship between the anal personality and the anal stage of development—without, however, ruling out the possibility of such a relationship (Kline, 1972, pp. 6–30; see also Eysenck and Wilson, 1973, pp. 96 ff.). These findings, clearly, cast grave doubts on the corresponding genetic clinical hypotheses.

[6]The effects Silverman (1975) has demonstrated of both sub- and supra-liminal presentation of psychoanalytically significant stimuli are adducible as experimental support for certain quite specific *special* motivational hypotheses. Silverman's experiments, however, are not relevant for the problem of the *general* motivational hypotheses.

ference, not as rules, but essentially as neurophysiological hypotheses formulated in the most general terms possible. Only thus do they become testable in any real sense. Seen in this light, our rules of inference—or rather the higher-level clinical hypotheses in which they are entailed—become comparable to theories in other sciences, such as the theory of genes, as this theory was understood some 15–20 years ago, and the big bang theory of cosmology that only quite recently crossed the border between sheer speculation and probable hypothesis. It may be good to remember that the gene theory was useful, both practically and theoretically, even at a time when the concept of a gene was still quite nebulous. It seems reasonable to expect that in the future at least a great many of our general and special clinical hypotheses and the rules of inference they entail will be judged in a similar manner.

The *fourth* point is meant to amplify a number of the claims I have made above. It is evident that, whereas rules of inference are involved in the inference and confirmation of the presence of unconscious events, mainly motives, they are not themselves inferred clinically and hence cannot be clinically confirmed. There are no superordinate clinical rules that we can apply to the rules we employ. It is of interest that, even though as such they do not have existential implications, we commonly use them *as if* they did. In other words, we regard the rules of inference not simply as rules but as in some way corresponding to *processes.* It seems reasonably clear that, as in the case of the rules, the occurrence of such processes can only be confirmed extraclinically. When in the case of P we infer unconscious hatred on the basis of observed excessive concern, we do that because the hatred and the concern, by virtue of their respective attributes, fulfill the main condition for application of the rule of inference entailed in the special clinical hypothesis of elimination by reaction formation of overt inner conflict. Now, if the presence of the unconscious hatred in the way indicated above is confirmed to a certain degree, we feel justified in regarding the hypothesis that the excessive concern is, in fact, a reaction formation against the hatred as confirmed to the same degree.

If we discount the conventionalist alternative, it seems fairly clear that here we reason *as if* our rule of inference had been validated by some extraclinical method (*as if* it had been *shown* to correspond on the extraclinical, neurophysiological level to a process [a "defense *mechanism*"] establishing a causal relationship between the two events, the unconscious hatred and the excessive concern). It is, of course, possible to regard the occurrence of such processes as representing in barest outline a basically neurophysiological hypothesis that is yet to be confirmed or refuted, as the case may be.

We are not in a position to understand more fully the claim I made earlier that, because of the paucity of our data, we cannot take the assumption very seriously that P has repressed her feeling rejected as a child by her mother. Seen in the light of the point I have just tried to make, the question here is not that we have insufficient data confirming the represssion *per se*, but that we have insufficient data confirming the hypothesis that as a child P felt rejected by her mother. *Clinically* we cannot *directly* confirm that something is repressed, only that this something, although it cannot be recalled, is likely to have been the case. In this situation it is proper, according to our rules of inference, to say that the something in question is repressed. We can then proceed, following extraclinical considerations, to posit *processes* that will account for the *relationship* we have inferred between the failure of recollection and the presumed occurrence of the something that is not recollected.

The *fifth* point concerns one particular aspect of Klein's formulation of clinical theory. It also provides an opportunity to correct a possible misconception of how the rules of inference are actually used. One of Klein's key concepts is that of meaning (1976, p. 26). As I have indicated on a previous occasion (Rubinstein, 1974, pp. 105f), in its psychoanalytic usage the word "meaning" has a number of meanings. I illustrated with the different ways we speak about meaning in reference to actions, symbols, and external situations. In these cases—and they are the ones Klein mainly has in mind—meaning is identifiable by the means-end rule and by rules entailed in the hypothesis of partial functional equivalence and various situational hypotheses. According to Klein, on the other hand, meaning is identified, not by inference, but by what he, following Polanyi, calls *indwelling* (p. 27). As used in this context, the word "indwelling" does not seem to differ appreciably from what analysts generally refer to as empathy and at one point (p. 39) Klein himself seems to equate empathy and indwelling.

It is here that a correction of a possible misconception of how our rules of inference are used is called for. It would be a mistake to think that, when, as I have done above, I speak about the rules of inference, I imply that what the rules identify is identified *in our experience* by clearly articulated logical steps. That is far from being the case. The application of the rules as well as the rules themselves are actually reconstructed in retrospect. I do, however, believe that, without our being aware of them, the rules are involved in our clinical understanding at least roughly as described above, much as, without our being aware of it, syntactic and other linguistic rules are involved in our everyday speech. This is relevant for a theory of empathy. Since it has a peculiar emotional as well as a purely cognitive aspect, empathy is not easy to describe in full detail. One feature, however, stands out, namely, the recognition of feelings, action tendencies, etc., on the basis, partly of their sometimes minimal expression, partly of the tacit operation of rules of inference of the kind discussed above. Thus, I cannot go along with the implicit view of many analysts, including Klein, that empathy is a not further analyzable mode of understanding. I may mention that Kohut (1977) has been quite explicit on this point. According to him, empathy is "as basic an endowment of man as his vision, hearing, touch, taste, and smell" (p. 144).

My *sixth* and last point is of an entirely different type. The above considerations all concern psychoanalysis as a science and one might claim that they *do not necessarily* carry implications regarding the efficacy of psychoanalytic therapy. Most contemporary analysts, I believe, would acknowledge that the relationship between psychoanalysis as a science and as a method of treatment is more complicated than Freud thought originally. It has, for example, never been shown that there is a positive correlation between the degree of patient improvement and the proportion of significant interpretations presented to the patient (in accordance with commonly accepted technical rules) that have been to a high degree confirmed clinically. Simple though it may seem, this statement is riddled with unanswered methodological questions. I cannot, however, in the present connection even begin to outline them.

REFERENCES

Eagle,M. (1973), Validation of motivational formulations: Acknowledgement as a criterion. *Psychoanal. & Contemp. Sci.,* 2:265–275. New York: Macmillan.

Escoll, P. J. (1977), reporter. The contribution of psychoanalytic developmental concepts to adult analysis. *J. Amer. Psychoanal. Assn.,* 25:219–234.

Eysenck, H. J., & Wilson, G. D. (1973), *The Experimental Study of Freudian Theory.* London: Methuen.

Freud, S. (1901), The psychopathology of everyday life. *Standard Edition,* 6. London: Hogarth Press, 1960.

———— (1908), Character and anal eroticism. *Standard Edition.* 9:168–175. London: Hogarth Press, 1959.

———— (1915), The unconscious. *Standard Edition,* 14:166–215. London: Hogarth Press, 1957.

———— (1938), Constructions in Analysis. *Standard Edition,* 23:257–269. London: Hogarth Press, 1964.

Hanson, N. R. (1958), *Patterns of Discovery.* Cambridge, Eng.: Cambridge University Press.

Hempel, C. G. (1965), *Aspects of Scientific Explanation.* New York: Free Press.

Hempel, C. G., & Oppenheim, P. (1948), The logic of explanation. In: H. Feigl & M. Brodbeck, ed. *Readings in the Philosophy of Science.* New York: Appleton-Century-Crofts, 1953:319–352. Reprinted with some changes and a postscript in Hempel, 1965:245–295.

Klein, G. S. (1976), *Psychoanalytic Theory.* New York: International Universities Press.

Kline, P. (1972), *Fact and Fantasy in Freudian Theory.* London: Methuen & Co.

Kohut, H. (1977), *The Restoration of the Self.* New York: International Universities Press.

Popper, K. R. (1962), *Conjectures and Refutations.* New York: Harper Torchbook, 1968.

Rubinstein, B. B. (1974), On the role of classificatory processes in mental functioning: Aspects of a psychoanalytic theoretical model. *Psychoanal. & Contemp. Sci.,* 3:101–185. New York: International Universities Press.

———— (1975), On the clinical psychoanalytic theory and its role in the inference and confirmation of particular clinical hypotheses. *Psychoanal. & Contemp. Sci.,* 4:3–57. New York: International Universities Press.

Schafer, R. (1976), *A New Language for Psychoanalysis*. New Haven & London: Yale University Press.

Silverman, L. H. (1975), On the role of laboratory experiments in the development of the clinical theory of psychoanalysis: Data on the subliminal activation of aggressive and merging wishes in schizophrenics. *Internat. Rev. Psychoanal.*, 2:43–64.

Suppe, F. (1974), *The Structure of Scientific Theories*. Urbana: University of Illinois Press.

Toulmin, S. (1953), *The Philosophy of Science: An Introduction*. New York: Harper Torchbook, 1960.

——— (1961), *Foresight and Understanding: An Enquiry into the Aim of Science*. Bloomington: Indiana University Press.

8 The Psychoanalytic and the Cognitive Unconscious

Morris N. Eagle

Freud's concept of the unconscious and the properties attributed to it represent the most interesting and the most conceptually challenging of psychoanalytic ideas and formulations. Although unconscious processes were discussed before Freud (see Ellenberger, 1970), there seemed to be at least since Descartes, an implicit equating of "mental" with "conscious." Hence, to speak of unconscious mental processes, as Freud did, seems to be a contradiction in terms, a logical absurdity. And, in fact, many philosophers did react in precisely that way to the concept of unconscious mental events (e.g., Field, Averling, and Laird, 1922).

It is unlikely that many philosophers or psychologists today would object on conceptual grounds to the idea of unconscious mental processes. Ironically, the concept of unconscious mental processes has gained a new respectability on the basis of recent experimental work in cognitive psychology and perception—work that demonstrates the existence of ubiquitous and remarkably complex and intelligent operations even in the absence of awareness.[1]

One purpose of this chapter is to examine the concept of unconscious mental processes emerging from cognitive psychology and compare it to the psychoanalytic concept of the unconscious. This comparison will reveal that while Freud's *general* claims regarding unconscious mental pro-

---

[1]See Shevrin and Dickman (1980) for a survey of experimental work in cognitive psychology that has bearing on the psychoanalytic concept of the unconscious. The issues dealt with in this chapter, however, are somewhat different from those with which Shevrin and Dickman are concerned.

cesses (e.g., that they are ubiquitous rather than exceptional, and that they show highly complex and purposive characteristics) are supported by recent work, there are important differences between his concept of the *dynamic* unconscious and the cognitive unconscious. These differences have to do with the role of repression and the issue of recoverability of unconscious contents and processes. I will also consider in this chapter some recent formulations within psychoanalytic theory that reduce those differences and render the psychoanalytic and the cognitive unconscious quite compatible. Let me begin with some concrete examples of phenomena that have suggested to cognitive psychologists the existence of complex unconscious cognitive processing.

EXAMPLES OF UNCONSCIOUS COGNITIVE OPERATIONS

If a triangle (or any other form) is flashed on at point A in a visual field and then, at an appropriate interval, at point B, one will experience the triangle moving from A to B, even though no actual movement has occurred. It is as if the viewer is making the "unconscious inference" (Helmholtz, 1867) that if an object is here in the field at time one, is there a short time later, then it must have moved. Of course, no conscious inference is experienced. But the apparent movement is just what would be experienced were the kind of inference I described above to be made. As Rock (1970) puts it, "movement will be perceived whenever the total information available adds up to the inference that an object has changed its location" (p. 9).

The inferential nature of induced movement is also demonstrated by the fact that the experience of movement can be eliminated by, so to speak, "forcing" a different inference. Thus, if simultaneously with the flashing on of B, A also reappears in its original location, one will experience no movement. Since A is in its original location, one need not "deduce" that it moved. Similarly, if a card with a window is moved back and forth revealing now A and then B, giving the impression of two objects being successively uncovered and covered, again no movement is experienced. As Rock (1970) notes, "It follows that if the first object is covered over, it has not moved to location B but remained where it is" (p. 9). Once again, the spontaneous perceptual experience will follow the inference that best fits the available data, or will be identical to what would occur if one engaged in a conscious, problemsolving inference that represented the most elegant solution to a problem.

As a second example of complex and intelligent operations underlying perceptions, consider the well-known Ames distorted room (Ittelson and Kilpatrick, 1951). Although the rear wall of the room is slanted from the frontal plane (so that ceiling and floor are not parallel, as they are normally), under appropriate viewing conditions, observers perceive the wall and room as normal. People standing in each corner of the wall are in fact at unequal distances from the observer and therefore project unequal images to the eye. As Rock (1983) explains, "According to the inference process concerning size, unequal visual angles equalized at equal distance from the observer will yield percepts of unequal size. Therefore, the people appear to be very different in size" (p. 301). It should be noted that the perceptual effect of two people objectively of the same size yet who appear markedly different in size is a striking and irresistible one and is unaffected by knowledge of how the room is constructed or that the effect is an illusion.

These examples illustrate the operation of inferential-like processes in perception. The existence of complex and intelligent cognitive processes outside awareness is not limited to inference and perception. For example, there is a good deal of evidence that we can process words along *semantic* dimensions prior to conscious and explicit knowledge of their specific identity. This is shown through a variety of techniques. For instance, Wickens (1972) reported that even though an observer may not be able to identify a stimulus word shown tachistoscopically for a brief duration and then followed by patterned masking (the pattern masks the word and prevents it from being perceived), the observer can choose, on a better-than-chance basis, words related to the stimulus word (along the dimensions of synonymity, taxonomic category, and semantic differential) when asked to select words to which the stimulus word is similar.

Employing a dichotic listening technique (the subject is given two different messages, one in each ear, and is instructed to attend to and "shadow" only one), Lewis (1970) reported that while subjects could not identify the words in the unattended channel, the reaction time for shadowing the material on the attended channel was slower when the word presented in the unattended channel was synonymous with its counterpart on the attended channel. In other words, although not consciously identified and not in awareness, the words on the unattended channel were processed up to the level of their semantic meaning, as indicated by their interference effects. In short, a highly complex and intelligent cognitive operation usually associated with conscious awareness—the analysis of semantic meaning—was being carried out at a level well below full conscious awareness.

Perhaps the most striking example of complex and intelligent cognitive operations being carried out below conscious awareness is provided by Turvey, Fertig, and Kravetz (1969), and Turvey and Fertig (1970). If in a task in which subjects are given short lists of words to remember, the words presented on the successive lists are drawn from the same category, recall performance across the lists will suffer. If, however, new words are presented from a category conceptually different from the immediately preceding one, there is a sharp recovery in recall performance. This is referred to as release from proactive interference. Turvey and his colleagues reported that one can obtain release from proactive interference when one switches words along dimensions *that are not even consciously recognizable.* Thus, if one has been presenting words that are all rated highly positive on one of the semantic differential dimensions—evaluation (good-bad), potency (strong-weak), and activity (active-passive) (Osgood,Suci and Tannenbaum, 1957)—and then switches to words highly negative on these dimensions, one will obtain release from proactive interference, that is, a significant improvement in recall. As noted, what is striking about this finding is that were one asked to examine carefully the list of words and to sort them in whatever way made most sense, it is doubtful that one could sort them according to the categories I have described above. In other words, subjects were processing and categorizing the stimulus words along very subtle and complex dimensions *implicitly and without awareness that they were so categorizing.* That these dimensions were *not* ones one would normally employ leads Turvey (1974) to raise the interesting question of whether "one may make distinctions tacitly that cannot be made explicitly, and, conversely, [whether] one may make distinctions explicitly that are not furnished tacitly" (p. 177). (How Turvey's comment relates to the psychoanalytic distinction between primary and secondary process is also an interesting question which cannot be pursued here).

As another example of complex cognitive processes that go on outside awareness, I refer to the linguistic "deep structures" that permit us to generate an indefinitely large number of coherent and gramatically correct sentences without necessarily being able to state explicitly the "rules" according to which we generate these sentences (Chomsky, 1957, 1980). This phenomenon seems clearly to be an example of having tacit unconscious knowledge of the rules we use when we generate certain behaviors, but which we may not know we have, and which we may not be able to describe explicitly. (As we shall see, the idea of behaving according to unconscious rules plays an increasingly important part in recent psychoanalytic formulations.)

Finally, I will report a number of experiments on unconscious processing that have made use of visual masking. As noted earlier, in this procedure, a stimulus (A) is presented briefly and after a brief interval is followed by a second stimulus (B). Under appropriate exposure and interval conditions, the A-stimulus is *masked* by the B-stimulus; that is, it cannot be detected. What is interesting about this technique is that under certain conditions, despite the absence of phenomenal experience of the A-stimulus, there is evidence that it has been processed at various levels of analysis. In an early study in this area (Eagle, 1959), the A-stimulus was a drawing of a boy engaged in either a benevolent act (handing a birthday cake to someone) or an aggressive act (knifing someone), and the B-stimulus was the boy himself with a neutral expression. Despite failure to detect the A-stimulus, the perceptions and judgments of the B-stimulus (as revealed in drawings and ratings on the semantic differential) were influenced by whether the A-stimulus was benevolent or aggressive. In other words, there was evidence that the A-stimulus was processed despite the absence of phenomenal experience.

In another masking study, Marcel (1983a) employed a variant of the Stroop (1935) color-word task in which subjects were asked to name a color that had been immediately preceded by a masked congruent color-word (e.g., the word "blue" when the color was blue), an incongruent color-word (e.g., the word "red" when the color was blue), or a control string of letters. Previous research with supraliminally presented words had demonstrated that color-naming reaction time decreases when the preceding word is congruent, and increases when the preceding word is incongruent. This is referred to as a priming effect. Marcel reported that even when the priming words were masked and presented at a level where subjects could not identify them, they nevertheless had a priming effect; that is, they influenced the reaction time to color-naming in the same way as supraliminally presented words do. In other words, the failure to achieve phenomenal experience did not prevent the processing of information up to the semantic level. Marcel reports a series of additional experiments, all of which indicate that complex information processing is possible despite the absence of phenomenal awareness.

On the strength of these studies, Marcel proposes a number of conclusions, some of which, although based on processing of perceptual information, are nevertheless remarkably similar to Freud's ideas regarding the nature of unconscious processes. Briefly they are: (1) Representations not represented in phenomenal awareness can nevertheless influence behavior and conscious experience. (2) Representations yielded by unconscious processing are different from those of which we are conscious. (3) While a perceptual event may be unconsciously processed along a number of dimensions simultaneously, only one interpretation at a time can be represented consciously. (4) A consciously experienced percept is not so much a retrieval or copy of an unconsciously processed event, but "the imposition of a qualitatively different structural description" (Marcel, 1983b, p. 256). That is, a conscious percept "is obtained by a constructive act of fitting a perceptual hypothesis to its sensory source" (Marcel, 1983b, p. 245). (5) Conscious representations can be reflected upon and reported, and serve as the basis for choice and intentional action, while none of these characteristics hold for unconscious representations. (6) Unconscious representations are best revealed indirectly, by their effects on other behavior and experience. Narrowing one's attention and focus to direct conscious identification and report of a stimulus may be inimical to revealing unconscious representations.[2]

In two very well designed experiments on the same variant of the Stroop color-naming test as the one employed by Marcel, Cheesman and Merikle (1984) present convincing evidence that at least some of the effects produced under conditions of visual masking reported by Marcel (1980, 1983a) and others are attributable to the fact that the masked stimuli were presented at exposure duration levels at which subjects can detect the masked stimuli at better than chance levels if very sensitive measures such as forced-choice responses are employed. However, as these authors note, all subjects reported that they could not perceive the masked words, despite their better than chance detection performances. In other words, although subjects may perform at clearly better than chance detection levels (at some exposure durations they perform at very high detection levels), their experience is that they are merely guessing.

This discrepancy between performance and subjective awareness led Cheesman and Merikle to distinguish between the exposure level at which detection performance is not greater than chance— the "objective threshold"—and the exposure level at which subjects *experience* that they cannot detect the stimulus and are merely guessing—the "subjective threshold." Cheesman and Merikle conclude and, as mentioned above, present convincing evidence that previous investigators reporting results in perception outside awareness were presenting stimuli at the subjective rather than the objective threshold level. Although Cheesman and Merikle intend to cast doubt on previous perception-without-awareness reports, their results actually *support* a more careful formulation of the perception-without-awareness phenomenon. Being able to discriminate the stimulus word in a forced-choice procedure at a better than chance level, while at the same time *not being consciously aware of the identity* of the word itself, indicates that semantic information has been processed without conscious awareness— that is, this ability itself indicates perception without awareness.

However, Cheesman and Merikle's results call for skepticism and caution in regard to those claims of perception without awareness in which stimuli are presented at or below the "objective" threshold—that is, at or below an exposure duration at which sensitive measures of response, such as forced choice, yield chance detection performances.

The finding reported by Cheesman and Merikle that is similar to the one reported by Marcel (1983a) is worth noting again. Despite the fact that subjects may report that they are guessing and that they have no confi-

---

[2]Although Marcel did not intend to do so, this conclusion can serve as a rationale for the use of free association to uncover unconscious material.

dence in their responses, these responses do, indeed, indicate that the subjects have processed information at the semantic level. Were someone to refuse to guess and to insist upon greater confidence in his response before issuing it, it would never be apparent that he knew much about the stimulus, even at the level where, subjectively, it felt that he was only guessing randomly.

There are many other examples of the cognitive processing and discriminations that occur prior to explicit recognition of stimuli—for example, affective discrimination prior to recognition (Kunst-Wilson and Zajonc, 1980). However, the foregoing examples should provide some idea of the range of complex cognitive processes that go on outside conscious focal awareness. In short, to cognitive psychologists, Freud's claim that complex unconscious mental processes are ubiquitous raises no special empirical or conceptual difficulties.

DIFFERENCES BETWEEN COGNITIVE AND PSYCHOANALYTIC UNCONSCIOUS

Whatever parallels there are between the cognitive and the psychoanalytic unconscious, there are also important differences. Perhaps the most obvious difference is suggested by the term "dynamic unconscious" in the psychoanalytic literature.[3] This conception describes a drama in which wishes are pushing for expression, and defensive processes are preventing full expression of these wishes. The Freudian "dynamic unconscious" consists mainly of id impulses, in Freud's (1933) words, "a cauldron full of seething excitations" (p. 73), whose primary nature is to strive peremptorily for immediate gratification, independent of consequences of reality and other constraints.

One must remember that for Freud cognition and thought develop out of the pressure of drive gratification. According to Freud (1900), if we were able to gratify our needs without cognitive activities, the latter would never develop. He writes:

All the complicated thought-activity which is spun out from the mnemic image to the moment at which the perceptual identity is established by the

---

[3]The psychoanalytic "dynamic unconscious" is, above all, an unconscious of aims, motives, and drives, in contrast to a cognitive unconscious of thought processes and ideas. This difference parallels an historical, one in which an exclusive emphasis on the logical, thoughtlike nature of unconscious mental life was supplemented by an emphasis on unconscious will and volition. Schopenhauer's (1881) "will to live" represents an obvious expression of the latter emphasis. It is well to remember, in speaking of historical antecedents to Freud's "dynamic unconscious," that for Schopenhauer, the will to live is most clearly expressed in sexual and self–preservative instincts.

external world—all this activity of thought merely constitutes a roundabout path to wish-fulfillment which has been made necessary by experience . . . . Thought is after all nothing but a substitute for a hallucinatory wish [pp. 605– 606].

Freud did not seem to take seriously the possibility that cognition and thought could be inherently programmed to reflect reality and could have their owns structure and development—an assumption basic to cognitive psychology.[4]

In any case, the important point is that in Freudian theory unconscious mental processes always reveal their links to drive gratification and are characterized by such primary process features as irrationality, illogicality, symbolization, condensation, displacement, and so on. By contrast, the unconscious mental processes of cognitive psychology are anything but irrational and illogical. As we have seen, these processes are intelligent, logical, and problem-solving.

Implied in the foregoing is another important, indeed basic, set of differences between the psychoanalytic and cognitive unconscious, having to do with the former's emphasis on repression and recoverability. What prevents full expression in awareness of instinctual wishes is the process of repression, which is itself unconscious. The "dynamic unconscious" is a repository of repressed contents. It is further claimed that when this active process is removed (e.g., through the therapeutic process), the contents that emerge and are consciously experienced are exactly those ordinary wishes and ideas which would have been experienced had not the active process of repression prevented it. In other words, what Freud claimed, and what the concept of repression also implicitly claims, is that unconscious contents are *recoverable* in conscious experience. In his description of unconscious mental states, Freud (1915) wrote:

We know for certain that they have abundant points of contact with conscious mental processes; with the help of a certain amount of work they can be transformed into, or replaced by, conscious mental processes, and all the categories which we employ to describe conscious mental acts, such as ideas, purposes, resolutions and so on, can be applied to them. Indeed we are obliged to say of some of these latent states that the only respect in which they differ from conscious ones is precisely in the absence of consciousness [p. 168].

In contrast to this view, the processes emphasized in cognitive psychology are generally not recoverable in conscious experience. For example, the

---

[4]One of the more important contributions of psychoanalytic ego psychology (e.g., Hartmann, 1939) is the idea that ego functions, such as cognition and thinking, can develop autonomously and independently of instinctual drive.

"unconscious inferences" discussed earlier are not expected, through any means, to be directly represented in conscious experience. While they can be described as if they were available to awareness, and while they are, so to speak, "reflected" in perceptual and cognitive products, these processes are simply not phenomenally present in conscious experience. Try as one might, one will never directly recover in experience the processes of "unconscious inference" that appear to underly the phenomenon of stroboscopic movement.

It seems to me that this difference in recoverability may, in part at least, be a function of the contrast between the psychoanalytic emphasis on contents (e.g., particular ideas and wishes) and the emphasis of cognitive psychology on processes. As Nisbett and Wilson (1977) have documented, one tends to consciously experience contents rather than the processes leading to these contents. The processes do not appear to be readily accessible to conscious experience. As Mullane (1983) points out, in psychoanalytic theory, too, while repressed unconscious contents such as wishes and ideas are held to be recoverable in consciousness, the *process* of repression is not recoverable in conscious experience. Similarly, while dream contents and symptoms are things we experience, the *processes* of dream formation and sympton formation function "automatically" and are not capable of becoming conscious.

Most important, a central assumption contained in the psychoanalytic ideas of repression and recoverability is what Marcel (1983a, b) refers to as the "identity assumption." The assumption is made that the wish or idea that is now experienced consciously is *identical* to the unconscious wish or idea that was repressed. The notion of the "timelessness of the unconscious" further supports the idea that a wish that emerges in consciousness, following the lifting of repression, is *identical* to the early, infantile wish rendered unconscious by repression. A wish *becomes* conscious, *forces* its way into consciousness. As Marcel has pointed out, the "identity assumption" has, in the past, also characterized conceptions of perception and memory. Thus, a percept was viewed as a *copy* of a physical object, and a memory was a *record* (e.g., an image, a replica, a trace) of an event that, when recovered through recall, produced that record.

In contrast to the "identity assumption" is the more contemporary constructivist view, which argues that consciousness and the phenomenal experiences that comprise it are *constructions*. Thus, perception is not a copy or replica of physical reality, but a constructive process that "attempt[s] to make sense of as much data as possible at the highest or most functionally useful level possible. . . ." (Marcel, 1983b). This is most apparent in the case of perceptual illusions. Induced movement, for example, as we have seen, is not a replica of reality, but a construction based on certain sets of cues. Similarly, a currently recalled memory is not a *reappearance* of an earlier recorded event, but a new construction of a disparate set of *features*. To give an illustration, there is a good deal of evidence that presented words are stored in memory as constellations of different features (e.g., the first letter of the word, the number of syllables it contains, the superordinate category to which it belongs, etc.). Further, the recall of a word is the "assembling," the construction of a set of features. This is shown by such phenomena as knowing the first letter with which a word begins when one cannot recall the word, as in the "tip-of-the-tongue" phenomenon (Brown and McNeil, 1966), or selecting an associatively or semantically related word when one makes a recognition error.

Freud (1937) himself recognized that memories are often constructions reflecting one's current state at least as much as the purported recorded event. Yet Freud did not extend this insight to unconscious wishes, ideas, and impulses. For these categories of mental life, Freud adhered to the "identity assumption," as if, somehow, unconscious wishes, ideas, and impulses were wholly formed and, following the removal of the repression barrier, simply made their appearance in consciousness, in unaltered form. This seems neither an especially accurate nor a useful way of under-standing and conceptualizing the relationship between unconscious and conscious processes and contents. A more likely assumption is, as Mandler (1983) and Marcel (1983b) suggest, that conscious experiences (including wishes and ideas) are constructions that depend on the particular uncon-scious and preconscious schemata that have been activated. In this concep-tion of the relationship between the unconscious and conscious, the unconscious (and preconscious) is not a storehouse of wishes and ideas waiting to become *conscious,* but a mental structure of features, schemata, and so on (perhaps ultimately to be linked to neurophysiological structures) that are, so to speak, drawn upon by, but not identical to, conscious experience.

Interestingly, the "identity assumption" is not present in Freud's *general* conception of the unconscious as the source of conscious experience, as the psychic *Ding an sich,* which can never be known directly, but which is indirectly known through the conscious experience to which it contributes and which it helps form. Freud's (1915) ideas that all "mental processes are in themselves unconscious" (p. 171), that only a portion of "psychical acts" reach consciousness, and that unconscious processes are qualitatively dif-ferent from conscious awareness do not appear to entail an "identity assumption."

The "identity assumption" makes its appearance when Freud discusses the so-called "dynamic unconscious" and the role of repression. Through these concepts, Freud was attempting to explain phenomena in which a wish or idea consciously (even if fleetingly) experienced at one time was then banished from consciousness but seemed to continue to influence experience and behavior (e.g., symptoms, slips, and dreams). That is, in some way (including symbolically), the person continued to behave *as if* he or she continued to harbor the banished wish or idea. Thus it is easy to understand why Freud thought of the repressed wish or idea as continuing to exist in its original form in the unconscious (just as it is easy to understand why one thinks of an unrecalled memory as the original record of an event, which simply appears in consciousness when recall occurs). However, this conception of an unconscious wish or idea has never been fully elucidated, nor have the difficulties it presents ever been fully resolved (e.g., see Rubinstein, 1980).

As noted earlier, the "identity assumption" view does not seem to be either accurate or profitable. What seems more accurate and more heuristic is a conception of unconscious wishes and ideas as *sets of schemata* that can be selectively activated. (It will be recognized that this is analogous to the idea discussed earlier—for which there is a good deal of evidence—that memories are stored as sets of features, any one or more of which can be selectively activated and "appear" in recall.) The particular schemata (and features) activated, their links to other schemata, and the different *organizations* of schemata possible can be related to Freud's (1911) conception of primary and secondary process and to Rapaport's (1951) concept of drive versus conceptual organization of thought and memory. These suggestions obviously need to be filled in and elaborated. However, it does seem clear that the relinquishment of the "identity assumption" and its replacement by the basic ideas of preconscious and unconscious schemata, of their selective activation (and deactivation), and of conscious experience as a constructive process that makes use of activated schemata, not only are likely to be more heuristic in their own right, but also represent a reformulation of psychoanalytic theory that will permit its integration with cognitive psychology. Such an integration is likely to entail, among other things, reformulations of certain basic psychoanalytic concepts, including the "cornerstone" concept of repression (see Rubinstein, 1967; 1974; Peterfreund, 1971; Bowlby, 1979, 1980, 1981; and Erdelyi and Goldberg, 1979 for some recent attempts to link psychoanalytic concepts to broader and current psychological approaches. These attempts are briefly discussed later.)

One may conclude that although recoverability may or may not be a real difference between the psychoanalytic and the cognitive unconscious, its importance is diminished when one rejects the "identity assumption." As I have tried to show, making the unconscious conscious is never a matter of direct recoverablilty. Furthermore, as I will now try to show, to the extent that the psychoanalytic unconscious is also made up of such processes as "rules," if-then propositions, implicit beliefs, and so forth, the issue of direct recoverability becomes less relevant and less important.

COMPATIBILITY BETWEEN PSYCHOANALYTIC AND
COGNITIVE UNCONSCIOUS

Despite the differences between the psychoanalytic and the cognitive unconscious, there are two broad considerations that reduce the conceptual incongruities and incompatibilities between them. One consideration concerns recent reformulations of certain clinical concepts in terms of unconscious beliefs and rules. The second consideration involves a recent psychoanalytic emphasis on unconscious representations (of self and object) which can perhaps constitute a link to the emphasis on representations in cognitive psychology.

UNCONSCIOUS "GRIM BELIEFS," "RULES," AND
SYMBOLIC EQUIVALENCES

In the context of presenting a new model of psychoanalytic therapy, Weiss, Sampson and their colleagues (e.g., Weiss, 1982; Weiss, Sampson, and the Mount Zion Psychotherapy Research Group, 1986) have argued that patients come to treatment with burdensome unconscious "pathogenic beliefs" they want to be rid of, rather than, as posited in traditional psychoanalytic theory, with infantile instinctual wishes they seek to gratify. Implicit in this reformulation of psychoanalytic theory is a reconceptualization of the psychoanalytic unconscious that includes beliefs, rules, and cognitive–affective schemata rather than simply instinctual wishes and impulses.

Consider, for example, the Freudian concept of castration anxiety. As Weiss (1982) suggests, in clinical understanding, a person suffering from castration anxiety can be said to be reacting in accord with the following complex, unconscious if-then proposition: If I openly pursue my ambitions and succeed, which is unconsciously equivalent to replacing father and therefore symbolically equivalent to committing incest, then I will be mutilated. As Weiss points out, understood in that way, castration anxiety rests on an unconscious "grim or pathogenic belief" in which ambitious strivings, and success in these strivings, are inevitably associated with the expectation of punishment and mutilation. What is involved here is a complex cognitive-motivational structure in which certain ordinary wishes and strivings, which, in themselves, are likely to be largely conscious, are "encoded" as if they were the equivalent of hostile and incestuous wishes and are then unconsciously *believed* and *expected* to warrant and bring severe punishment. In this cognitive-motivational complex, it is not so much wishes and strivings that are unconscious, but the cognitive components of both the symbolic meaning of these wishes and the belief and expectation that they are inevitably followed by punishment.

Consider, as another example of a cognitive–affective schema including a "pathogenic belief," Modell's (1983) description of what he calls "survivor guilt" and "separation guilt." These are patients whose anxiety and guilt suggest the following unconscious if-then proposition: If I separate from my parent(s) and survive (and even prosper) as a separate and autonomous person, it will be at the expense of my parent(s). Or, as a variant of this theme, Masterson (1976) suggests that commonly found in the history of borderline patients is an early pattern in which mother withdraws her emotional availability in response to the child's efforts at separation and autonomy and emotionally rewards the child's regressive and clinging be-havior. Obviously, this pattern of response is likely to shape behavior, so that the positively reinforced regressive behavior is strengthened, and inde-pendent behavior is discouraged. But, in the present context, this pattern of response constitutes implicit messages that separation from mother dis-pleases her and leads to the danger that love and support will be with-drawn. This response pattern can also be seen as leading to the establishment of such messages as implicit rules: If I try to separate and become independent, it will be at the expense of mother, or I will be abandoned, or some kind of disaster will follow.

I believe that a "pathogenic belief" similar to the ones discussed is often characteristic of agoraphobic patients. In the last few years, I have treated four agoraphobic women in whom separation guilt and anxiety appeared to be primary. In these cases, the initial insight and awareness, quite close to their actual phobic experience, was that they had been living according to the proposition, or rule, that "if I separate I will not survive." Later in treatment came the more startling and surprising insight that they had been living according to the further if-then proposition, or rule that "if I separate, mother (or father) will not survive."

For one agoraphobic patient, this insight was dramatically facilitated by a particular incident, which I will describe. But first some brief background information: Following the birth of her first baby (and a difficult pregnan-cy, which included toxemia) and the prospect of moving to a new town, the patient developed severe agoraphobic symptoms, which resulted in her, her husband, and their new baby moving in with her parents. For many years, the patient had always prepared the filters for her mother's kidney dialysis machine. She continued to do this even after she had married and moved into her new apartment (before returning to her parents subsequent to the outbreak of the agoraphobic symptoms). Some time during the course of therapy, the patient decided that she would no longer be respon-sible for this task, and she so informed her mother, who appeared to accept her decision with equanimity. Shortly after this, the patient came to the session and reported that at the end of the previous week her mother had gone to visit a relative a few hundred miles away and had to return suddenly because she had not brought enough filters with her and thereby had literally endangered her life. While relating this incident, the patient suddenly and emotionally exclaimed: "No wonder I had to move back home. This way I can oversee *both* my mother and Mark [her new baby]." During the course of therapy, the patient became more and more aware of the degree to which she had internalized her mother's message, "If you leave me and live your own life, I will not survive." From the time of the incident with the dialysis filters, the patient began to make steady progress, eventually became symptom free and, with her husband and baby, moved into her own apartment.

To remind the reader of the main point of this example, in some of Freud's own clinical concepts (e.g., castration anxiety) as well as in the recent clinical formulations noted earlier, the unconscious is implicitly conceptualized, not as a repository of instinctual impulses and wishes but as a cognitive-affective structure that includes implicit "rules" and propositions and associated dispositions to experience certain affects (e.g., guilt and anxiety).

When concepts such as castration anxiety are understood as implicit or unconscious rules, the similarities between the cognitive and psychoanalytic unconscious become even more apparent. For example, just at "unconscious inferences" and "deep structures" do not need to be made explicit in order for them to be descriptive of certain behaviors, so castration anxiety, understood as an unconscious rule, does not need to be explicit in order for it to account for certain behaviors. Thus, a person need not consciously and explicitly entertain the belief that if he pursues certain strivings, certain threatening consequences will follow. And yet, the person's pattern of overt behavior, thoughts, and affects will be as if he had the above belief and *as if* he were following that "rule" in certain areas of his life.[5]

---

[5]Although not acknowledged by them, "pathogenic beliefs" discussed by Weiss (1982), Weiss, Sampson and their colleagues (1986) are similar, in important respects, to the schemata and "rules of living" invoked by Beck and his colleagues (e.g., Beck, Rush, Shaw, and Emery, 1979) to account for the cognitive distortions associated with depression. Both involve implicit assumptions and belief systems that are dysfunctional and are associated with maladaptive behaviors and dysphoric affects (above all, anxiety and depression). However, there are important differences between the two views, mainly arising out of the fact that Weiss and Sampson and Modell (1983) derive their concept of "pathogenic beliefs" from a psychoanalytic context. Beck and his colleagues write about dysfunctional cognitions and schemata in general terms, with little or no reference to the object-rational, dynamic, and developmental contexts in which these cognitions and schemata arise and in which they are enacted. Thus, Beck discusses the "cognitive triad" of negative concepts about one's self, the future, and the external world in a general sense; that is, he does not link it to unconscious meanings, to

A further discussion of parallels between the Freudian unconscious and Chomsky's "deep structures" can be found in Nagel (1974).[6]

Unconscious Representations

Another consideration that renders the psychoanalytic unconscious more compatible with the cognitive unconscious is the psychoanalytic emphasis on unconscious representations (e.g., see Sandler and Rosenblatt, 1962;

---

specific wishes and aims, to specific interactions, to specific developmental issues, or to specific origins, other than to say that these negative cognitions are "developed from previous experience" (Beck et al., 1979, p. 3). Consider, by contrast, Weiss's discussion of the pathogenic belief on which castration anxiety is based: Certain aims (ambitious strivings) that are particularly associated with developmental issues in interaction with parental figures, take on unconscious meanings and are then linked to anxiety and associated dysfunctions and inhibitions. Or, as another example, consider the survivor guilt and separation guilt discussed by Modell: Based on implicit messages communicated in specific interactions, developmentally appropriate aims and strivings for separation and autonomy assume certain unconscious meanings and become associated with anxiety and guilt.

Another important difference between cognitive-behavior therapy and the psychoanalytic approach of Weiss (1982) and Weiss, Sampson, and their colleagues (1986) is the recognition on the part of the latter group that pathogenic beliefs are both enacted in, and relinquished through, the ongoing relationship with the therapist. According to this group, patients test their "pathogenic beliefs" in their interaction with the therapist and work through their pathogenic beliefs and expectations by the aid of the establishment of therapeutic *conditions of safety*.

Recently, Safran (1983) observed that cognitive-behavior therapists typically neglect the information available from their interactions with the patient, in particular their own feelings and reactions, and argues that the cognitive-behavior therapist should be "actively using the therapeutic relationship to disconform the client's dysfunctional expectations about interpersonal relationships" (p. 17). He has also noted—and this is, of course, taken for granted in psychoanalytically oriented therapy—that the patient's pattern of behavior with the therapist, and the reactions that that pattern evokes in the latter, are indicative of the patient's behavior pattern with other people, and the reactions he or she evokes in them. Safran also echoes the criticisms by others (e.g., Mahoney, 1980) of cognitive therapists' overly narrow view of the role of affect (particularly anxiety) in behavior and in treatment. While Safran's comments are made in the context of demonstrating the relevance and importance of Sullivan's Interpersonal Theory to cognitive-behavior therapy, they are also relevant in the present context. For, certain similarities notwithstanding, the areas of relative neglect noted by Safran also serve to highlight the differences between cognitive-behavior therapy and the approach of Weiss (1982) and Weiss, Sampson, and their colleagues (1986).

[6]Nagel raises the question of what it means to follow or have knowledge of a rule. He argues that in order for one to attribute knowledge of a rule to a person, that person must be able to *recognize* that rule as an expression of his understanding of a particular domain. For example, according to Nagel, to claim that a person has knowledge of linguistic "deep structures," means that one must show that the person, as an expression of his understanding of language, must come to recognize certain grammatical rules embedded in these "deep structures." And if one extended this to the case of castration anxiety, Nagel would be understood as insisting that, if we are to speak in terms of following rules, it would mean that the person

Blatt, 1974; Bowlby, 1980; Blatt and Lerner, 1983). The concept of representations, although appearing with great frequency in current psychoanalytic
literature, is often vague and undefined. As far as I can see, as it is used in
that literature, the concept of self-/ and object representations is intended
to refer to the implicit schemata, images, working models—whatever lan-

---

must come to recognize the rule, "if certain strivings, then threatening consequences," as an
expression of his understanding of his behavior.

It seems to me that Nagel insists on a person being able to recognize a rule because he
wants to distinguish—following Rubinstein's (1977) distinction—a *person* following a rule, and
an *organism*, a brain, or a central nervous system following a rule. Nagel makes clear his view
that in the latter case, speaking of rule-following is only a *metaphoric* way of talking. Thus, in
the perception of induced movement, references to "unconscious inferences" being "made"
and "rules" being followed are only *as-if* ways of talking. It is only *as if* one were making an
"unconscious inference" or following a rule. But, *as a person*, one is not making an inference or
following a rule. And the fact that no inference or rule is recoverable in conscious experience
would, to Nagel, represent evidence for this conclusion. The person experiencing induced
movement will never come to recognize the inference or rule as an expression of his understanding or his or her experience of induced movement. This is similar to the perceptual-
distortion experience in the Ames room experiment. One will never come to consciously
experience the "inference" concerning the relationship among visual angles, distances, and
resulting percepts of size. Nor will one come to understand the "inference" as an expression of
one's understanding or of one's experience. If, upon given a theoretical account, one does
understand the explanation of one's perceptual experience in terms of the above "inference,"
one's understanding is not in terms of something that one, as person, has done, or in terms of
some rule that one, as person, has understood and followed, but is rather an understanding
that is not essentially different from comprehending the complex "rule-following" operations
of a sophisticated piece of machinery.

In further support of Nagel's distinction, the evidence indicates, as noted earlier, that
experiences such as induced movement and the Ames room perceptual distortions are entirely
uninfluenced by knowledge given to the observer—for example, knowledge regarding how
the Ames room is constructed, or knowledge that one's experience of induced movement is
illusory. This suggests, although not conclusively that the rules that generate such phenomena
as induced movement and the Ames room perceptual distortions are expressions of rigidly
determined, preprogrammed properties of the central nervous system rather than learned
relationships acquired by a person.

For Nagel, the critical factor in permitting one to talk legitimately about a person following
a rule appears to be the potential recoverability of the rule. Even if, at any given time, the rule
that one is following is a tacit one, unavailable to conscious experience, it must be capable of
being recovered in conscious experience if one is to be legitimately entitled to say that one is
following a rule in a sense that is not simply metaphoric. Thus, one may be unaware of, and
unable at a given time to articulate, the grammatical rules underlying one's grammatically
correct sentences. However, in order to be able to say that, as person, one is following such
and such grammatical rules, one must, according to Nagel, be capable of recognizing and
articulating those rules, understanding their connection to the sentences one has generated,
and perhaps even intentionally using them to generate new sentences.

A similar point can be made with regard to the unconscious "rules" of interest to psychoanalysis discussed here. Even if, at any given time, the rules implied in castration anxiety,
separation guilt, and survivor guilt are tacit and are not available to conscious experience,
these rules are capable of being recovered in conscious experience. That is, one is capable of

guage one chooses to use—one implicitly has of oneself and of others. Related concepts include self-image, body-image, identity, and object constancy.

Self-/ and object representations can vary according to their degree of articulation as well as their differentiation from each other. For example, to speak of poor ego boundaries is essentially to say that one's implicit sense of oneself is not clearly articulated and is not sharply differentiated from others and from the environment. Self-/ and object representations can also vary according to their qualitative contents (e.g., poor versus good self-image) and the degree to which these contents are internally consistent and internally integrated. For example, one's different representations of another can be integrated to yield a complex, coherent, and stable image. Or they can remain unintegrated and yield temporally unstable alternations of all-good and all-bad images (a phenomenon referred to as "splitting" in the literature). The latter case is as if two different people—one all good and the other all bad—were being represented. Furthermore, the affective reactions associated with these different object representations also remain unintegrated, so that all-loving alternate with all-hating responses.

Much more can be said about the concept of self-/ and object representations, but in the present context, the main point is that a psychoanalytic unconscious constituted by representations, schemata, images, and working models is much closer to the unconscious of cognitive psychology than is the traditional unconscious of instinctual wishes and impulses. Insofar as the basic conceptual elements of cognitive psychology are also representations, schemata, and images, cognitive psychology shares a common con-

---

experiencing consciously that these are the rules that one is or was following, and one is capable of understanding certain past and new behaviors as expressions of these rules. Hence, by Nagel's criterion, it is legitimate to say that, as person, one is following the unconscious rules referred to by concepts such as castration anxiety, separation guilt, and survivor guilt.

It should be noted that to say that one must be capable of understanding and consciously experiencing a rule if it is to be applicable to a person does not mean, as Mischel (1963, 1966) has argued, that in order to validate an attribution of unconscious motives (or, in the present case, unconscious rules) to another person, that *particular individual* must come to acknowledge and consciously experience that motive (or that rule). For, as I have argued elsewhere (Eagle, 1973), that particular individual may never come to acknowledge the attribution (just as a particular individual may never come to understand an unconscious rule as descriptive of his behavior, or perhaps just as a particular individual may never be able to articulate explicitly the grammatical rules he or she is following in generating a wide range of sentences). What is involved in Nagel's criterion is not the acknowledgements of particular individuals, but whether attributions of unconscious motives and rules are the kinds of things one can, as person, consciously experience and understand as descriptive of one's behavior. Hence, while a particular individual may never become conscious of an unconscious desire attributed to him, desires are the kinds of things that he, as person, can understand as accounting for certain of his behaviors.

ceptual language with the recent reformulations of the psychoanalytic unconscious.

THE ROLE OF REPRESSION

A primary and traditional goal of psychoanalysis and psychoanalytic therapy has been to make the unconscious conscious, and this, in turn, has meant to undo repressions. This makes sense in the context of the traditional conception of the dynamic unconscious, with its emphasis on instinctual wishes and impulses. That is, a primary goal of therapy was to bring to conscious awareness and experience the instinctual wishes one has repressed, but which nevertheless had continued to strive for and find expression in various behaviors, including, of course, neurotic symptoms. What does it mean, however, to undo repressions when one is speaking of unconscious representations and unconscious "grim beliefs" and "rules"? More specifically, when one refers to unconscious representations and grim beiefs, does one require the concept of repression and the entire theoretical network in which it is embedded, including instinct, theory, cathexis, and countercathexis? Can one even meaningfully think of beliefs being repressed, and still retain the original, basic meaning of repression?

Within psychoanalytic theory, beliefs are not the kinds of phenomena that are repressed. Nor does it even make sense, in that context, to speak of beliefs being able to be repressed. Since the anxiety to which the conscious awareness of a particular content would lead is the immediate cause of its repression, one would have to say that in order for beliefs to be repressed, beliefs themselves are associated with anxiety, or that beliefs themselves will bring horrible consequences. But, as we have seen, in a concept like castration anxiety, it is not beliefs but certain strivings and wishes that are associated with anxiety. If I believe that certain strivings are equivalent to murder and incest and will therefore bring severe punishment, it is understandable that I would repress these strivings. But what sense would it make to talk about repressing my beliefs about these strivings? One can also ask a similar question with regard to unconscious self-/ and object representations. While these representations may be unconscious, they, too, do not easily fit the Freudian model of repression. For example, one can hardly speak meaningfully of unconscious representations that are constantly striving for expression and gratification and are being kept from conscious awareness by countercathexis. (This issue will be discussed more fully later in this paper.) If it is not very meaningful to speak of unconscious representatons, rules, and beliefs being repressed, in the traditional sense of repression, how is one to understand their unconscious status?

THE ACQUISITION OF UNCONSCIOUS "PATHOGENIC BELIEFS" AND REPRESENTATIONS

The answer to the above question, I suggest, includes the following considerations:

Images, schemata, and working models of oneself and others generally form the background of our interactions and experiences, rather than being themselves focal and explicit. They are akin to what Polanyi (1958) calls "tacit knowledge." Like all "tacit knowledge," they are not normally present in our conscious experience, not because they are repressed, but because they are implicit and not spelled out. For example, to say that one represents others as hostile, ungiving parents does not mean that this representation is either in one's conscious awareness or, because it is not, repressed. Rather, it means that one reacts to others *as if* one expected them to be hostile and depriving, and *as if* one's implicit schemata and image of them were of a hostile, depriving parent. In short, one reason implicit representations and rules remain implicit is that they often were acquired early in development and have never been made explicit. Also, as Bowlby (1979) points out with regard to unconscious representations—and, I would add, unconscious rules and beliefs—there is a commitment by all not to examine them or make them explicit.

Consider the example of my agoraphobic patient described earlier. The unconscious belief that if she becomes an autonomous person and leaves mother, the latter will not survive is not acquired directly and explicitly. Rather, such "messages" are typically enacted and communicated implicitly and nonverbally—as, for example, in the mother's failure to take a sufficient number of dialysis filters with her, after the daughter refused to assume that task. Indeed, one can expect that were the message explicitly spelled out, it would be denied by the person communicating it. Furthermore, such messages are also there to be learned, through the observations of interactions of other members of the family.

In short, the "pathogenic beliefs" on which separation guilt, castration anxiety, and other maladaptive responses are based are learned mainly nonverbally and implicitly, and in an interpersonal and affective context in which the very rule or message being learned is never made explicit. The impact and influence of these implicit messages are then maintained through a number of processes. As Freud (1923) pointed out about superego formation, prohibitions and taboos that were once external become internalized as part of one's own personality. Similarily, the implicit messages I am discussing become internalized, so that their maintenance no longer depends upon external sources. Further, as seems to be the case with much tacit knowledge, in contrast to explicit knowledge, these implicit rules are not "damaged by adverse evidence" (Polanyi and Prosch, 1975). That is, they are never directly subjected to test and criticism. In short, one continues to operate on the basis of these early acquired implicit "rules."

It should be noted that in traditional Freudian theory, ordinary strivings are symbolically equated with incest and murder because—given the universality of the oedipal complex—ordinary strivings do constitute partial, indirect, and disguised gratifications of sexual (incest) and aggressive (murderous) wishes. Hence, as noted earlier, castration anxiety is a quasi-rational instance of the punishment fitting the (psychological) crime. If, however, one does not uncritically accept this view, the question of how certain ordinary strivings come to be symbolically equivalent to incest and murder, remains a particularly apt one.

INSTINCTUAL WISHES VERSUS SYMBOLIC EQUIVALENCE

When Modell (1983) discusses the "pathogenic belief" underlying "survivor guilt" and "separation guilt"—to the effect that if I separate and become an independent person, I will destroy mother (or father)—he does not suggest that a person experiencing survivor guilt or separation guilt necessarily harbors the *actual wish* to destroy mother. Rather, such a person is reacting *as if* strivings for separation and autonomy were *symbolically equivalent* to destroying mother. And similarly, when Weiss (1982) describes the "pathogenic belief" underlying castration anxiety, he does not suggest that the person experiencing such anxiety necessarily harbors *actual* unconscious death wishes toward father and *actual* incestuous wishes toward mother. Rather, he suggests that castration anxiety stems from the "pathogenic belief" that if I achieve certain ambitious strivings, my success will entail the destruction of father. In other words, as noted earlier, Weiss suggests that one does not actually wish the destruction of father, but that certain developmentally normal and ordinary strivings are experienced, at some level, as *symbolically equivalent* to the destruction of father.[7]

---

[7]I am not suggesting that children never have death wishes and incestuous impulses toward their parents. What I am questioning, and what seems to me to be implicitly questioned by the concept of pathogenic belief, is the claim that certain clinical phenomena, such as castration anxiety and separation guilt, are a consequence of the biologically based *universality* of such wishes and impulses. I am suggesting, instead—and, it seems clear, so are Weiss (1982) and Modell (1983)—that these "grim beliefs" and their associated anxiety and guilt are based on symbolic equivalences facilitated by parental implicit communications.

It is also possible that parental hostility towards the child's achievements and competitive strivings may itself be the stimulus that creates hostile, even murderous, impulses in the child towards the parents. Without regard for the particular history and origin of these hostile impulses, their very existence is taken as further confirmation of what is already assumed—namely, the universality of the oedipal complex.

Two important questions arise in connection with this idea of symbolic equivalences: How are they acquired? And why do they (and other rules and beliefs) remain inaccessible to conscious awareness? As for the question of acquisition of unconscious symbolic equivalences, I have already suggested that they may be based on implicit and early parental messages communicated to the child. But, contrary to Weiss's and Modell's claims, that explanation is unlikely to represent the entire story and, in any case, does not take adequate account of the child's developmental level.

I suggest that unconscious meanings and symbolic equivalences are acquired through an interaction between early and implicit messages com-

---

A similar point can be made with regard to the "separation guilt" and "survivor guilt" discussed earlier. The child who is repeatedly given the implicit message that his or her ordinary strivings for autonomy and separation from the family are equivalent to abandoning and destroying members of the family may come to feel and fantasize that only by actually destroying them can he or she become truly autonomous, and may come to harbor murderous wishes. But there is no inherent and necessary connection between strivings and for autonomy and murderous wishes.

As Milton Klein (1981) and others (e.g., Sheleff, 1981) have pointed out, after abandoning his seduction theory, Freud displayed a striking and persistent blindness towards the aggressive and sexual behavior of adults towards children. Klein observes that at the very time that Freud reported, in a letter to Fliess (May 31, 1897) his own dream in which he experienced sexual feeling towards his 11-year-old daughter, he also wrote in his notes: "Hostile impulses against parents (a wish that they should die) are also an integral part of neuroses" (Freud, 1887–1902, p. 207). As Klein states, "What is striking is that Freud made a theoretical turnaround by theorizing about the child's impulses toward the parent on the same day that he gave a personal account of the parent's impulses toward the child" (p. 197). Freud's exclusive focus on the child's fantasies and impulses is also seen in a number of other ways noted by Klein. In his paper, "A Child Is Being Beaten," Freud (1919) interprets a patient's reports of being beaten, not as veridical memories, or not as memories at all, but as libidinal fantasies. And although Freud studied the Oedipus trilogy and borrowed one of his central concepts from it, he ignores the striking fact that Laius, the father, ordered that the infant Oedipus be put to death. (In this connection, see also Sheleff, 1981, who describes an old Persian myth in which the father kills the son.) Other examples of Freud's neglect of, and disinterest in, the role of actual adult behavior towards children include his failure to note and give weight to the degree to which Dora was being used as a pawn by her father in his affair with Frau K.

Freud's neglect of the effects of adult and parental behavior, and his exclusive emphasis on the libidinal and aggressive impulses and fantasies of the child, were necessitated by a theory that placed the origins of pathology almost entirely in intrapsychic instinctual impulses and the conflicts that surrounded them. Hence, actual events (e.g., being beaten) serve only as "releasers," or perhaps facilitations, of what are, in any case, universal, biologically laid down, vicissitudes. As Freud (1919) puts it at one point, "It is in the years of childhood between the ages of two and four or five that the congenital libidinal factors are first awakened by actual experiences and become attached to certain complexes" (p. 184). Or, as Jones (1953) states, "Freud had discovered the truth of the matter: that irrespective of incest wishes of parents towards their children, and even of occasional act of the kinds, what he had to concern himself with was the general occurrence of incest wishes of children towards their parents" (p. 322). In other words, whatever parents did or did not do in reality, incestuous and aggressive wishes of children towards parents are congenitally established.

municated to the child and the child's relatively primitive affective-cognitive schemata and operations. That is, mother's anxious or depressed reaction to the child's autonomous behavior may be *experienced* by the child as equivalent to destroying her. Of course, such an interpretation of mother's reaction seems more likely in the context of a pathological symbiotic relationship. Nevertheless, the acquisition of such symbolic equivalences may be, in part at least, a function of more developmentally primitive cognitive-affective categories and processes in which clear differentiations are not made between displeasing mother and destroying her. Similarly, father's reaction to the son's competitive and ambitious strivings may be *experienced and interpreted* by the son as equivalent to destroying father. Again, although this interpretation of father's reaction seems to be facilitated by a chronic competitive and hostile relationship, it may also be a function of a more primitive primary process mode of thought in which clear distinctions are not made between competition and destruction. I do not deny that some parents might come quite close to conveying the direct message that separation and autonomy or ambitious strivings are equivalent to destroying them (see the earlier discussion of my agoraphobic patient). Rather, I suggest that normal developmental processes may facilitate the acquisition of certain unconscious meanings and symbolic equivalences.

The point here is that the unconscious symbolic equivalences I have been discussing need not be *entirely* attributable to either environmentally induced events (i.e., parents' implicit communications) or universal, instinctually derived libidinal (incestuous) and aggressive (death wishes) impulses. An important contributing factor, I have been arguing, is the child's relatively primitive cognitive-affective developmental level, which facilitates the interpretation and experience of certain strivings and wishes (e.g., desire for physical closeness with mother; desire for separation and autonomy) as equivalent, say, to incest and murder.

The second question posed was why certain unconscious meanings and symbolic equivalences (as well as related "rules" and beliefs) remain unconscious. Here, too, I believe the answer lies in the interaction between, on the one hand, parental denial and commitment not to "spell out" certain messages and, on the other, normal developmental process. I noted earlier that the child's cognitive-affective processes are different from the adult's and can be characterized as more primitive and more primary process in nature. It is this difference between adult and childhood cognitive modes that accounts partly for the inaccessibility in adulthood of early acquired rules, beliefs, and symbolic equivalences.

Schachtel (1959) has made the point that we remember relatively little about the rich experiences of childhood because "the categories (or schemata) of adult memory are not suitable receptacles for early childhood experiences and therefore not fit to preserve these experiences and enable their recall" (p. 284). He also noted that as we develop, our perceptual modes of experience shift from an autocentric to an allocentric orientation. Relating and extending these observations to the present context, one can say that one reason certain "rules" and beliefs are and remain unconscious is that they are based on cognitive categories and modes of experience that have significantly altered in the course of development and therefore are no longer accessible to adult experience. In some sense, the inaccessibility of certain rules and beliefs is a developmental example of state-dependent memory—that is, the inability to remember in one state (e.g., a nondrug state) what one had learned in another state (e.g., a drug state). Our clinical accounts of unconscious "rules" and beliefs in terms of the if-then propositions implicit in castration anxiety, survivor guilt, and separation guilt are adult *as if* versions of primitive cognitive-affective schemas that can only be approximated through verbal descriptions. As adults, we may describe and understand with reasonable accuracy the unconscious rules and beliefs on which castration anxiety is based in if-then propositional form. However, it is likely that the early acquired rules and beliefs and the cognitive-affective experiences and schemata on which they are based were much more inchoate and confused. In short, one reason for the unconscious status in adulthood of certain early acquired rules, beliefs, and symbolic equivalencess has to do with the different modes of experience and cognition characteristic of childhood and adulthood.

Whatever the reason for these unconscious symbolic equivalences, there is a critical distinction to be drawn between, on one hand, actual incestuous and murderous impulses and strivings and, on the other, ordinary impulses and strivings that are experienced as *symbolically equivalent* to incestuous and murderous impulses. Modell (1983) and Weiss (1982) do not deal with the full and profoundly different implications for central aspects of psychoanalytic theory of these two different points of view. Freud's (1914) repression hypothesis, which he viewed as the cornerstone of psychoanalysis, is appropriate only to the first view. Thus, if castration anxiety is understood to involve unconscious wishes and impulses that are *actually* incestuous and murderous, then understandably these wishes and impulses themselves would need to be repressed—in the traditional sense in which impulses are constantly striving for expression and constantly need to be held down by an active counter force. Furthermore, it is understandable that anxiety would accompany the lifting of the repression of these wishes and impulses. If, however, the wishes and impulses in castration anxiety are understood as ordinary strivings—competitive and exhibitionistic ones, drives toward success—which have come to *mean unconsciously* and become *symbolically equivalent* to, incest and murder, then the model of irrational, id impulses constantly striving for expression and requiring repression does not seem apt. Furthermore, what appears to require uncovering is not the repressed (instinctual) impulses themselves, but the *unconscious meanings* given to ordinary, consciously experienced strivings. As Klein (1976) notes, repression is "the refusal to acknowledge the *meaning* of a tendency" (p. 247). In other words, what are unconscious but need to be made conscious are not only instinctual impulses, but also meanings and symbolic equivalences associated with ordinary strivings, which themselves can be conscious.

The contrast between the two points of view can be drawn in still another way. In traditional Freudian theory, were the unconscious to become conscious, one would consciously experience incestuous and murderous desires and aims—for these desires and aims have been repressed and come to conscious experience when repressions are lifted. Indeed, according to the traditional view, sexual and aggressive wishes (including incestuous and murderous wishes) are, in part, gratified (even if in a sublimated form) by ordinary competitive strivings. In the alternate conception I have outlined, however, were the unconscious to become conscious, one might also realize that competitive and success strivings unconsciously have come to mean and are symbolically equivalent to incestuous and murderous impulses and hence, are associated with incomprehensible and irrational anxiety. As noted earlier, the latter seems to me what G. S. Klein (1976) had in mind when he defined repression, not in terms of failure of awareness of certain wishes, but in terms of failure to make connections and lack of comprehension of the significance of an experience.

A Modified Conception of Repression

Earier I argued that it does not make too much theoretical or clinical sense to speak of the repression of rules and beliefs when repression is defined as an active force that prevents instinctual impulses and wishes from reaching conscious awareness. However, there is another, in my view more meaningful, way to conceptualize repression—as *diasvowed* and *disowned* aspects of the personality. The question I want to examine is to what extent one can account for the unconscious status of rules and beliefs through this modified concept of repression. First, I will briefly elaborate on the dynamic unconscious as the *disavowed*. It is true, as noted earlier, that whereas the psychoanalytic dynamic unconscious is a *motivational* unconscious of drives and impulses, the cognitive unconscious is an unconscious of information processing, rules, and cognitive structures. If this were all there is to this basic difference, one could say that just as there is cognitive processing that goes on unconsciously, so there are broad aims and biological imperatives that, in some sense, motivate our behavior wihout our awareness. The latter is an assumption common, for example, to current sociobiology, to

Freud's concept of instinctual drives, and to Bowlby's (1969) idea of an attachment system. That is, the claim is made that certain functional bio-logical-behavioral systems have evolved which, in some sense, direct our behavior, whatever our stated conscious motives and reasons may be.[8] What is distinctive about Freud's claims, however, is the idea that these unconscious forces could be represented in consciousness but are pur-posively *disavowed* and *extruded* from consciousness or, perhaps more im-portantly, are disavowed and extruded from one's concept of who one is, from one's self-organization (see Klein, 1976). These unconscious forces— whether one thinks of them as wishes, impulses, or behavioral tenden-cies—are then experienced as an ego-alien *it* rather than as an avowed part of oneself, as *I*. It is this distinction, rather than that between instinctual drive and controlling structure, that is held by some (correctly, I believe) to be the essence of Freud's division of the personality into id and ego (see Brandt, 1966; Bettelheim, 1982; Eagle, 1984).[9]

The ego-alien *it* quality of the disavowed is captured by people's descrip-tion of their disturbing obsessive thoughts as events that happen to them ("they keep occurring to me") rather than as something *I do;* of their com-pulsive rituals as behaviors they must carry out; of phobic fears as irrational dreads despite knowing better. The ego-alien quality of the disavowed is also seen in fully conscious experiences—uncanny experiences, for exam-ple; or unbidden obsessive thoughts; or experiences of depersonalization or unreality; or even bodily sensations in people who experience their body as alien to their (disembodied) self.

If the Freudian id and ego are understood as being disowned, ego alien, and outside the self (experienced as an *it*), in contrast to being owned and integrated into oneself (experienced as an *I*), the conscious versus uncon-scious becomes of secondary importance to integrated versus unintegrated, owned versus disowned. Unawareness of a mental content (e.g., a wish) is only one means of disowning and only one possible symptom of failure of integration. Others are becoming intellectually and impersonally aware of an idea without the accompanying affect; experiencing generalized affects (moods) without connecting them to one's thoughts, wishes and expecta-tions; as Klein (1976) notes, failure to comprehend the personal significance of events or to make connections between them; failure to make a personal

---

[8]The underlying forces that are believed to direct our behavior are not limited to biological imperatives, but include also other, external factors. For example, Marx (Marx and Engels, 1848) maintained that economic class membership shapes our very consciousness and, there-fore, our behavior and actions. And recently, Nisbett and Wilson (1977) have presented impressive evidence that stimulus characteristics of situations that do influence our behavior are often not cited in the reasons given for that behavior. These reasons instead reflect our mini "causal theories" regarding what is *supposed* to occur.

[9]I do not agree with Bettelheim's general claims regarding the purported mistranslations of Freud's writings into English.

commitment to projects and aims pursued passively or symptomatically; or simply failure to experience certain sensations, goals, desires, emotions, wishes as familiar, characteristic of oneself, and one's own. All these means have in common a failure to acknowledge and integrate certain mental contents into one's self-organization. This, I believe, is the full import of Freud's shift from making the unconscious conscious as the goal of psychoanalysis to "where id was, there should ego be." In the statement of the goal of psychoanalysis, the emphasis is not primarily on expanding the contents of that which one is aware (although it may include that) nor is it primarily, as it has unfortunately come to be understood, a matter of increasing *control* over instinctual impulses (although it may also include that). Rather, it entails an expansion of one's self-organization, so that where the impersonal, disowned, integrated *it* was, there should the personal, owned, integrated *I* be. That is, one's sense of self comes to include more and more what was previously experienced as ego alien and not part of the self.

One implication of the foregoing discussion is that the essence of repression is not the relegation of mental contents to the unconscious, to unawareness, but, as Klein (1976) emphasized, the failure of those contents to be integrated into one's overall sense of personal identity. In this view, repression is defined, not as instinctual impulses pressing for expression and held down by counter forces, but as the failure to integrate into an executive self-structure all the cognitive and affective contents, desires, plans, evaluative schemas, "rules", representations, predispositions, and schemas that are part of one's overall personality.

With repression so defined, it becomes clear that a problem central to psychoanalytic theory—and one that should also be of major interest to cognitive psychology—is not only how mental contents enter consciousness, but the processes through which these contents become owned and acknowledged as part of oneself, that is, how they become part of one's autobiography. We have accepted the possible disjunction between information processing and conscious experience, but we have not as easily accepted the possible disjunction between what is in conscious experience and what is owned as part of oneself. While whatever enters conscious awareness is usually experienced as ego-syntonic, as we have seen, it is possible for fully conscious mental contents to be experienced in a variety of ways as ego alien, as not belonging to oneself. In other words, removing contents from conscious experiences is only one means, albeit the most heavily emphasized one, of dealing with unintegrated mental contents. It is the failure of ownership and integration, however, that is crucial in the central id-ego paradigm of psychoanalysis. It turns out, therefore, that a consideration of the psychoanalytic dynamic unconscious inevitably leads to the central issue of integration, of ego-syntonic versus ego-alien mental contents. The centrality of this issue is not apparent from the perspective of cognitive psychology, a perspective that concerns itself mainly with the processing of information rather than with the integration of such "information" into one's self-organization.

To return to the original theoretical issue of interest: Although, as we have seen, the unconscious rules and beliefs I have discussed cannot be said to be repressed in the usual sense of the term, can they be thought of as repressed in the modified sense just discussed, insofar as they are often experienced in an ego-alien fashion? It will be useful to approach this question by considering the status of superego prohibitions in psychoanalytic theory, for the same question applies to superego phenomena. Superego prohibitions, taboos, and guilt are also held to be unconscious, and yet one cannot say they are repressed if one defines repression in the traditional way. Indeed, as Weiss (1982) suggests, the unconscious "pathogenic beliefs" and "rules" he discusses are phenomena that can be subsumed under the concept of superego. The earlier discussion of castration anxiety and "separation guilt" (or "survivor guilt") should make clear the degree to which such concepts involve the basic idea of violation of taboos and anticipated fitting punishments.

A central fact of superego prohibitions, as well as of the unconscious "rules" and "pathogenic beliefs" I have been discussing, is that they were initially external—that is, in some way communicated by others—and in varying degrees and over a period of time became internalized. However, although internalized, they are not fully integrated into one's self-organization. With regard to the superego, this is seen in a number of ways. In popular descriptions, conscience is often visualized as a homunculus standing outside oneself and evaluating one's thoughts and actions. Also, people often employ the locution, "My conscience tells me," as if it were an agency separate and apart from oneself. These visualizations and ways of speaking of conscience reveal, subtly, its heritage from and remaining links to an external source. This notion of conscience is to be contrasted with a fully integrated set of moral values and ideals in which it is more natural to speak of "I believe . . . ."

That the superego is internalized (is, in some sense, part of the self) and yet not fully integrated (is in another sense, not part of the self) is precisely why it served as a model for Fairbairn's (1952) concept of "internalized object" and for the largely synonymous concept of "archaic introject." If we cut through the jargon and often obscure writing, the essence of those concepts, it seems to me, is the idea of internalization without full integration. As Schafer (1968) notes, the clinical and behavioral evidence for such internalization often consists of reports of felt "presences" that influence one's experiences and behavior. Ideas of demons and dybbuks residing within oneself and influencing one's feelings and actions are particularly vivid expressions of "internalized objects" and "archaic introjects." The feeling underlying such fantasies is that one is, so to speak, inhabited by a foreign body/mind.

A less dramatic example is illustrated by a former patient whose presenting symptom was severe dyspareunia. The patient reported the obsessive and recurrent thought prior to sexual intercourse: "If they could see me now," the "they" being her parents, who still thought of her as an innocent virgin. Without getting into the details and complexities of the case, I want to point out that through the obsessive thought, the patient's parents were carried with her as "presences" before she carried out the forbidden and defiant act of sexual intercourse.

It can be seen, then, that superego prohibitions can be as ego alien and as unintegrated as unacceptable instinctual wishes. Hence, the disowned status of the id or the "it" cannot be limited to instinctual wishes, for, as we have seen, the superego can also be a disowned and unintegrated part of the personality. An important difference, however, between instinctual wishes and superego prohibitions and "internalized objects" is that the former are originally and intrinsically internal, whereas the latter were originally and by their very nature external. Hence, the basic defense against instinctual wishes is to render external—into an "it"—what is essentially internal. To put it another way, the basic defense against instinctual wishes is to disown something that, from a broader point of view, is an inherent part of one's self or, at least of one's personality.[10] It is the reversal of this externalization process to which Freud was referring when he defined the aim of psychoanalysis as "Where id was, there should ego be." In other words, when repression and other defenses are lifted, one can own that which was, in some sense, always part of oneself but which was disowned and rendered an "it." That instinctual wishes are an inherent and inescapable part of one's personality is what made them for Freud prime candidates for repression. Because one could not physically escape or flee or eliminate them, as one could external stimuli, one denied them access to consciousness and psychologically rendered them external, that is, not part of oneself.

By contrast, "internalized objects," "archaic introjects," and primitive superego prohibitions are essentially external representations, rules, and beliefs that have become internalized, but remain unintegrated and unmetabolized "foreign bodies." That is, they have become inappropriately and incompletely internalized and, in an important sense, *should* have an ego-alien, "it" status. Hence, the basic aim of psychotherapy, in Fairbairn's

---

[10]One can, I believe, meaningfully, distinguish between the broader concept of personality, which includes disowned or unrecognized trends and features, and the narrower concept of self or self-organization, which is made up primarily of endorsed or owned aspects of one's personality. (See Eagle, 1983, for a further discussion of the issue.)

(1952) view, is not to transform an "it" into an "I," but to reverse the process. If Fairbairn's conception of the basic goal of therapy can be summarized in an aphorism, one could paraphrase Freud: Where "I" was, there shall "it" be. That is, given the destructive effects of internalized objects, archaic objects, and primitive superego prohibitions and punishments within the personality, the main task of therapy is, so to speak, to exorcise them—or, to state it less dramatically, to soften and modulate their impact so that the patient can pursue his or her internally generated and developmentally and personally appropriate needs, desires, ambitions and goals. Hence, while for Freud, the main goal of therapy is to own or to make internal (to make part of the "I") what has been defensively externalized, the main goal of therapy for object-relations theorists is to return to external status what has been defensively and pathologically internalized.

One can now fashion an answer to the original question. Although the rules and pathogenic beliefs of which Weiss and Modell write, along with superego prohibitions, are unconscious, they cannot, in any simple sense, be said to be repressed in *either* the traditional or the modified senses of repression. Rather, as noted earlier, their unconscious status is attributable mainly to such factors as early implicit learning, developmental level at which the learning took place, and parental denial. It was noted earlier that unconscious rules and grim beliefs are unconscious because they are learned implicitly and nonverbally in an interpersonal and affective context in which they are never made explicit. Also as noted earlier, this is accomplished partly by parental denial that such rules obtain (the parents are often themselves unaware of the messages they convey). For example, someone who has learned the rule, "If I become autonomous I will destroy you," will most certainly confront denial rather than confirmation if he or she makes this rule explicit.

As far as I can see, in only one sense can one say that certain rules and pathogenic beliefs are rendered unconscious by active processes that are at least *akin* to repression. And that is the idea that unawareness and failure of acknowledgment of certain rules and belief are, at least in part, *motivated* by the desire to avoid the psychic pain that awareness and acknowledgment would entail.

Also, Weiss (1982) has suggested that "pathogenic beliefs" are rendered and kept unconscious in the service of not endangering vital ties to parents. And Bowlby (1979, 1981) has observed that children learn implicitly not to question or review the "official" parental image of representation. Family therapists too (for example, have reported that families often collude to maintain and refuse to examine certain family myths. All this suggests that people who live by certain unconscious rules and pathogenic beliefs were early on given the metamessage not to become aware of, not to examine, and not to acknowledge those rules and beliefs. In other words, in accord with one core characteristic of repression, the unconscious status of super-ego prohibitions, "rules," and "pathogenic beliefs" is motivated by the need to avoid anxiety and guilt—in particular, by the need to avoid parental displeasure and endangering parental ties. However, other key aspects of the repression process do not appear to be at all applicable to superego prohibitions and "pathogenic beliefs." For example, as argued earlier, it makes little sense to think of such prohibitions and beliefs as constantly pressing for discharge or conscious expression.

TRANSLATION OF REPRESSION INTO INFORMATION-PROCESSING TERMS

A number of attempts have been made to translate the psychoanalytic concept of repression into information-processing terms (e.g., Peterfreund, 1971; Erdelyi & Goldberg, 1979; Bowlby, 1980, 1981). In these translations, repression is viewed as the failure to process information or, in Bowlby's (1980) terms, "defensive exclusion." Relying on the concept of "perceptual defense" (see Eagle & Wolitzky (1977) for a brief explication of this concept), Bowlby (1980) has redefined repression as the defensive exclusion of external and internal input "together with the thoughts and feelings to which such inflows give rise . . ." (p. 65). Furthermore, since, according to Bowlby, behavioral systems, such as attachment, are activated by signals, the defensive exclusion of such signals or input leads to the deactivation of the systems. As Bowlby puts it, "In traditional terms the system thus deactivated is said to be repressed. Or, put the other way about, the effects of repression are regarded as being due to certain information of signifi-cance to the individual being systematically excluded from further process-ing" (Bowlby, 1980, p. 65).

On two important counts, this description of defensive exclusion does not seem to be consistent with what is traditionally meant by repression. First, in the traditional meaning of repression, rather than being deacti-vated, instinctual impulses continue to press for direct expression in be-havior and experience (even perhaps at an intensified level) and find indirect expression in symptoms, dreams, parapraxes, and indeed if one also includes sublimation, in *all* behavior. Second, the essence of repression is not that information is not processed, but that information that is pro-cessed is not experienced in conscious awareness and, as I have tried to show above, is not integrated into one's self-organization.

Finally, what is not made clear in the analogy between information processing and repression is why information processing should play a central role in psychopathology. In the context of Freudian theory, given such ideas as the relationship between instinctual impulse and excessive excitation and the consequent importance of drive discharge (e.g., Freud, 1923, 1926), one can understand that repression would be seen as the primary pathogen of neurosis. But why should "deactivation," for example, be strongly associated with psychopathology? One can imagine a variety of answers to this question, but Bowlby (1980) does not make entirely clear what *his* answer is. Bowlby's answer is that there are biologically based instinctual systems, such as the attachment system, and that were it not for defensive exclusion and deactivation, one would normally experience feelings, needs, and desires related to these instinctual systems. Bowlby (1981) describes Mrs. G, who because of defensive exclusion of signals linked to attachment and consequent deactivation of the attachment system, does not experience normal feelings of loss, of missing or needing someone, or the like. The effect of all this on Mrs. G in that she experiences her life as empty, flat, and devoid of feeling. Here (and elsewhere) Bowlby is suggesting that the link between defensive exclusion and deactivation on the one hand and psychopathology on the other lies in the effect the former have on the range and richness of one's feelings and on one's ability to relate deeply and closely to others. Note that Bowlby's account seems especially relevant to schizoid kinds of pathology, in which isolation, lack of affect, or flat affect are prominent symptoms. It is not clear how Bowlby's ideas of "defensive exclusion" and "deactivation" would account for other kinds of pathology and symptoms. Also not clear in Bowlby's scheme is the role of such factors as anxiety and guilt in contributing to pathology.

In short, reformulations of repression in terms of information processing and cognitive theory often omit the properties essential to repression. They also often do not make clear, on theoretical grounds, the purported connection between the stipulated cognitive processes (e.g., defensive exclusion, lack of full processing) deemed to be analogous to repression and the development and maintenance of pathology. While, as I have tried to show, the concept of repression is embedded in a theoretical context that justifies its central role in pathology, this is often not the case with cognitive processes held to be analogous to repression. Further, of critical psychoanalytic concern is not so much information processing, but the "fate" of the information processed, that is, the extent to which the information is integrated into one's self-organization and the processes underlying the degree of success or failure in accomplishing such integration. So far, cognitive psychology has had relatively little to say regarding these issues.

CONCLUSION

The recent clinical and theoretical psychoanalytic formulations I have discussed deal less with repressed instinctual contents than with such concepts as "pathogenic beliefs," implicit "rules" governing one's emotions and actions and unconscious symbolic equivalences between certain strivings and desires on the one hand and forbidden and frightening meanings on the other. These formulations also deal with the central issue of the degree to which mental contents—whatever their source—are owned and integrated into one's conception of oneself. It is hoped that what is uncovered in cognitive psychology will elucidate how symbolic equivalences, "grim beliefs," and implicit "rules" are acquired and operate and how mental contents come to be endorsed as part of oneself. If psychoanalytic clinicians and theorists are to be able to use the findings in cognitive psychology, it will be necessary for them to formulate their ideas in terms of ordinary cognitive processes about which there is some understanding. And, conversely, one should also expect that the more affective, motivational, and vital material with which psychoanalysis deals will challenge concepts of the cognitive unconscious.

REFERENCES

Beck, A. T., Rush, A. J., Shaw, B. F., & Emery, G. (1979), *Cognitive Theory of Depression*. New York: Guilford Press.

Bettleheim, B. (1982), Reflections on Freud and the soul. *The New Yorker*, March 1, pp. 52–93.

Blatt, S. J. (1974), Levels of object representation in anaclitic and introjective depression. *The Psychoanalytic Study of the Child*, 29: 107–158. New Haven: Yale University Press.

—— & Lerner, H. (1983), Investigations in the psychoanalytic theory of object relations and object representations. In: *Empirical Studies of Psychoanalytic Theories, Vol. 1*, ed. J. Masling. Hillsdale, NJ: The Analytic Press.

Bowlby, J. (1969), *Attachment and Loss, Vol. I: Attachment*. London: Hogarth Press.

—— (1979), On knowing what you are not supposed to know and feeling what you are not supposed to feel. *Canad. J. Psychiat.*, 24: 403–408.

—— (1980), *Attachment and Loss, Vol. III: Loss*. New York, Basic Books.

—— (1981, February), Defensive processes in light of attachment theory. Paper presented at meeting of Association of Child Psychotherapists.

Brandt, L.W. (1966), Process or structure. *Psychoanal. Rev.*, 53: 50–54.

Brown, R., & McNeill, D. (1966), The "tip of the tongue" phenomenon. *J. Verb. Learn. Verb. Beh.*, 5: 325–337.

Cheesman, J., & Merikle, P. M. (1984). Priming with and without awareness. *Perception and Psychophysics, 36(4)*, 387–395.

Chomsky, N. (1957), *Syntactic Structures*. The Hague: Mouton

—— (1980), *Rules and Representations*. New York: Columbia University Press.

Eagle, M. (1959), The effects of subliminal stimuli of aggressive content upon conscious cognition. *J. Pers.*, 27:

—— (1973), Validation of motivational formulations: Acknowledgment as a criterion. In: *Psychoanalysis and Contemporary Science, Vol. 2*, ed. B. B. Rubinstein. New York: Macmillan, pp. 331–337.

—— (1983), Anatomy of the self in psychoanalytic theory. In: *Nature Animated*, ed. M. Ruse. Dordrecht, Holland: D. Reidel, pp. 133–161.

_____ (1984), *Recent Developments in Psychoanalysis: A Critical Evaluation.* New York: McGraw-Hill.

_____ & Wolitzky, D. (1977), Perceptual defense. *International Encyclopedia of Psychiatry, Psychology, Psychoanalysis and Neurology:* Vol. III. New York: Human Sciences Press.

Ellenberger, H. (1970), *The Discovery of the Unconscious.* New York: Basic Books.

Erdelyi, M. H., & Goldberg, B. (1979), Let's not sweep repression under the rug: Toward a cognitive psychology of repression. In: *Functional Disorders of Memory,* ed. J. F. Kihlstrom & F. J. Evans. Hillsdale, NJ: Lawrence Erlbaum Associates.

Fairbairn, W. R. D. (1952), *Psychoanalytic Studies of the Personality.* London: Routledge & Kegan Paul.

Field, G. C, Averling, F., & Laird, J. (1922), Is the Conception of the unconscious of value in psychology? A Symposium. *Mind,* 31: 413–442.

Freud, S. (1887–1902), *The Origins on Psychoanalysis: Freud's Letters to Wilhelm Fliess.* New York: Basic Books, 1954.

_____ (1900), The interpretation of dreams. *Standard Edition,* 4 & 5. London: Hogarth Press, 1953.

_____ (1911), Formulations of the two principles of mental functioning, *Standard Edition,* 12: 218–226. London: Hogarth Press: 1958.

_____ (1914), On Narcissism; An Introduction. *Standard Edition,* 14: 67–102. London: Hogarth Press, 1957.

_____ (1915), The unconscious. *Standard Edition,* 14: 159–216. London: Hogart Press, 1957.

_____ (1919), A child is being beaten: A contribution to the study of the origins of sexual perversions. *Standard Edition,* 17: 175–204. London: Hogarth Press, 1955.

_____ (1923), The ego and the id. *Standard Edition,* 19: 1–59. London: Hogarth Press, 1961.

_____ (1926), Inhibitions, symptoms, & anxiety. *Standard Edition,* 20: 87–172. London: Hogarth Press, 1959.

_____ (1933), New introductory lectures in psycho-analysis. *Standard Edition,* 22: 1–182. London: Hogarth Press, 1964.

_____ (1937), Constructions in psycho–analysis. *Standard Edition,* 23: 255–269. London: Hogarth Press, 1964.

Hartmann, H. (1939), *Ego Psychology and the Problem of Adaptation,* New York: International Universities Press, 1958.

Helmholtz, H. L. F. (1867), *Treatise on Physiological Optics.* Transl. from the 3rd German ed., Ed. J. G. C. Southall. New York: Dover, 1962.

Ittelson, W. H., & Kilpatrick, F. P. (1951), Experiments in perception. *Scient. Amer.,* 185: 50–55.

Jones, E. (1953), *The Life and Work of Sigmund Freud, Vol. I,* New York, Basic Books.

Klein, G. S. (1976), *Psychoanalytic Theory: An Exploration of Essentials.* New York: International Universities Press.

Klein, M. I. (1981), Freud's seduction theory. *Bull. Menn. Clinic,* 45: 185–208.

Kunst–Wilson, W. R., & Zajonc, R. B. (1980), Affective discrimination of stimuli that cannot be recognized *Science,* 207: 557–558.

Lewis, J. L. (1970), Semantic processing of unattended messages during dichotic listening. *J. Exp. Psychol.,* 85: 225–228.

Mahoney, M. J. (1980), Psychotherapy and the structure of personal revolutions. In: *Psychotherapy Process: Current Issues and Future Directions,* ed. M. J. Mahoney. New York: Plenum Press.

Mandler, G. (1983, August), Cognition, schemas, and Freud. Paper presented at Symposium on "Psychoanalysis and Cognitive Psychology: Convergences and Divergences," at Annual Meeting of the American Psychological Association, Anaheim, CA.

Marcel, A. J. (1980), Conscious and preconscious recognition of polysemous words: Locating the selective effects of prior verbal context. In: *Attention and Performance VIII,* ed. R. Nickerson. Hillsdale, NJ: Lawrence Erlbaum Associates, pp. 435–457.

Marcel, A. J. (1983a), Conscious and unconscious perception: Experiments on visual masking and word recognition. *Cognitive Psychology*, 15: 197–237.

―――― (1983b), Conscious and unconscious perception: An approach to the relations between phenomenal experience and perceptual processes. *Cognitive Psychology*, 15: 238–300.

Marx, K., & Engels, F. (1848), *The Communist Manifesto*. New York: International Publishers, 1948.

Masterson, J. F. (1976), *Psychotherapy of the Borderline Adult: A Developmental Approach*. New York: Brunner/Mazel.

Mischel, T. (1963), Psychology and explanations of human behavior. *Philosophical and Phenomenological Research*, 23: 578–594.

―――― (1966), Pragmatic aspects of explanation. *Philosophy of Science*, 33: 40–60.

Modell, A. (1983, May), Self presentation and the presentation of the self: An overview of the more recent knowledge of the narcissistic personality. Paper presented at Symposium on "Narcissism, Masochism, and the Sense of Guilt in Relation to the Therapeutic Process," Letterman General Hospital, San Francisco, 1983.

Mullane, H. (1983), Defenses, dreams, and rationality. *Synthese*, 57: 187–204.

Nagel, T. (1974), Linguistics and epistemology. In: *On Noam Chomsky: Critical Essays*, ed. G. Harman. Garden City, NY: Anchor Press/Doubleday.

Nisbett, R. E., & Wilson, T. D. (1977), Telling more than we know: Reports on mental processes. *Psycholog. Rev.*, 84: 231–259.

Osgood, C. E., Suci, G. J. & Tannenbaum, P. H. (1957), *The Measurement of Meaning*. Urbana: University of Illinois Press.

Peterfreund, E. (1971), Information, systems, and psychoanalysis. *Psychological Issues*, Monogr. 25/26. New York, International Universities Press.

Polanyi, M. (1958), *Personal Knowledge*. Chicago: University of Chicago Press.

Polanyi, M., & Prosch, H. (1975), *Meaning*. Chicago: University of Chicago Press.

Rapaport, D. (1951), *Organization and Pathology of Thought*. New York: Columbia University Press.

Rock, I. (1970), Perception from the standpoint of psychology. In *Perception and its Disorders*. Association for Research in Nervous and Mental Disease, Vol. 68.

―――― (1983), *The Logic of Perception*. Cambridge, MA: The M.I.T. Press.

Rubinstein, B. B. (1967), Explanation and mere description: A metascientific examination of certain aspects of the psychoanalytic theory of motivation. In: Motives and thoughts: Psychoanalytic Essays in Honor of David Rapaport, ed. R. R. Holt. *Psychological Issues*, Monogr. 18/19, Vol. 5. New York: International Universities Press.

―――― (1974), On the role of classificatory process in mental functioning: Aspects of a psychoanalytic theoretical model. *Psychoanal. Contemp. Sci.*, 3: 101–185.

―――― (1976), On the possibility of a strictly clinical psychoanalytic theory: An essay in the philosophy of psychoanalysis. In: *Psychology versus Metapsychology: Psychoanalytic Essays in Memory of G. S. Klein*, ed. M. M. Gill & P. S. Holzman. New York: International Universities Press.

―――― (1977), On the concept of a person and of an organism. In: *Science and Psychotherapy*, ed. R. Stern, L. S. Horowitz, & J. Lynes. New York: Haven.

―――― (1980), On the psychoanalytic theory of unconscious motivations and the problem of its confirmation. *Psychoanal. Contemp. Thought*, 3: 3–20.

Safran, J. D. (1983), Some implications of Sullivan's Interpersonal Theory for Cognitive Therapy. In: *Cognitive Psychotherapies: Recent Developments in Theory, Research, and Practice*, ed. M. A. Reda & M. J. Mahoney. Cambridge, MA: Ballinger.

Sandler, J., & Rosenblatt, B. (1962), The concept of the representational world. *The Psychoanalytic Study of the Child*, 17: 128–145.

Schachtel, E. G. (1959), *Metamorphosis*. New York: Basic Books.

Schafer, R. (1968), *Aspects of Internalization.* New York, International Universities Press.

Schopenhauer, A. (1883), *The World as Will and Idea,* trans. R. B. Haldane & J. Kemp, 11th ed. London: Routledge & Kegan Paul, 1964.

Sheleff, L. S. (1981), *Generations Apart: Adult Hostility to Youth.* New York: McGraw-Hill.

Shevrin, H., & Dickman, S. (1980), The psychological unconscious: A necessary assumption for all psychological theory? *American Psychologist,* 35: 421–434.

Stroop, J. R. (1935), Studies of interference in serial verbal reactions. *J. Exp. Psychol.,* 18: 643–662.

Turvey, M. T. (1974), Constructive theory, perceptual systems, and tacit knowledge. In: *Cognition and the Symbolic Processes,* ed. W. W. Weimer & D. S. Palermo. Hillsdale, NJ: Lawrence Erlbaum Associates.

_____ & Fertig, J. (1970), Polarity on the semantic differential and release from proactive interference in short–term memory. *J. Verbal Learning and Verbal Behavior,* 9: 439–443.

_____, Fertig, J., & Kravetz, S. (1969), Connotative classification and proactive interference in short–term memory. *Psychonomic Science,* 16: 223–224.

Weiss, J. (1982), *Psychotherapy Research: Theory and Findings, Theoretical Introduction.* The Psychotherapy Research Group. Department of Psychiatry, Mount Zion Hospital and Medical Center, Bulletin #5.

Weiss, J., Sampson, H., & the Mount Zion Psychotherapy Research Group (1986), *The Psychoanalytic Process: Theory, Clinical Observation, and Empirical Research.* New York: Guilford Press.

Wickens, D. D. (1972), Characteristics of word encoding. In: *Coding Processes in Human Memory,* ed. A. W. Melton & E. Martin. Washington, DC: Winston.

9 Affect and the Unconscious: A Cognitive Perspective

Jeremy D. Safran
Leslie S. Greenberg

Our objective in this chapter is to examine the concept of the "unconscious" from the perspective of a cognitive metapsychology. As Meichenbaum and Gilmore (1984) point out, "No other concept so clearly divides the traditional behavioral from the psychodynamic camps" (p. 273). The increasing interest in the theoretical integration of different therapeutic approaches has, however, recently stimulated an attempt by some cognitive behaviorists to analyze the concept of the unconscious from a cognitive perspective (e.g., Mahoney, 1982; Meichenbaum and Gilmore, 1984).

These authors, while agreeing that some form of unconscious processing takes place, are quick to point out that this does not necessarily constitute an acceptance of the psychoanalytic concept of the "unconscious." Meichenbaum and Gilmore (1984), for example, state that ". . . in a cognitive behavioral model, there is no commitment to an "energy model" of psychodynamic conflict or to a particular mental or motivational model of the mind (i.e. id, ego, super ego processes). Instead there is an attempt to develop a taxonomy of cognitive events, processes, and structures and to develop a testable theoretical model of how these processes interact with each other as well as with feelings, behaviors and environmental consequences" (p. 291).

Mahoney (1982), in his discussion of the unconscious, makes reference to Hayek's (1978) notion of the primacy of the abstract, and conceptualizes the unconscious as consisting of tacit, higher–level organizing principles that shape conscious cognitive processes and behavior. This notion appears to be reasonably convergent with the concept of "core organizing principles," which Meichenbaum and Gilmore (1984) conceptualize as unconscious structures that determine conscious cognitive processes and behavior.

A fundamentally important difference between *these* cognitive formulations of the unconscious and the Freudian psychoanalytic concept of the unconscious is that while the Freudian concept of the unconscious is inextricably linked to considerations regarding the role of affect in the psychic economy, the cognitive formulations are essentially affect–free. The fact that contemporary cognitive–behavior therapists would conceptualize the unconscious without reference to emotional or motivational considerations is consistent with the general trend in experimental psychology to ignore the role of emotion and motivation in human functioning (cf. Greenberg and Safran, 1986). Dawes (1976), for example, has termed the social psychologist's traditional interest in the role of affective and motivational processes in influencing human behavior as "deep" psychology, and contrasts it with the increasing tendency in contemporary experimental psychology to account for human behavior in information–processing terms. He characterizes this contemporary trend as a "shallow" psychology. The cognitive–behavioral concept of the unconscious articulated by Mahoney (1982) and Meichenbaum and Gilmore (1984) is consistent with the information–processing model of man that views maladaptive behavior as resulting from dysfunctional rules and heuristics rather than from nonrational, affective processes.

For Freud, the unconscious and affect were central in understanding pathology (Nemiah, 1984). Freud believed that under normal circumstances events activate both ideas and associated affect. Typically, the associated affect is spontaneously discharged, thus allowing the idea to move into the background and to cease to play an important role in the individual's functioning. However, when the associated affect is too threatening for the individual, it is warded off and becomes separated from the idea, before the normal process of discharge can take place, thereby creating dysfunction. In the cognitive–behavioral conceptualization of the unconscious articulated by Mahoney (1982) and Meichenbaum and Gilmore (1984), the pathogenic element is not the warding–off of affective processes, but rather dysfunctional rules that operate at an unconscious level. There is thus a fundamental difference between psychoanalytic and cognitive–behavioral formulations of the role of unconscious factors in psychopathology.

Freud's understanding of the role of unconscious emotional processes in psychopathology is linked to his drive metapsychology. We can distinguish, however, between some of Freud's basic insights about the relationship between emotion, the unconscious, and psychopathology, on one hand, and the drive metapsychology within which they are embedded, on the other. We will argue that Freud's essential intuition—namely, that the role of the unconscious in psychopathology and psychotherapy is best understood in conjunction with its relationship to emotional processes—is an important one, and that this perspective is lacking in contemporary cognitive–behavioral formulations, which have been influenced by experimental psychology. We will argue that a major class of psychological dysfunction arises from the failure to fully process internally generated information that is consistent with the conscious experience of emotion. This internally generated information can be thought of as action/disposition information, which under normal conditions constitutes a vital component in the construction of emotional experience (Greenberg and Safran, 1984b). This perspective, which will be elaborated later, integrates "shallow" and "deep" psychology, by dealing with information–processing, affect, and motivation in the same model.

We will begin by comparing some of the metapsychological assumptions upon which the psychoanalytic model of the unconscious is based, with the metapsychological assumptions guiding both theory and research in contemporary cognitive psychology. As we shall see, this task will be somewhat complicated by the fact that "cognitive theory" is not a single coherent set of ideas, but rather a number of different approaches to the study of cognition that are typically classified together under the rubric of cognitive theory (Neisser, 1980).

We will then review some research evidence and associated theory emerging from experimental cognitive psychology, which is relevant to the topic of the unconscious. Our review will be a selective one. We will not, for example, review the extensive literature on subliminal perception or the literature on perceptual defense, both of which are relevant to the topic. We will instead focus primarily upon research and theory in the area of selective attention. Our objective in doing so is twofold. First, it is to provide the reader with a historical perspective on the fashion in which the investigation of unconscious processes has gradually come to assume legitimate status amongst experimental cognitive psychologists. Second, it is to provide some idea of the picture of unconscious processes, as well as the relationship between unconscious and conscious processes that is emerging from this research.

THE DRIVE METAPSYCHOLOGY

Freud's fundamental vision of the human condition is embodied in the drive model or psychic–energy model. As Greenberg and Mitchell (1983) articulate, the fundamental principles underlying the drive metapsychology are as follows:

(1) The unit of analysis is the individual as a discreet individual. Man is not viewed as an intrinsically social animal. Society is imposed upon individuals who are already complete within themselves. People accept the protection of society at the cost of renunciation of many of their most personal goals. It is possible to speak about the individual outside an interpersonal context.

(2) Because it *is* possible to speak of the individual divorced from an interpersonal context, it is also possible to speak about a "constancy principle," which deals with the regulation and distribution of psychic energy within the organism. The constancy principle, in stipulating that the purpose of the psychic apparatus is to keep the level of stimulation within the individual as close to zero as possible, is thus the fundamental motivational postulate of drive theory.

(3) The origin of all human activity can thus be ultimately traced to the demands of instinctual drive. The origin of this drive is not influenced by social context. It is inherited biologically.

(4) There is no inherent object, no preordained tie to the human environment.

Embedded as it is within the drive metapsychology, Freud's view of the unconscious is as a "seething cauldron" of primitive impulses, which ultimately must be tamed or renounced in order to allow the individual to live within society (Eagle, 1984). It is readily apparent that this concept of the unconscious has little in common with the cognitive–behavioral models we have discussed.

In his earlier writings, Freud considered the failure to make conscious and to discharge affect as being the central pathogenic process (Breuer and Freud, 1895). While later psychoanalytic writings deemphasized the importance of catharsis as a critical ingredient of psychoanalysis, Freud never abandoned the view that the fundamental psychic danger facing the organism is excessive excitation (Eagle, 1984). This notion is conceptually dependent upon the drive metapsychology, which views the regulation of psychic energy as the fundamental motivational principle.

Although subsequent interpreters of Freud have different opinions about the true nature of psychic energy, and whether or not it should be thought of as a real entity or a metaphorical concept, it is at least implicit in much of Freud's writing, as well as psychoanalytic writing in general, that psychic energy or drive can be thought of as a quasi–physiological entity, which exercises force upon the mind and the body in a mechanistic fashion. Critics of the drive metapsychology from within the psychoanalytic community (e.g., Gill, 1976; Holt, 1976; Klein, 1976, Schafer, 1976) argue that it is impossible to link a psychology built on concepts of energy and structure with a psychology of meaning, and that for this reason the drive metapsychology constitutes an inadequate metapsychology for understanding human beings. Gill (1976), for example, argues that Freud clearly intended the drive metapsychology to be taken in biological and mechanistic terms, and that this biological/mechanistic metapsychology constitutes an inadequate psychology, because it is in a different universe of discourse from that of meaning.

The second major criticism of the drive metapsychology has been that Freud fails to take into account the inherently interpersonal nature of people (Fairbairn, 1952; Sullivan, 1953; Eagle, 1984). In constructing the drive model, Freud drew upon the biological metaphors which were available in the intellectual climate of late–nineteenth–century Vienna. It is thus based on neurological conceptions and hydraulic metaphors that are now outmoded. Freud's drive theory is founded on the Darwinian assumption that all behavior must be understood in terms of its survival function. This is the same assumption that is central to contemporary ethologists (e.g., Bowlby, 1969; Lorenz, 1977). Freud, however, equates survival or adaptation with the avoidance of the danger of excessive excitation, resulting from a failure to discharge affect (Eagle, 1984). For Freud, establishing psychoanalysis as a biological science and incorporating biological considerations into psychoanalytic theory, meant that man is fundamentally a biological organism and only secondarily an interpersonal creature. Biology and the environment are viewed as two independent and often opposing forces.

THE COGNITIVE METAPSYCHOLOGY

As Neisser (1980) has pointed out, there is no one "cognitive psychology." The metatheoretical perspective that has dominated the field of cognitive psychology since its inception, however, can best be characterized as the information–processing approach. This approach draws heavily upon the brain–computer analogy. Proponents of this approach have applied concepts stimulated by advances in the field of computer sciences to construct models that can clarify with a high degree of specificity the way in which information is encoded, represented, stored, and retrieved from memory. According to Neisser (1967), "The term 'cognition' refers to all processes by which the sensory input is transformed, reduced, elaborated, stored, recovered and used. It is concerned with these processes even when they operate in the absence of relevant stimulation, as in images and hallucinations. Such terms as sensation, perception, imagery, retention, recall, problem solving and thinking, among many others, refer to hypothetical stages or aspects of cognition" (p. 4).

The brain–computer analogy has played an important role in the emergence of the developing cognitive science. As Shaw and Bransford (1977) point out, it has been instrumental in liberating theorists and researchers from the excessive restrictions imposed upon them by behavioral psychology. Computer technology has stimulated the development of modeling techniques and experimental procedures that allow cognitive scientists to develop and test fine–tuned predictions about internal processes not directly observable. This has been an important aspect of the development of cognitive psychology as an empirically based science.

Information–processing theories are explicitly concerned with the fashion in which incoming stimulus information is processed in order to extract meaning from it. In theory, then, they should be less vulnerable to the previously articulated criticisms of drive theory, which state that it is incompatible with a psychology of meaning. As we shall see, however, when we discuss the ecological approach to cognitive psychology, this is not completely so.

A major criticism of the information–processing approach is that people are conceptualized as disembodied computing machines, rather than as active organisms that interact with their environment in an adaptive fashion. In the information–processing model, cognition is considered independent of emotion and action. Critics of the information–processing approach, however, question whether it is possible to truly understand the nature of human cognitive processes if we consider them out of context of action and emotion. Shaw and Bransford (1977), for example, make the following comments:

> It is wise to remember that computer scientists' systems are artificially contrived while ours are naturally evolved; their systems are passive while ours are active; their systems are purposeless (except in a second–hand way) while ours pursue primary goals of self–survival and adaptation; their systems, as complex as they are, are still astonomically simpler than those psychologists must understand. And what of the role of emotional, personality and social factors in determining the questions appropriate to humans but as yet undefined for artificial systems? [p. 3]

The major metatheoretical disputer of the information–processing approach in cognitive psychology is the ecological approach to perception, initially advanced by Gibson (1966, 1979). In contrast to the information–processing approach, the ecological perspective emphasizes the role of biological/evolutionary factors in human functioning. It thus shares the biological orientation of drive metapsychology. However, unlike drive theory, which equates survival and adaptation with the avoidance of excessive psychic excitation, the ecological perspective understands the survival of the species in terms of the adaptation of the organism to its ecological niche. One of the major objections that ecological theorists have to the information–processing metaphor is that once we begin hypothesizing about stages of information–processing activity that are necessary for transforming information into meaningful form, we end up in a process of infinite regress. Thus, if we theorize that the organism transforms sensory information into a usable form through a series of information–processing stages, the question then becomes: Who is the agent who uses this information in the final stage? From an ecological perspective, it is therefore seen as more parsimonious to assume that evolution, by designing perceptual systems that are adapted to extract meaning directly from the environment, has rendered a complex process of information–processing unnecessary. As Shaw and Bransford (1977) state:

> Hence, when asked where the buck of knowledge ceases to be passed, or where the epistemic regress ends, the ecological psychologist responds: At the beginning of the process; it stops with perception, the process upon which the intrinsic meaning of man's relationship to his world is founded. It is the perceiver who knows and the knower who perceives, just as it is the world that is both perceived and known. Neither memory, nor inference, nor any other epistemic process other than perception intervenes between the knowing–agent and the world it knows, for knowing is a direct rather than an indirect process [p. 10].

Ecological theorists thus question whether an epistemology based on the person–computer analogy can provide us with a theory of meaning.

Proponents of the ecological perspective also criticize the information–processing perspective because of its failure to conceptualize the human being as an organism that is adapted to its ecological niche. They argue that there is no way in which we can begin to understand human psychological functioning without a detailed understanding of the environment in which this functioning takes place. In the ecological approach, then, the emphasis is much more on the interface between people and their environment than the information–processing stages that are hypothesized to be taking place inside the individual's head. Traditionally, the focus of investigation in ecological psychology (as in information–processing psychology) has been on object perception rather than person perception. An attempt has thus been made to characterize the geometric structure underlying the more important physical properties of the world (e.g., rigidity, nonrigidity, shape, size) and to understand the perceptual process in this context (e.g., Gibson, 1966). The extension of an ecological perspective to the realm of "social knowing" suggests, then, that we cannot fully understand the nature of human functioning without a detailed understanding of the interpersonal context in which it takes place. Viewed from this perspective, it becomes apparent that the information–processing metatheory is no less guilty of failing to conceptualize people as fundamentally interpersonal creatures than is drive metapsychology.

In discussing the conceptualization of the relationship between cognition and action that emerges from the traditional information–processing perspective, Weimer (1977) makes the following comment: "Common to these positions is an implicit notion that cognition is to be understood 'from the outside inward', that it is a matter of the structuring and restructuring of sensory information by intrinsically sensory systems and that the product of cognition has to somehow subsequently be married (in a peculiar sort of shotgun wedding) to action. Thus cognition has a puzzling, dualistic character for sensory theorists" (p. 270).

In contrast, the conceptualization of the relationship between cognition and action that emerges from an ecological perspective is that cognition is essentially a skilled action. As Weimer (1977) explains: "The mind is intrinsically a motor system and the sensory order by which we are acquainted with external objects as well as ourselves, the higher mental processes which construct our common sense and scientific knowledge, indeed everything mental, is a product of what are, correctly interpreted, constructive motor skills" (p. 272). The processes underlying human knowledge are thus conceptualized as skilled actions. This is consistent with Piaget's (1954) position that the child initially comes to know the world, not through passive observation, but through the observation and internalization of his or her actions upon objects.

While our comparison of information–processing and ecological metatheories has been brief, it has, we hope, been sufficiently detailed to highlight some of the conceptual strengths and weaknesses of the two approaches. As we have argued elsewhere, the concerns that the ecological perspective attempts to address can add a useful corrective influence to the information–processing perspective (Safran and Greenberg, 1986). We advocate a combined information–processing/ecological perspective, which holds that while it is useful to develop and empirically test models describing the fashion in which information is processed, it is vital not to overdraw the brain–computer analogy. Any approach that attempts to understand cognitive processes by temporarily bracketing them off from emotion, action, and the ecological niche in which they operate, is in danger of yielding a distorted picture of the phenomenon of interest. This holds true in the case of conscious as well as unconscious cognitive processes.

In the next section we will provide a historical review of the developments in the area of selective attention that have led to a preliminary conceptualization of the distinction between conscious and unconscious processes from a cognitive perspective. Research and theory development in this area have been primarily influenced by the information–processing metatheory. Following this we will briefly review some recent theoretical and empirical developments in cognitive psychology, which we believe are more in line with the type of information–processing/ecological perspective we are advocating. We believe that the incorporation of these developments into our understanding of the nature of unconscious processes provides a more complete and clinically useful understanding of human psychological processes.

SELECTIVE ATTENTION

The study of attentional processes was a central topic of investigation in early academic psychology. Titchener (1908), for example, stated that ". . . the doctrine of attention is the nerve of the whole psychological system, and that as men judge of it, so shall they be judged before the general tribunal of psychology (p. 173)." Similarly, William James (1890) considered attention to be the central organizing principle in human experience, as reflected in his statement: "My experience is what I agree to attend to. Only those items which I notice shape my mind—without selective interest my experience is utter chaos" (p. 402). While James considered attentional processes to be a suitable topic for investigation in scientific psychology, he warned that "The unconscious is the sovereign means of believing whatever one likes in psychology and of turning what might become a science into a tumbling ground for whimsies" (p. 163).

With the ascendence of the behavioral tradition in experimental psychology, the study of conscious psychological processes became as unacceptable as the study of unconscious psychological processes, and the topic of attention lost its legitimate status in the scientific community. As Kahneman (1973) points out, Osgood (1953) published an important text that covered the entire field of experimental psychology without mentioning the topic of attention more than once. That same year, a study was published by Cherry, which heralded the relegitimization of the topic of attention amongst experimental psychologists, as well as the emergence of the new cognitive psychology.

Cherry (1953) employed a dichotic listening task in order to investigate the nature of selective attention. In this procedure, subjects are presented with two messages to different ears, using earphones, and asked to monitor one of the two channels. The researcher can then investigate the way in which information that is not in focal awareness is processed, by assessing recognition or memory for characteristics of the unattended message. Cherry found that while subjects were aware of the presence of the unattended message, they could recall virtually nothing about it when subsequently questioned, with the exception of gross characteristics such as sex of the speaker. Subjects were thus unable to identify considerations more relevant to the meaning of the unattended–to stimulus.

This finding led Broadbent (1958) to propose his initial filter theory of selective attention. Broadbent theorized that incoming information is processed through a single channel. He hypothesized that selective attention operates by setting a filter in this channel to select a certain class of stimuli and to reject all others. According to Broadbent, this filtering process takes place early in the process of perception. He also theorized that the criteria for message selection are exclusively of a physical nature (e.g., message intensity, pitch, or location in space). In his model, any analysis of a message for meaning takes place only subsequent to the initial filtering process.

While Broadbent's model is commonly acknowledged as having played an important role in repopularizing the investigation of attentional processes, it was quickly realized that there are certain phenomena that it simply cannot account for. For example, the "cocktail party phenomenon" described by Cherry (1953), in which one suddenly becomes aware of a previously unattended–to conversation upon overhearing one's name, suggests that information that is not in focal awareness is nevertheless being analyzed on more than the basis of simple physical characteristics. This selective attention for one's name was demonstrated using a dichotic listening task, by Moray (1959), who found that subjects responded to their name spoken in the unattended ear while shadowing or repeating the message delivered to the other ear.

A simple study by Gray and Wedderburn (1960) also demonstrated the inadequacy of Broadbent's filter model. They found that when words were divided into syllables that were presented simultaneously to two different ears, subjects attended to both ears to extract meaning, rather than selecting one physical channel, thereby processing the information as meaningless syllables. This evidence suggests that subjects must be initially processing the unattended channel for meaning rather than for simple physical characteristics.

Evidence of this type led Treisman (1960; 1969) to propose her attenuation theory of selective attention. Treisman essentially suggested that the filtering process that takes place is not an all–or–nothing process and that the rejected meaning is really only attenuated. She hypothesized that the attenuated signal is matched against "dictionary units" in memory. These units have different thresholds of activation. If a specific attenuated signal exceeds the threshold of activation for the relevant unit or analyzer in memory, the unit becomes activated and the signal becomes conscious. While Treisman maintained the concept of a filter or "bottleneck" that exists early in the process of perception, she departed significantly from Broadbent by postulating that a signal can be processed by many analyzers simultaneously. This is a departure from the single–channel processing assumption of Broadbent's (1958) model and, as we shall see, anticipated subsequent theorizing about the multichanneled nature of preattentive processing.

Deutsch and Deutsch (1963) proposed an important alternative to Treisman's filter/attenuation model, as a way of accounting for the fact that the criteria for message selection are not limited exclusively to physical characteristics. According to them, all incoming information is subjected to a complex, higher–level analysis, on the basis of which only a subset of the information is selected for processing in focal awareness. Also according to Deutsch and Deutsch (1963), information is multichanneled in nature until much later in the process than Broadbent's (1958) model suggests.

Neisser (1967) was perhaps the first theorist in the area of selective attention to reject the notion of a filter altogether. He described perception as a process of analysis by synthesis. He maintained that one understands spoken messages by covertly reproducing them, and that visual perception takes place by an analogous synthetic process. He thus saw perception as a constructive set. This notion of analysis by synthesis anticipated subsequent conceptualizations of the relationship between perception and action advanced by theorists writing within the ecological tradition (e.g., Turvey, 1977; Weimer, 1977). According to Neisser (1967), unattended–to information is not "filtered out." It is simply not selected for further perceptual synthesis. He maintained that all conscious awareness is preceded by a preliminary, preattentive process that organizes the perceptual field into coherent units, thus separating the stimuli into figure and ground. This preattentive processing is simultaneous and holistic in nature, in contrast to focal attentional processing, which is logical and sequential in nature. Although he theorized that preattentive processes perform a preliminary sorting and organization of sensory data, Neisser identified detailed perceptual analysis with focal attention, and focal attention with awareness.

A classic and often–cited study conducted by Corteen and Wood (1972) provided evidence that challenged this position. They demonstrated that subjects who received shocks during a dichotic listening task, subsequently demonstrated significant galvanic skin response in reactions to words (which had never been presented before) that were semantically related to shock–associated words that had been presented to the "unattended" ear. It is to be noted that this emotional conditioning to semantically associated words took place despite the fact that the words or stimuli that were conditioned were at first not perceived consciously. The study thus suggests that emotional reactions can take place in response to a sophisticated semantic analysis that takes place outside conscious awareness.

Informed by this and similar evidence, Kahneman (1973) developed a model of attention that was similar to Neisser's (1967), insofar as he conceptualized attention as an active process of elaboration, rather than a filtering or selecting–out process. Kahneman, however, hypothesized that more detailed meaning analyses can take place outside awareness. According to him, the critical factor that determines whether or not information is processed in focal awareness is the amount of attentional capacity that is focussed upon it. Awareness or consciousness is thus identified with information that is allocated greater amounts of attentional capacity. Detailed meaning analyses, however, are not restricted to conscious processing. Kahneman (1973) also sees preattentive processing as multichanneled in nature, rather than single–channeled or sequential. Norman and Bobrow (1975) articulated a model of selective attention that is similar in many ways to Kahneman's.

UNCONSCIOUS VERSUS CONSCIOUS PROCESSING

Research continues to demonstrate that complex, semantic processing takes place outside awareness, and that preconscious processing is qualitatively different from conscious information–processing. The Corteen and Wood study (1972) was successfully replicated by Corteen and Dunn (1974) and Von Wright, Anderson and Stenman (1975). More recently Dawson and Schell (1982) replicated the Corteen and Wood (1972) findings, using even more stringent experimental controls.

Underwood (1977) found that subjects in a dichotic listening task who were required to shadow words in one ear, showed a reduced latency in shadowing time if semantically related words had previously been presented to the unattended ear. This suggests that words that are not *consciously* processed are nevertheless able to activate a perceptual set for semantically related words. Spence (1980) demonstrated that response latencies for discrimination between words and nonwords were significantly reduced by a subliminal stimulus, which, while too brief to permit conscious representation, was nevertheless able to activate a perceptual set that facilitated the recognition of a target word.

On the basis of her research, Conrad (1974) concluded that in unconscious processing, all possible meanings of a perceived input are activated and processed in parallel. In one condition, she presented subjects with potentially ambiguous words that were disambiguated by the sentences in which they were embedded. In the second condition, she presented words embedded in sentences that did not disambiguate them in the manner described above. Subsequently, she found that the ambiguous word interfered with the process of naming a visually presented word, as long as this word was semantically related to any of the possible meanings of the ambiguous word. This was true even in the condition in which the ambiguous word had been disambiguated by a sentence. These results suggest (a) that multiple meanings of the ambiguous word were indeed activated for subjects, even if only one meaning of the word was conscious for the individual when the word was disambiguated by the sentence; and (b) that processing of information and perception of information are integrally tied to responding. Similar findings have emerged from studies conducted by Neely (1977) and Marcel (1980).

According to Posner and Snyder (1975a, b), sensory input automatically activates a variety of different pathways in the nervous system. As long as this information is not processed at the conscious level, minimal demands are made upon attentional capacity. From a survival perspective this can be seen as benefitting the organism, since a wide array of information is constantly being processed, in parallel, in a variety of different ways. Since conscious processing is serial in nature rather than parallel, however, the admission of one stimulus, or one aspect of a stimulus, to consciousness automatically prevents other signals from becoming conscious. Conscious processing thus plays an inhibiting or restricting role with respect to signals that are not currently in conscious awareness.

Posner and Snyder (1975a) argue that unconscious processes operate not only at the level of perception but also at the level of preparation of responses in memory. The Stroop test, for example, provides a classic illustration of this observation. When the name of a specific color (e.g., blue) is printed in ink of a different color (e.g., red) the individual shows an increased response latency when asked to name the color of the ink. The semantic information provided by the written word thus appears to interfere with the person's performance on the task despite the fact that he or she attempts to ignore this information. Posner and Snyder (1975a) suggest that this phenomenon demonstrates that (a) a stimulus automatically activates multiple meanings, despite the fact that only one meaning may be conscious at a given point in time; (b) those meanings which are not conscious may nevertheless affect performance; and (c) the presentation of a stimulus (in this case the name of the color) automatically activates a pathway that includes not only semantic components but also a motor program associated with the output (in this case the naming of the color).

As the foregoing review suggests, the evidence acquired from research has gradually shifted the focus of theory away from an exclusive preoccupation with the question of how information is selectively admitted to awareness, to a more broad–scope attempt to understand the difference between the principles that characterize unconscious and conscious processing, as well as the nature of the interplay between the two. As Van Den Bergh and Eelen (1984) suggest, the reintroduction of consciousness into the framework of experimental psychology has functioned like the Trojan Horse, carrying unconscious cognitive processes in its belly.

Dixon (1981) argues that a biological frame of reference can be useful, if not absolutely necessary, for purposes of understanding the nature of, and relationship between, conscious and unconscious processes. Both types of processing activity can be understood in terms of their survival function.

They can be conceptualized as complementary processing activities with different but equally important survival features. Conscious processing is more restrictive than unconscious processing, with respect to the amount of sensory inflow that can be registered at one time. It has the advantage, however, of being more flexible in nature, allowing for sophisticated learning and for the formulation of action plans in response to sophisticated problem–solving activity. According to LaBerge (1981), the research evidence suggests that several properties are associated with unconscious processing. These include an unlimited attentional capacity; a lack of awareness, or absence of intentionality; a high degree of efficiency; and a resistence to change. Unconscious processing, because of its large capacity in contrast to conscious processing (cf. Kahneman, 1973; Schiffrin and Schneider, 1977), allows for the processing of multiple channels of information at the same moment. This allows the organism to register a large amount of information that may be important for purposes of survival. It also allows for rapid and immediate responses to a variety of stimuli in situations that are potentially threatening to the organisms of survival.

UNCONSCIOUS PROCESSING, ACTION AND EMOTION

The experimental evidence emerging from research on selective attention and related areas is making it increasingly evident that any conceptualization of conscious cognitive processes is necessarily inadequate without an understanding of the nature of unconscious cognitive processing. As Shevrin and Dickman (1980) conclude, following their review of a number of relevant experimental studies, there is evidence both that information–processing does take place at an unconscious level and that conscious and unconscious processing are characterized by different organizational features.

An important finding is the evidence that the unconscious processing of information is in some way integrally tied to responding, or at least to action disposition (e.g., Conrad, 1974; Posner and Snyder, 1975a, b). This evidence is consistent with Trevarthen's (1968) observation that "visual perception and the plans for voluntary action are so intimately bound together that they may be considered products of one cerebral function" (p. 391). It is also consistent with the ecological metatheoretical perspective, which views cognition and action as inextricably linked (Turvey, 1977; Weimer, 1977).

In an attempt to recognize the essentially motoric nature of cognition, a number of theorists from within the cognitive tradition have recently postulated the existence of structures in memory that represent, in a common locus, autonomic arousal, expressive motor behaviors, and memories or images of events that have elicited expressive motor behaviors. (Bower, 1981; Leventhal, 1982; Lang, 1983). Although there are differences in the specific details of these various models, which we will not go into here (for example, some theorists conceptualize these structures as semantic networks, whereas others conceptualize them as schemalike structures), a hypothesis common to all is that these memory structures operate at an unconscious or a preattentive level, and that the activation of one element in the memory structure (e.g., a specific image) has the potential for activating other elements in that memory structure (e.g., a particular configuration of autonomic responses and expressive motor behaviors). It is thus hypothesized that a particular pattern of expressive motor behaviors and autonomic responses can automatically be activated without conscious awareness. Although at first glance it may appear that this conceptualization is little different from a classical conditioning account of automatic response activation, the characteristics of the proposed memory structures, as we have argued elsewhere (Safran and Greenberg, 1986), are specified in a fashion that accounts for relationships of meaning between concepts. The model thus goes beyond a simple associative one.

Some theorists (e.g., Bower, 1981) stipulate that the memory structures also contain nodes for specific emotions, and that in this fashion emotion becomes tied to ideas and expressive motor behaviors in memory and plays an organizational function. We believe that this type of formulation begs the question as to what "emotion" is. Our position, which has been influenced by Leventhal (1979, 1982), is that the subjective experience of emotion is the result of the processing of action–disposition information that emerges when expressive motor, autonomic, and imagery codings from these schematic structures are accessed and combined with information processed from the environment (Greenberg and Safran, 1984a, b). Again, we wish to emphasize that this information is synthesized at a *preattentive* or *unconscious* level.

Elsewhere we reviewed the evidence consistent with the hypothesis that the expressive motor behavior accompanying specific basic emotional experiences are constant across developmental ages, across cultures, and are wired–into the main organism (Greenberg and Safran, 1986). Following evolutionary theorists such as Izard (1977) and Tomkins (1980), we hypothesize that this wired–in expressive motor substrate for emotional experience has evolved through a process of natural selection and that it has survival value. Thus, for example, the expressive motor configuration associated with anger is hypothesized to be compatible with a self–protective fight response. The expressive motor configuration associated with fear is hypothesized to be compatible with a flight response.

The act of processing this type of information at an unconscious level provides the individual with action–disposition information, which he or she can then process at a conscious level and elaborate into an action plan, if he or she so chooses. The preattentive synthesis of emotional information thus takes advantage of the multichanneled nature of unconscious processing, in order to provide the individual with a multitude of information, potentially relevant for survival, in the form of an efficient and economical emotional signal. The type of cognitive–affective–behavioral system we are describing (Greenberg and Safran, 1986) is thus seen as having the following characteristics: (1) The conscious experience of emotion is the product of an unconscious or preattentive synthesis of subsidiary components. (2) Emotional experience involves a synthesis of information from sources both external and internal to the organism. (3) The cognitive–affective system is adapted to the ecological niche. (4) Emotion has an adaptive function, and (5) Emotional experience tells us what events mean to us as biological organisms. With regard to this final point, Leventhal (1982) argues that emotions ". . . can be regarded as a form of meaning. They have significance for the person experiencing and expressing them. Their meaning has two aspects: they 'say' something about our organismic state (i.e., they meter its moment–to–moment readiness), and they 'say' something about the environment" (p. 122).

The model we have been discussing is consistent with an information–processing metatheory in that it specifies definite cognitive operations through which information is processed, and combines with other information to provide information that is utilizable by the organism. At the same time, however, it is also consistent with an ecological metatheory in that (a) it conceptualizes people as biological organisms rather than as disembodied computing machines; (b) an attempt is made to understand psychological functioning from an evolutionary perspective: emotional and cognitive processes are viewed as having evolved to meet the demands of a particular ecological niche; and (c) cognition, emotion and action are viewed as fused, or as different aspects of the same process, rather than as independent processes.

We will conclude this section by articulating two themes that have been implicit, if not explicit, in our discussion so far. The first is that by expanding the cognitive conceptualization of the unconscious to include concerns of ecological relevance, we are offering a cognitive alternative to a drive theory of *motivation*. Cognitive psychologists have, for the most part, conscientiously stayed away from dealing with motivational issues. However, there is no intrinsic reason for cognitive psychologists to avoid dealing with motivational issues. If we wish to have a truly adequate understanding of both conscious and unconscious psychological processes, it is necessary that we look at them in relationship to emotion and action. As Weimer (1977) asserts: "We must acknowledge that motivation is intrinsic to the operation of the CNS [central nervous system] and that the extrinsic sources of motivation that can be retained from classic motivation theory have their 'source' in the intrinsic motivation of nervous systems; that is, cognitive psychology must develop a 'motor theory' of motivation" (p. 295).

The second theme is that the conceptualization of emotional processing along the lines we have articulated, will ultimately permit us to develop a model of human functioning that is truly compatible with a psychology of meaning. We view our analysis of emotional processing as consistent with, and extending, Gibson's (1979) concept of affordances. According to Gibson people perceive objects and events in the world in terms of what they *afford* to them as organisms. A flat surface is thus perceived in terms of its walk–on–ability. A stick is perceived in terms of its grasp–ability. We, on the other hand, argue that we know objects and events in the world in terms of their *meaning* for us as biological organisms. This meaning is apprehended through the action dispositions that they evoke in us, and these action dispositions are the core of emotional experience. We thus conceptualize these action tendencies as a form of tacit knowledge, which is made explicit when the action–tendency information is synthesized and elaborated consciously.

As we have detailed elsewhere (Greenberg and Safran, 1984b, 1986; Safran and Greenberg, 1986), the model we have articulated has some important clinical implications. Perhaps one of the most important ones is that psychological problems can result from a failure to fully synthesize potentially adaptive action–disposition information. For example, the person who fails to synthesize action–disposition information consistent with anger may fail to protect himself or herself from a destructive interpersonal situation. The person who fails to synthesize action–disposition information consistent with loneliness may fail to engage in intimacy–seeking behaviors that could lead to the establishment of an adaptive interpersonal relationship.

The model also facilitates the generation of hypotheses regarding the specific information–processing deficits from which this failure to synthesize adaptive action–disposition information results, as well as therapeutic interventions that can potentially remedy these deficits. We hypothesize that deficits of this type can result from a failure to *attend* to action–disposition information or expressive motor behaviors consistent with a specific emotion. As Underwood (1978) states, attention may be viewed as the "major control process in the passage of information into and out of the memory system and indeed through the human information–processing system as a whole" (p. 325). In this respect, the conceptualization emerging from the perspective we have outlined is closer to Sullivan's (1953) notion of selective inattention than it is to Freud's notion of repression.

Also consistent with Sullivan (1953), we hypothesize that anxiety–provoking interpersonal encounters can obstruct the processing of information both around and within the individual (Safran, 1984a, b). This can result in a failure to develop elaborated schematic structures appropriate to certain classes of emotional experience that have been associated with anxiety–fraught interpersonal encounters. This, in turn, can result in what is essentially a structural inability to synthesize certain classes of emotional experience in any kind of refined or mature fashion. And consistent with Eagle (1984), we hypothesize that in some cases, the failure to develop mature schematic structures associated with specific classes of emotions can result in accessing very primitive, explosive, and age–inappropriate emotions when they *are* synthesized. This can have the secondary complication of increasing the amount of fear an individual has in experiencing certain classes of emotion, thus making it all the more difficult to access those emotions.

CONCLUSION

The view of the unconscious that arises from the cognitive perspective we have outlined can ultimately be contrasted with the Freudian conception of the unconscious in the following fashion. Whereas Freud saw the unconscious as a "seething cauldron" of instinctual drives, which must be controlled or renounced in order to adapt to reality, the current perspective views the unconscious as providing action–disposition information that has not been synthesized and elaborated in focal awareness. In this respect, the concept of the unconscious derived from a cognitive perspective is much closer in nature to the more recent psychoanalytic developments articulated by theorists such as George Klein (1976), Schafer (1976, 1983), and Eagle (1984) than it is to the traditional psychoanalytic conception. In both the more recent psychoanalytic perspective and the cognitive perspective we have outlined, the goal of psychotherapy is one of owning disclaimed action tendencies, rather than one of acknowledging, and then taming or renouncing chaotic instinctual drives.

The cognitive perspective presented here augments current psychoanalytic thinking by elaborating upon the mechanisms through which actions can be disclaimed, as well as by articulating, in information–processing terms, what it means to acknowledge a disclaimed action. We believe that this results in more than a mere translation of concepts from one language to another. Understanding the processes of owning and disowning action tendencies in information–processing terms can provide us with insights as to how to facilitate the synthesis of adaptive emotional processes when this synthesis is not taking place. A variety of examples can be found in Greenberg and Safran (1986) and Safran and Greenberg (1986).

The cognitive framework we have outlined shifts our understanding of the unconscious from a clinical/descriptive level to the level of theory that is strongly grounded in, and linked to, experimental research. It shifts the level of analysis from a descriptive level to an explanatory one. As Toulmin (1972) and Weimer (1979) point out, explanation is at the core of science. In this respect, both the topographic and structural models of the mind that Freud initially developed, were, because of their explanatory nature, important attempts to frame the phenomenon of the unconscious in a scientific context. Drive theory is to be faulted, not on the basis of its attempt to explain, but rather on the basis of the inadequacy of the explanation. This failure may result, at least in part, from the fact that Freud attempted to establish psychoanalysis as a biological science, by using concepts that were prominent in the scientific climate of his time, but are now outdated.

More recent psychoanalytic developments (e.g., Klein, 1976, Schafer, 1976; Eagle, 1984) have, in our opinion, provided a descriptive analysis with a greater degree of verisimilitude than Freud's metapsychology. However, these recent developments lack the explanatory power that is an essential part of a true scientific theory. We believe that casting the unconscious within a cognitive framework is an important step in this direction. Information–processing theory is an explanatory theory with the scientific merit of having important aspects of the nomological net grounded in observables. This enables us to modify theory in response to new evidence yielded by scientific investigation.

Along with critics of Freud from within the psychoanalytic community (e.g., Klein, 1976; Eagle, 1984), we are critical of certain aspects of Freud's drive metapsychology. We are, however, sympathetic to his attempt to understand humankind from a biological perspective and to view both conscious and unconscious processes in relationship to human passions. In contrast, the picture of the unconscious emerging from a purely information–processing approach is a sterile one and provides an incomplete picture of human functioning. A metatheory completely devoid of biological considerations is ultimately no more satisfactory than a metatheory that incorporates biology in a mechanistic fashion. As we have emphasized, however, there is no intrinsic reason for cognitive psychologists to continue to study cognition out of context of emotion, action, and environment. Our hope is that the information–processing/ecological perspective we have offered (Greenberg and Safran, 1984b, 1986; Safran and Greenberg, 1986) will provide cognitive psychologists with a way to talk about emotions and the unconscious, and psychoanalytic theorists, with a way to talk to cognitive psychologists.

REFERENCES

Bower, G.H. (1981), Mood and memory. *American Psychologist*, 36: 129–148.
Bowlby, J. (1969), *Attachment and Loss, Vol 1: Attachment*. New York: Basic Books.
Breuer, J., & Freud, S. (1895), Studies on hysteria. *Standard Edition*, 2: 1–170. London: Hogarth Press, 1955.

Broadbent, D.E. (1958), *Perception and Communication*. London: Pergamon.

Cherry, E.C. (1953), Some experiments on the recognition of speech, with one and with two ears. *J. Acoustical Society of America*, 25: 975–979.

Conrad, C. (1974), Context effects in sentence comprehension: A study of the subjective lexicon. *Memory and Cognition*, 2: 130–138.

Corteen, R.S., & Dunn, D. (1974), Shock associated words in a nonattended message: A test for momentary awareness. *J. Exp. Psychol.*, 102: 1143–1144.

Corteen, R.S., & Wood, B. (1972), Autonomic responses to shock associated words. *J. Exp. Psychol.*, 94: 308–313.

Dawes, R.M. (1976), Shallow psychology. In: *Cognition and Social Behavior*, ed. J.S. Carroll & J.W. Payne. Hillsdale, NJ: Lawrence Erlbaum Associates.

Dawson, M.C., & Schell, A.M. (1982), Electrodermal responses to attended and nonattended significant stimuli during dichotic listening. *J. Exp. Psychol.: Human Perception and Performance*, 8: 315–324.

Deutsch, J.A., & Deutsch, D. (1963), Attention: Some theoretical considerations. *Psycholog. Rev.*, 70: 80–90.

Dixon, N. (1981), *Preconscious Processing*. New York: Wiley.

Eagle, M.N. (1984), *Recent Developments in Psychoanalysis*. New York: McGraw-Hill.

Fairbairn, W.R.D. (1952), *An Object–relations Theory of the Personality*. New York: Basic Books.

Gibson, J.J. (1966), *The Senses Considered as Perception Systems*. Boston: Houghton Mifflin.

———— (1979), *The Ecological Approach to Visual Perception*. Boston: Houghton Mifflin.

Gill, M.M. (1976), Metapsychology is not psychology. In: *Psychology Versus Metapsychology: Essays in Memory of George S. Klein*, ed. M.M. Gill & P.S. Holzman. New York: International Universities Press.

Gray, J.A., & Wedderburn, A.A. (1960), Grouping strategies with simultaneous stimuli. *Quart. J. Exp. Psychol.*, 12: 180–184.

Greenberg, J.R., & Mitchell, S.A. (1983), *Object Relations in Psychoanalytic Theory*. Cambridge, MA: Harvard University Press.

———— & Safran, J.D. (1984a), Hot cognition: Emotion coming in from the cold. A reply to Rachman & Mahoney. *Cognitive Therapy and Research*, 8: 591–598.

———— & Safran, J.D. (1984b), Integrating affect and cognition: A perspective on therapeutic change. *Cognitive Therapy and Research*, 8: 559–578.

———— & Safran, J.D. (1986), *Emotion in Psychotherapy*. New York: Guilford Press.

Hayek, F.A. (1978), *New Studies in Philosophy, Politics, Economics and the History of Ideas*. Chicago: University of Chicago Press.

Holt, R.R. (1976), Drive or wish? A reconsideration of the psychoanalytic theory of motivation. In: *Psychology Versus Metapsychology: Essays in Memory of George S. Klein*, ed. M.M. Gill and P.S. Holzman. New York: International Universities Press.

Izard, C.E. (1977), *Human Emotions*. New York: Plenum Press.

James, W. (1890), *The Principles of Psychology*. New York: Holt.

Kahneman, D. (1973), *Attention and Effort*. Englewood Cliffs, NJ: Prentice-Hall.

Klein, G.S. (1976), *Psychoanalytic Theory: An Exploration of Essentials*. New York: International Universities Press.

LaBerge, D. (1981), Automatic information processing: A review. In: *Attention and Performance, Vol. 9*, ed. J. Long & A. Baddeley. Hillsdale, NJ: Lawrence Erlbaum Associates.

Lang, P.J. (1983), Cognition in emotion: Concept and action. In: *Emotion, Cognition and Behavior*, ed. C. Izard, J. Kagan, & R. Zajonc. New York: Cambridge University Press.

Leventhal, H. (1979), A perceptual motor processing model of emotion. In: *Advances in the Study of Communication and Affect, Vol. 5: Perception of Emotions in Self and Others*, ed. P. Pliner, K.R. Blankstein, & I.M. Spigel. New York: Plenum Press.

———— (1982), The integration of emotion and cognition: A view from the perceptual–motor theory of emotion. In: *Affect and Cognition*, ed. M.S. Clarke & S.T. Fiske. Hillsdale, NJ: Erlbaum.

Lorenz, K. (1977), *Behind the Mirror*. New York: Harcourt Brace Jovanovich.

Mahoney, M.J. (1982), Psychotherapy and human change processes. *Psychotherapy Research and Behavior Change*, 1. Washington, DC: American Psychiatric Association.

Marcel, A.J. (1980), Conscious and preconscious recognition of polysemous words: Locating the selective effects of prior verbal context: In: *Attention and Performance, Vol. 8*, ed. R.S. Nickerson. Hillsdale, NJ: Lawrence Erlbaum Associates.

Meichenbaum, D., & Gilmore, J.B. (1984), The nature of unconscious processes: A cognitive-behavioral perspective. In: *The Unconscious Reconsidered*, ed. K.S. Bowers & D. Meichenbaum. New York: Wiley.

Moray, N. (1959), Attention in dichotic listening: Affective cues and the influence of instructions. *Quart. J. Exp. Psychol.*, 11: 56–60.

Neely, J.H. (1977), Semantic priming and retrieval from lexical memory: Roles of inhibitionless spreading activation and limited–capacity attention. *J. Exp. Psychol.*, 106: 226–254.

Neisser, U. (1967), *Cognitive Psychology*. New York: Appleton–Century Crofts.

———— (1980), Three cognitive psychologies and their implications. In: *Psychotherapy Process*, ed. M.J. Mahoney. New York: Plenum Press.

Nemiah, J.C. (1984), The unconscious and psychopathology. In: *The Unconscious Reconsidered*, ed. K.S. Bowers & D. Meichenbaum. New York: John Wiley.

Norman, D.A., & Bobrow, D.G. (1975), On data–limited and resource–limited processes. *Cognitive Psychology*, 7: 44–64.

Osgood, G.E. (1953), *Method and Theory in Experimental Psychology*. New York: Oxford University Press.

Piaget, J. (1954), *Construction of Reality in the Child*. New York: Basic Books.

Posner, M.I., & Snyder, R.R. (1975a). Attention and cognitive control. In: *Information Processing and Cognition*, ed. R.L. Solso. Hillsdale, NJ: Lawrence Erlbaum Associates.

———— & Snyder, R.R. (1975b), Facilitation and inhibition in the processing of signals. In: *Attention and Performance*, ed. P.M.A. Rabbitt & S. Dornic. New York: Academic Press.

Safran, J.D. (1984a), Assessing the Cognitive-interpersonal cycle. *Cognitive Therapy and Research*, 8: 333–348.

———— (1984b), Some implications of Sullivan's interpersonal theory for cognitive therapy. In: *Cognitive Psychotherapies: Recent Developments in Theory, Research and Practice*, ed. M.A. Reda & M.J. Mahoney. Cambridge, MA: Ballinger.

———— & Greenberg, L.S. (1986), Hot cognition and psychotherapy process: An information processing/ecological approach. In: *Advances in Cognitive–Behavioral Research and Therapy* Vol. 3., ed. P. C. Kendall. New York: Plenum Press.

Schafer, R. (1976), *A New Language of Psychoanalysis*. New Haven: Yale University Press.

———— (1983), *The Analytic Attitude*. New York: Basic Books.

Shaw, R., & Bransford, J. (1977), *Perceiving, Acting and Knowing: Toward an Ecological Psychology*. Hillsdale, NJ: Lawrence Erlbaum Associates.

Shevrin, H., & Dickman, S. (1980), The psychological unconscious. *American Psychologist*, 35: 421–434.

Shiffrin, R.M., & Schneider, W. (1977), Controlled and automatic human information processing: II. Perceptual learning, automatic attending, and a general theory. *Psycholog. Rev.*, 84: 127–190.

Spence, D.P. (1980), Lawfulness in lexical choice—A natural experiment. *J. Amer. Psychoanal. Assn.*, 28: 115–132.

Sullivan, H.S. (1953), *The Interpersonal Theory of Psychiatry*. New York: Norton.

Titchener, E.B. (1908), *Lectures on the Elementary Psychology of Feeling and Attention*. New York: Macmillan.

Tomkins, S.S. (1980), Affect as amplification: Some modifications in theory. In: *Emotion: Theory, Research and Experience, 1*, ed. R. Plutchik & H. Kelerman. New York: Academic Press.

Toulmin, S. (1972), *Human Understanding*. Princeton, NJ: Princeton University Press.

Treisman, A.M. (1960), Contextual cues in selective listening. *Quart. J. Exp. Psychol.*, 12: 242–248.

—— (1969), Strategies and models of selective attention. *Psycholog. Rev.*, 76: 282–299.

Trevarthen, C.B. (1968), Two mechanisms of vision in primates. *Psychologische Forschung*, 31: 299–337.

Turvey, M.T. (1977), Preliminaries to a theory of action with reference to vision. In: *Perceiving, Acting and Knowing: Toward an Ecological Psychology*, ed. R. Shaw & J. Bransford. Hillsdale, NJ: Lawrence Erlbaum Associates.

Underwood, G. (1977), Contextual facilitation from attended and unattended messages. *J. Verbal Learning and Verbal Behavior*, 16: 99–106.

—— (1978), Attentional selectivity and behavioral control. In: *Strategies of Information Processing*, ed. G. Underwood. London & New York: Academic Press.

Van Den Bergh, O., Eelen, P. (1984), Unconscious processing and emotions. In: *Cognitive Psychotherapies: Recent Developments in Theory, Research and Practice*, ed. M.A. Reda & M.J. Mahoney. Cambridge, MA: Ballinger.

Von Wright, J.M., Anderson, K., & Stenman, V. (1975), Generalization of conditioned GSR's in dichotic listening. In: *Attention and Performance*, ed. P.M.A. Rabbitt & S. Dornic. New York: Academic Press.

Weimer, W.B. (1977), A conceptual framework for cognitive psychology: Motor theories of the mind. In: *Perceiving, Acting and Knowing: Toward an Ecological Psychology*, ed. R. Shaw & J. Bransford. Hillsdale, NJ: Lawrence Erlbaum Associates.

—— (1979), *Notes on the Methodology of Scientific Research*. Hillsdale, NJ: Lawrence Erlbaum Associates.

10

From the Subjectivity of Science to a Science of Subjectivity*

Robert D. Stolorow
Geoge E. Atwood

In our earlier psychobiographical studies of Freud, Jung, Reich, and Rank (Stolorow and Atwood, 1979), we demonstrated that the psychological life of a psychological theorist is inevitably imported into the structure of his or her theories, shaping them according to the organizing principles of the theorist's own personal subjectivity and lending them a coloration expressive of his or her personal history and existence as an individual. Most important for psychoanalysis, we found that Freud's picture of the unconscious as a "seething cauldron" of infantile instinctual drive derivatives was heir to his lifelong need to maintain a defensively idealized vision of his mother. By locating the sources of "badness" and psychopathology in the child's innate instinctual drives—the nucleus of the Freudian unconscious—he symbolically purified his image of his mother of her disappointing and enraging qualities, thereby preserving her as an untarnished source of love, devotion, and goodness. Through this crypto-biological view of the unconscious, Freud also sought to ground psychoanalysis in the natural science of his day. Our studies of the subjective origins of such theorizing have led us to propose a purely psychological framework to guide psychoanalytic inquiry, freed of the encumbering mechanistic imagery of Freudian metapsychology. As we will describe in greater detail below, such a framework includes a significantly altered view of the unconscious, one that brings into focus the prereflective structuring activity that both restricts the

*An earlier version of this paper was presented at the convention of the American Psychological Association, Washington, D.C., on August 23, 1982.

213

field of a person's awareness and thematizes the contents of his or her conscious experiences.

Emerging from our demonstrations of the subjective origins of psychological theories are two broad questions that are of great importance for the science of personality psychology. The first of these concerns the significance of demonstrating the subjective origins of a theory for assessing the validity of that theory. One extreme position that might be taken on this issue would be to consider the explication of psychological origins as a means of completely invalidating the theory. The extreme opposite position would be to claim that the origins and validity of a theory are entirely separate problems, having no bearing on each other whatsoever. While avoiding the reductionistic fallacy of the first position, the second position imposes an artificial and intellectually deadening conceptual barrier between the theorist as a person and the products of his or her work.

Our own position on the relationship between subjectivity and validity is different from the two extreme positions just described. The analysis of origins, while not constituting an invalidation, nevertheless *reveals a theory's particularization of scope*. Thus, such an analysis both delimits the generality of the theory's applicability and points to the empirical domain to be accounted for by more embracing theoretical viewpoints.

It is here that we encounter the second broad question for a science of personality: How can we arrive at a psychological theory that is more general and inclusive—one that can account not only for the phenomena that other personality theories address, but also for these other theories themselves? The answer to which we have been led by our work is that such an inclusive and unifying perspective can be attained only by a theoretical framework that takes human subjectivity itself as its principal domain of inquiry.

We refer to our effort in this direction as "psychoanalytic phenomenology." Being a depth psychology of human subjectivity, it seeks to illuminate the structure, significance, origins, and transformations of personal subjective worlds in all their richness and diversity. In the present paper we can only sketch this framework with the broadest brushstokes,[1] while attempting to show that it holds great promise in providing a coherent perspective from which to view the array of issues that have formed the traditional concerns of personality theory. These issues include the notion of personality structure, the concept of motivation, the idea of unconscious mental processes, the theory of psychological development, the problem of defining psychological health and pathology, and the nature of therapeutic change.

---

[1]This theoretical framework is elaborated in detail in Atwood and Stolorow (1984).

PERSONALITY STRUCTURE

From the perspective of psychoanalytic phenomenology, personality structure is the *structure of a person's experiencing*. Thus, the basic units of analysis for our investigations of personality are *structures of experience*—the distinctive configurations of self and other that shape and organize a person's subjective world. We conceptualize these structures as systems of ordering or organizing principles—cognitive–affective schemata through which a person's experiences of self and other assume their characteristic forms and meanings. Such structures of subjectivity are disclosed in the thematic patterning of a person's subjective life.

In psychoanalytic phenomenology the concept of character is coextensive with the structure of a subjective world. A person's character is his psychological organization, and character analysis is an elucidation of the nature, developmental vicissitudes, and multiple purposes of the configurations that are its constituents. This conception of character analysis assumes that recurrent patterns of conduct serve to actualize the nuclear configurations of self and other that constitute a person's character. Such patterns of conduct may include inducing other people to act in predetermined ways, so that a thematic isomorphism is created between the ordering of the subjective and interpersonal fields.

MOTIVATION

Psychoanalytic phenomenology does not postulate a theory of the nature of personality as an "objective entity." Instead, it consists in a methodological system of interpretative principles to guide the study of *meaning* in human experience and conduct. Its explanatory concepts thus emphasize not "psychic determinism" and a natural-science view of causality, but rather a *subjective contextualism* that brings to focus the nexus of personal meanings in which a person's experience and conduct are embedded. Rather than formulating impersonal motivational prime movers of a mental apparatus, psychoanalytic phenomenology seeks to illuminate the multiple conscious and unconscious *purposes* or personal reasons that lead a person to strive to actualize his or her psychological structures. The configurations that a person strives to actualize may, in varying degrees, fulfill cherished wishes and urgent desires, provide moral restraint and self-punishment, aid adaptation to difficult realities, and repair or restore damaged or lost self-and other images. They may also serve a defensive purpose, in preventing other, subjectively dangerous configurations from emerging in conscious experience. It is extremely important for conceptualizing a personality structure to determine the relative motivational salience or priority of these multiple purposes in the organization of experience and conduct.

The evolution of our framework has led us to propose an additional, more general, supraordinate motivational principle: that the *need to maintain the organization of experience* is a central motive in the patterning of human action. The basic psychological process that mediates this functional relationship between experience and action is *concretization*—the encapsulation of structures of experience by concrete, sensorimotor symbols. We have come to believe that the concretization of experience is a ubiquitous and fundamental process in human psychological life and that it underlies a great variety of psychological activities and products. Concretization can assume a number of forms, depending on what pathways or modes of expression it favors. For example, when motor activity predominates in the mode of concretization, then behavioral enactments are relied upon to actualize required configurations of experience. When motor activity is curtailed, as in sleep, then perceptual imagery may become the preferred pathway of concretization, as in dreams.

Our motivational principle can be understood to apply in two senses. One the one hand, a pattern of action may serve to maintain a *particular* organization of experience, in which specific required configurations of self and other are actualized, and dangerous ones are precluded. On the other hand, a pattern of action may serve to maintain psychological organization per se, as when concrete enactments are required to sustain the structural cohesion and continuity of a fragmenting sense of self or other. So-called sexual and aggressive "acting out" is conceptualized not in terms of a defective "mental apparatus" with a lack of "impulse control," but rather in terms of the need for behavioral enactments to shore up an imperiled subjective world.

REPRESSION AND THE UNCONSCIOUS

In psychoanalytic phenomenology, repression is understood as a process whereby particular configurations of self and other are prevented from crystallizing in awareness. Repression may thus be viewed as a *negative organizing principle*, operating alongside the positive organizing principles underlying the configurations that do repeatedly materialize in conscious experience. The "dynamic unconscious," from this standpoint, consists in that set of configurations which consciousness is not permitted to assume, because of such configurations' association with emotional conflict and subjective danger. Particular memories, fantasies, feelings, and other experiential contents are repressed because they threaten to actualize these dreaded configurations. Other psychological defenses are conceptualized as further transformations of the subjective world that by radically altering and restricting the person's experience of self and other, prevent dreaded configurations from emerging.

In addition to the "dynamic unconscious" viewed as a system of negative organizing principles, another form of unconsciousness has increasingly assumed a position of importance in our framework. The organizing principles of a person's subjective world, whether operating positively (giving rise to certain configurations in awareness) or negatively (preventing certain configurations from arising), are themselves unconscious. A person's experiences are shaped by his or her psychological structures, without this shaping becoming the focus of awareness and reflection. We have therefore characterized the structure of a subjective world as *prereflectively unconscious*. This form of unconsciousness is not the product of defensive activity, even though great effort is required to overcome it. It derives from the circumstance that, in the absence of reflection, a person is unaware of his or her role as constitutive subject in elaborating his or her personal reality.

An understanding of the form of unconsciousness that we have designated as prereflective sheds light on the unique importance of dreams for psychoanalytic theory and practice. The prereflective structures of a person's subjective world are most readily discernible in his or her relatively unfettered, spontaneous productions, and there is probably no psychological product that is less fettered or more spontaneous than the dream. As human subjectivity in purest culture, the dream constitutes a "royal road" to the prereflective unconscious—to the organizing principles and dominant leitmotivs that unconsciously pattern and thematize a person's psychological life.

PERSONALITY DEVELOPMENT

In psychoanalytic phenomenology, personality development refers to the *structuralization of personal experience*. Efforts to construct a developmental psychology of the subjective world are still in their infancy. They have been significantly hampered by the persistent psychological tradition of artificially dividing human subjectivity into cognitive and affective domains. We have proposed a mending of the rift between cognition and affect, and a focus on the ontogenesis of unitary configurations of (cognitive–affective) experience. Our particular interests have been the vicissitudes of psychological differentiation and integration, and the role of psychosexual symbols in the articulation of the subjective world. We view the developmental process as an *intersubjective* one throughout, shaped at every point by the unique interplay between the vulnerable, evolving subjectivity of the child and the more complexly organized and firmly consolidated subjectivities of caregivers.

The particular thematic structure of a child's subjective world evolves organically from the critical formative experiences that mark his or her unique early history, and from the individualized array of personal motivations that develops as the result of these experiences. Once the child has established a relatively stable psychological organization, it serves as a prereflective frame of reference, into the structure of which he or she will unconsciously assimilate subsequent experiences. Developmental change occurs when this structure is altered and expanded to accomodate new constellations of experience.

PSYCHOLOGICAL HEALTH, PATHOLOGY, AND THERAPY

A theory of personality development centering on the structuralization of experience will seek a conception of psychological health in some formulation of *optimal structuralization*. This ideal can be conceptualized in terms of the healthy person's ability to achieve an optimal balance between the maintenance of his or her psychological organization, on the one hand, and his or her openness to new forms of experience, on the other. On the one hand, the person's psychological structures have become sufficiently consolidated so that they can assimilate a wide range of experiences of self and other and still retain their integrity and stability. His or her subjective world, in other words, is not unduly vulnerable to disintegration or dissolution. On the other hand, the person's psychological structures are sufficiently flexible to accomodate new configurations of experience of self and other, so that the organization of his or her subjective life can continue to expand in both complexity and scope.

Correspondingly, we can conceptualize two broad classes of psychopathology that reflect the two types of failure to attain this optimal balance. One class is composed of those psychological disorders which reflect the consolidation of *pathological structures* that operate rigidly to restrict a person's subjective field. Examples are found in persons whose lives are severely constricted by defensive structures that inflexibly order their experiences to prevent the emergence of emotional conflict and subjective danger. The other class consists of those psychological disturbances that reflect *insufficient or faulty structuralization*—developmental deficiencies and arrests in the formation and consolidation of the subjective world (Stolorow and Lachmann, 1980). Examples are found in persons who are prone to self-fragmentation and require immersion in archaic modes of relatedness to sustain the cohesion and continuity of their precarious self-experiences (Kohut, 1971, 1977).

From the perspective of psychoanalytic phenomenology, the therapeutic situation may be viewed as a set of facilitating conditions that permit the structure of a person's subjective world to unfold maximally and find illumination in relatively pure culture. Analogously to the process of psychological development, the therapeutic process is seen to be embedded in a specific *intersubjective field* created by the interplay between the differently organized subjectivities of patient and therapist. The mode of therapeutic action within this field will differ, depending on the extent to which either pathological structures or remnants of insufficient structuralization predominate in the treatment at any particular juncture.

When pathological structures predominate, therapeutic change can be conceptualized as a gradual process of *structural transformation*: The ossified, pathological forms that have heretofore structured the patient's experiences are progressively broken up and reorganized, making it possible for a new and enriched personal reality to open up before him or her. When remnants of faulty structuralization predominate, treatment aims not for the breaking up and reorganization of existing pathological structures, but rather for the *growth* of psychological structure that is missing or unsteady as a consequence of developmental voids and interferences. The patient is permitted to establish a matrix of archaic relatedness from within which arrested developmental thrusts can be revitalized, and formerly abandoned developmental tasks can be resumed and completed.

CONCLUSIONS

Our studies of the subjective origins of psychological theories have led us to propose that a more general, inclusive, and unifying theory must take human subjectivity itself as its principal domain of inquiry. Our own framework, psychoanalytic phenomenology, seeks to illuminate the structure, significance, origins, and transformations of personal subjective worlds. This framework provides a coherent perspective from which to view the array of issues that have formed the traditional concerns of personality psychology.

Psychoanalysis is, and always has been, a science of the structure of subjectivity, concerned with the patterns that unconsciously organize personal experience and conduct. Its contribution has been in the placing of various psychological phenomena (symptoms, dreams, transferences) in the structural contexts of meaning to which they belong. However, its formulations have long been encumbered by a biological determinism with roots both in Freud's personal subjective life and in nineteenth-century natural science. Our aim has been to free the phenomenological knowledge of psychoanalysis from its procrustean bed of mechanism and determinism. Hence, the point of departure for our psychoanalytic phenomenology has been the concept of an experiencing subject, and at the deepest level of our theoretical constructions we operate within the sphere of subjectivity, abjuring assumptions that reduce experience to a material substrate. This central focus on the unconscious structuring of experience defines the unique place of psychoanalysis among the sciences.

REFERENCES

Atwood, G., & Stolorow, R. (1984), *Structures of Subjectivity: Explorations in Psychoanalytic Phenomenology.* Hillsdale, NJ: The Analytic Press.
Kohut, H. (1971), *The Analysis of the Self.* New York: International Universities Press.
_____ (1977), *The Restoration of the Self.* New York: International Universities Press.
Stolorow, R., & Atwood, G. (1979), *Faces in a Cloud: Subjectivity in Personality Theory.* New York: Jason Aronson.
_____ & Lachmann, F. (1980), *Psychoanalysis of Developmental Arrests: Theory and Treatment.* New York: International Universities Press.

11 Perversion and the Desire to Harm

Robert J. Stoller

The main issue in the following discussions—the desire to humiliate as an essential theme in erotics—needs considerable scrutiny. In light of this, I would like to make two preliminary observations.

(1) This study presents a number of conclusions, as well as a question I cannot answer: what specific piece of any individual's erotic behavior is *not* a perversion? My hypotheses provide an account, if somewhat sketchy, of what a perversion is, but the scope of the present work does not permit us to provide analysis of what does not count as a perversion.

(2) I shall present hypotheses, clinical vignettes, and impressions; as a result, the study will, appear rather informal.

DOES PERVERSION EXIST?

In the universities, in the literature on erotics, in the literature for psychologists, psychiatrists, and psychotherapists, we find a tendency to avoid the use of the word "perversion." "Perversion" is a pejorative term. It reeks of sin, accusation, vindictiveness, and righteousness. The term evokes an absolute morality—in it are heard the thunder of God and his agents on earth. How then could anyone familiar with psychodynamics, cultural relativity, social inequities, and the cruelty of the law still hope to use the term in any theoretical context? In the name of decency, "perversion" has dropped out of modern psychiatric and psychoanalytic discourse. Part of the difficulty lies in the social background—it has stood in the way of research into the origins of sexual behavior, and it denies social realities, namely, the sexual frankness unfolding in the modern world. The criteria for the use of the term were in the hands of authorities such as psychiatrists, courts, and officialdom, and judgments were made not on the basis of what an individual was doing—what his or her act meant to himself or herself—but on the basis of the anatomic parts used, and the mores of the culture.

And so, in reaction against such dictionary meanings as "corrupt" and "debased," a gentler, enlightened position has emerged. As an example of this social progress, let me sketch that shift in attitude as it developed in official psychiatric circles in the last thirty years.

The American Psychiatric Association began its efforts to consolidate diagnoses with the publication of the *Diagnosis and Statistical Manual— Mental Disorders* (DSM I) (APA, 1952). Before that time, there was no official nomenclature for psychiatric disorders; or, rather, different social institutions—for example, the Veterans Administration—each had its own. In that era, as *DMS I* notes, the diagnosis "Psychopathic Personality with Pathologic Sexuality" was available. Then, with *DSM I* came "Sociopathic Personality Disorders—Sexual Deviation (Specify Supplementary Term)," with the following elaboration: "type of pathologic behavior such as homosexuality, transvestism, pedophilia, fetishism and sexual sadism (including rape, sexual assault, mutilation)" (p. 39). Toward the back was the listing "Supplementary Term—Sexual Perversion."

A humanitarian movement was under way: "psychopathic personality," with its powerful defamatory sense, had been rendered more objective by the change to "sociopathic personality." But as happens when we try to change beliefs by changing labels, old meanings infect new words: "sociopath" did not clean up "psychopath." Besides, the former "perversions" were still called "disorders," though the accusation was softened with the rather neutral "deviation." Even calling these conditions "pathologic behavior" (Stoller, 1974, 1979) was a weighty judgment.

In 1968 the APA released *DSM II* (APA, 1968). The category was now: "Personality Disorders and Certain Other Non-Psychotic Mental Disorders. Sexual deviations: homosexuality, fetishism, pedophilia, transvestitism, exhibitionism, voyeurism, sadism, masochism, other sexual deviations, [unspecified sexual deviations]" (p. 41, 44). But still, there was the word "disorders."

Then, following battles in which homosexuality *per se* was removed as a diagnosis, *DSM III* (APA, 1980), listed, under "Psychosexual Disorders," two categories of what, in ancient days, had been the perversions: "Gender Identity Disorders" and "Paraphilias." In other classifications these disorders are referred to as Sexual Deviations. The term paraphilia is preferable because it correctly emphasizes that the deviation (para) is in that to which the individual is attracted (philia)" (pp. 266–267). *DSM III* lists fetishism, transvestism, zoophilia, pedophilia, exhibitionism, voyeurism, sexual masochism, sexual sadism, and atypical paraphilias: "Coprophilia (feces), Frotteurism (rubbing), Klismophilia (enema), Mysophilia (filth), Necrophilia (corpse), Telephone Scatalogia (lewdness), and Urophilia (urine)" (p. 275).

Paraphilia: how clean and tidy, science triumphant. Change the labels and the activities change.

Nonetheless, I want to retain the term "perversion" because of its connotations. "Perversion" is a sturdy word, throbbing with assumptions, while "paraphilia" is a wet noodle; it is too neutral, and, in fact, says nothing. It does not contain the quality the person we would call "perverse" finds essential. That quality is the sense of sin, of sinning.

The concept of sin is at the center of "perversion." In science, however, there is no place for such a concept. Please understand: (a) I am not claiming there is such a thing as sin; I am only saying that people believe in it; (b) it may be unscientific to believe in sin, but it is also unscientific to believe that people do not believe in sin.

I advocate a different criterion from name calling, even though in practice the criterion is difficult to apply. I would, for example, ask: Does the actor, at the time he acts, feel that he is sinning. I wish to let this motivate a definition: An activity is perverse if the erotic excitement depends on one's feeling that he or she is sinning. If such a dynamic is present, then using weak terms such as "deviation," "variant," or "paraphilia" obscures the most significant feature of the act. I insist, then, that in perversion, the desire to sin is essential.

But what, exactly, is the sin? It is the same as for all sins: the desire to hurt, harm, be cruel, degrade, humiliate someone (including, at levels of lesser awareness, the desire to harm oneself). In the case of perversion, the person to be harmed is one's sex object (including oneself).

The psychoanalytic literature, from Freud on, has not used these criteria. Instead, whatever an analyst felt was aberrance was called "perversion." That is too diffuse, for it assumes that all sexually aberrant people share crucial common dynamics. (From Freud on, the term "sexual" is used without distinguishing whether erotic or gender behavior is intended.) For me, such an assumption is too much like the other methods of thinking that were used when someone was labelled perverse. The classifying process was effortless. We did not have to search out what was going on inside the person. Our theory of behavior or of diagnosis did the work, saving us the trouble of listening to patients.

I would like, therefore, to offer a different system for defining perversion. Essentially, we would ask: What is the person's intention? I explored these ideas several years ago (Stoller, 1975) and have since studied them to see whether they hold up clinically, theoretically, and logically. I think they do, but they have never been used by anyone else.

By *aberration* here I mean an erotic technique or constellation of techniques that one uses as one's complete sexual act and that differs from one's culture's traditional, avowed definition of normality. Sexual aberrations can be divided into two classes: variants (deviations) and perversions. By *variant* I mean an aberration that is not primarily the staging of forbidden fantasies, especially fantasies of harming others. Examples would be behavior set off by prenatal hormones; abnormal brain activity, as with a tumor, experimental drug, or electrical impulse from an implanted electrode; or an aberrant act one is driven to *faute de mieux*; or sexual experiments one does from curiosity and finds not exciting enough to repeat. *Perversion*, the erotic form of hatred, is a fantasy, usually acted out but occasionally restricted to a daydream (either self-produced or packaged by others, that is, pornography). It is a habitual, preferred aberration necessary for one's full satisfaction, primarily motivated by hostility. By "hostility" I mean a state in which one wishes to harm an object; that differentiates it from "aggression," which often implies only forcefulness. The hostility in perversion takes form in a fantasy of revenge hidden in the actions that make up the perversion and serves to convert childhood trauma to adult triumph. To create the greatest excitement, the perversion must also portray itself as an act of risk-taking. [Stoller, 1975, pp. 3–4].

In other words, perversion is an erotic neurosis. (In making this claim, I take issue with Freud and the whole analytic literature except Gillespie, 1956, which considers perversion a form of behavior different from that in neuroses, being powered by a different constellation of drives and defenses and serving different purposes.) Perversion is a response to—an attempt to cure the effects of—traumas, frustrations, conflicts, and other painful conditions that could not be handled without one's changing one's development. The visible manifestation of the cure is the story line of the perversion—the cast of characters with their assigned parts, the action, the *mise en scène*. The script is then played out as daydream, in pornography, or in the real world.

At this point I must, even this early in the argument, address the question as to whether there is an essential difference between the person who performs a perversion; the one who keeps from doing it but needs to fantasize it (by daydreams or pornography) to be well-satisfied; and the person who does not need or prefer that portrayal but who, nonetheless, when chancing on it, gets excited. To say that the difference is a matter of degree is not helpful until we know what factors determine those differences in degree. We are probably as far from being able to take that measure as we are for any other aesthetic decision (i.e., any other matter of taste). We are a long way from knowing, for instance, to what extent inherited or other constitutional factors play their part directly in erotic choice, or indirectly—as when one infant can inherently withstand a noxious parental factor more easily than can another infant—or what parts of a constellation of postnatal psychologic influences are more present in one person's history than another's. The best I can do is unravel certain dynamics, such as the desire to do harm, or the theater of risk. A word of caution: finding these dynamics in a person does not enable one to predict when an individual will be pushed beyond fantasy into action. These are judgments theory cannot yet make.

As stated before, perversion is a "habitual, preferred aberration necessary for one's full satisfaction." There are probably few people who do not recognize their favorite script, once they meet it. The definitions imply that everyone is erotically aberrant, and most people most of the time are a bit perverse.

Perversion may in part be difficult to study because the gross cases blind us to underlying subtleties. If you are the sort of person I used to be, you are so struck by the absurdity or monstrousness of the behavior that you stop thinking, comfortable with "perversion" in its accusatory sense. We need no explanation in the gross cases, for we feel that the person must be mad, or that the behavior is unnatural, and these rubrics substitute for explanation. The complex dynamics of the neurosis do not seem to apply. An example:

> L., labourer, was arrested because he had cut a large piece of skin from his left forearm with a pair of scissors in a public park.
>
> He confessed that for a long time he had been craving to eat a piece of the *fine white skin of a maiden*, and that for this purpose he had been lying in wait for such a victim with a pair of scissors; but, as he had been unsuccessful, he desisted from his purpose and instead had cut his own skin. His father was an epileptic, and his sister was an imbecile. Up to his seventeenth year he suffered from *enuresis nocturna*, was dreaded by everybody on account of his rough and irascible nature, and dismissed from school because of his insubordination and viciousness.
>
> He began onanism at an early age, and read with preference pious books. His character showed traits of superstition, proneness to the mystic, and showy acts of devotion.
>
> When thirteen his lustful anomaly awoke at the sight of a beautiful young girl who had a fine white skin. The impulse to bite off a piece of that skin and eat it became paramount with him. No other parts of the female body excited him. He never had any desire for sexual intercourse, and never attempted such.
>
> He hoped to achieve his end easier with the aid of scissors than with his teeth, for which reason he always carried a pair with him for years. On several occasions his efforts were nearly successful [Krafft-Ebing, 1906, pp. 238–240].

As illustrations of the less bizarre behavior, I include below advertisements from pornography magazines. They represent thousands of ads in hundreds of magazines published each year. We cannot know how many people practice each of the behaviors advertised, but it is safe to say that there are many. I shall start by quoting a few such ads and listing some of their titles.

Skye Publishing

Fact and fiction about dominant women, everything illustrated. Panties, foot worship, smother, killer girls, mixed wrestling . . .

Wanted: Panty Poopers

W/M loves to poop in panties. Would love to have correspondence with young ladies with same interest. Will pay for any photos sent.

Pictures of My Little Girls

Momma needs to pick up some fast money selling naked pictures of her Three Little Girls ages 8–16.

Titles:

"Scissor Stories," "Cigar-smoking Females," "Barefoot Girls who Never Wear Shoes," "White Male Slave," "Saddle Shoe Fetish," "Oral Service Given Free," "Pussy Galore" . . .

I hope this list will create the impression, in lieu of better data, that perversion may be more commonplace than is generally acknowledged and that there are more categories than are dreamed of in our manuals. In addition, these perversions are for men, not women, and almost all are heterosexual and offer women as the sex object.

Some of the ads offer pornography, yet they do not appeal to all of us . . . But how can we conceptualize pornography that does not excite? I do so by means of the following definitions: Pornography is that product manufactured with the *intent* to produce erotic excitement. Pornography is pornographic when it does excite. Not all pornography is pornographic to all.

I wish to support, at least to some extent, the view that perversions exist, by listing various fetishes: boots, underwear, raincoats, leather, rubber, painted fingernails, penises, protruding veins on erect penises, plucked eyebrows, dead bodies, and so on, for we can extend the list to an astonishing degree, until we get to pipes, collar studs, artificial eyes, hearing aids, and many more.

SAD TALES

These fetishes are benign enough. No one is killed, mutilated, or raped. In fact, the action is played out with an object, not a whole person, and whatever that action is, the object—the fetish—is either inanimate or a body part not liable to feeling devastated. Why, then, should society not respond benignly, "Do not call these acts mental diseases or disorders, or perversions. Do not talk of sin"? The modern, enlightened stance aims at reducing the priggish, defensive, projecting, hypocritical rules that treat deviations, including erotic ones, as fundamental attacks on the body politic. Our present instances, fetishes, are only symbols, highly compacted stories that subliminally signal their fuller meanings; they do not stab, bite, poison, smother, crush, or demolish. Nonetheless, hidden in these symbols, I suggest and shall soon discuss, are scripts that portray hostile acts. That fetishists really harm no one must not be confused with the fact that their behavior hides, among other things, this hostility dynamic. (A dynamic is not an action; you cannot even measure the intensity of a wish by knowing the script that carries the dynamic.)

Perhaps this is easier to see if we turn to another excitement—humor (jokes, the comic, wit, irony, caricature, sarcasm—to suggest a continuum of increasingly expressed hostility). I do not believe you can tell a witty, comic, or humorous story without there being a quality, as there is in caricature, of an implied or visible victim being insulted. Still, a slapstick movie in which someone slips on a banana peel and breaks a leg is different from seeing the same event actually occur in the street. (I suppose that those who laugh in the street—or who consciously set out to create accidents—are the equal of the erotically perverse.)

We advance into the thesis that perversion is created from a story in which someone is harmed. That is easy to see in the madder excitements, but now we need examples, beyond fetishism, of perversion where hostility is present but invisible. Let three examples serve: exhibitionism, voyeurism, and transvestism.

Here is a typical exhibitionist episode. If we use "exhibitionist" in the restricted meaning that refers to perversion (not the broader meaning, where "exhibitionistic" is more or less synonymous with "histrionic," without implying erotic excitement), then we are talking about a man, heterosexual, married (if in his twenties or beyond), not effeminate, not consciously warding off homoerotic desires. He is likely to have been arrested before, for exhibiting his genitals (Krafft-Ebing, 1906). Someone disparages him—a superior at work, a stranger, his wife. He feels bad, and, though he cannot articulate the form of the bad feeling, questioning him would help him describe anxiety, anger, depression, and disgust that is not clearly focused on anyone, including himself. This tensely unpleasant state builds up until he decides, usually without seeing that his deciding is related to the bad feeling, to put his modus operandi into effect. He goes to another part of town, to a public area he knows is not his own territory, where he can silently draw the attention of women by exposing his genitals. The witnesses of his act must be strangers, or at least women he hardly knows.

As he positions himself, he awaits the women's response. When they are angry or otherwise shocked, he is not upset but is either excited or unexpectedly calm. Though it may be obvious that the woman is going to call the authorities, he is unmoved, in the sense that he does not rush away. He may be as if in a state of suspended animation, not wanting to escape and not understanding why. Because of this he is likely to be arrested, and this is the proximate reason for the high recidivist rate. Not only does he wait to be caught after the act, but the act itself has *being caught* built into it: as the strange woman watches, he feels that her watching consists of her catching him doing wrong. He needs to believe she is thinking that he is doing wrong, or the behavior fails.

The scene, however, may go a different way in these modern times, with a modern woman. If she is not shocked, not offended, not outraged— if he knows she is not violated but is simply amused or unconcerned—the man is left feeling puzzled, unfulfilled, uneasy, embarrassed, humiliated.

The explanations for the behavior are at hand; one need only talk with the exhibitionist, in a situation of trust, to see what he is up to. First, you should recognize that his going to a strange part of town and exposing his genitals to strange women is not itself the perversion but only the first of two parts, the foreplay. The second part, which has never been recognized as part of the erotic activity, is the woman's shock, the ensuing fuss with the police and bystanders, the arrest, the court appearance with its potential for ruining the man's life. You—rational you—ask the same question as the judge: "Why do you do this, why do you repeat this, why—when you know the possible terrible consequences—do you not refrain?" And the poor devil can only answer, "I do not know." That is: "I do not know what I know." (The last applies, of course, to almost everyone, any time.)

"What I do not know I know is that I was humiliated earlier today; I have not quite taken in that I felt worthless. I felt that, and then transformed it by detaching myself from my awareness. I went from precise awareness of my pain to vague discomfort. In that way, I could forget I was made to feel unmanly and have always worried about that. I am nobody worthwhile, and someone made me know it again. But I discovered a cure for this most awful of failures. I can restore my sense of value, of self, of identity, of being, with that most essential of all definers of maleness and masculinity: my penis. Look what happens when I display my penis (at the right time, in the right place, of course). People are schocked, the police arrest me, society—through its agents, the courts—reaffirms the terrible thing I have done, and the price that I pay is ruination. And I was able to do all that just by showing my penis. By God, what a cock."

All perverse acts—not all aberrations, just the perversions, (here we see the purpose of trying for a more precise definition)—are instant cures. That, even beyond body pleasure, is reason enough for repeating the acts.

The sad part is that, without insight into what he does, the perverse person must repeat his destructive "cures" endlessly; aspirin for a brain tumor.

And why a stranger? Because a familiar, such as his wife, could not possible be shocked at the view of something so domesticated. In our culture, a woman—and her husband knows this—is not assaulted by the vision of his penis.

Now let us try this mode of explanation on voyeurism. The voyeur, too, goes to a strange place and is excited only by strange women. Even if he is married to the most gorgeous woman in the world, he is elsewhere, passionate to glimpse secretly a stranger, but bored with the view of his wife. The common factor, once again, is violation, hostility, the desire to harm. The voyeur imagines that he is robbing the woman of her privacy, forcing her to give up what she wouldn't give *him* voluntarily. When he cannot manage malice, boredom sets in. How can he, if married, abuse his wife by looking, when the marriage contract, in our society at any rate, gives him rather free access?

Transvestism is the third example of a perversion in which the hostility is not manifestly visible. By "transvestism" I mean dressing in, or otherwise handling, clothes of the opposite sex in order to be excited.

Let us begin to examine this by a nonclinical route: pornography is a published daydream. Perversion is a performed daydream. Pornography is a *forme fruste* of a perversion. When you are researching excitement, pornography has the advantage of being a dependable daydream; it is visible, can be examined over and over, and, because it is produced for sale, we are guaranteed it represents a genre, that it is the preferred daydream for lots of people.

Imagine before you the cover of a piece of transvestite pornography, to be described shortly. What does it say to the transvestite that he will know it is worth the high price charged? Why does it arouse him and leave nontransvestites untouched?

The first rule in daydreams is that each detail counts. Each has an effect, even if its assigned effect is that it be unimportant. Though the illustration says little to the nontransvestite, for a susceptible man, a lot is communicated. Let us start with the printed words and pick out some of the information, concealed from the nontransvestite but erotic to the transvestite.

The title is "Panty Raid." That will erotically signal men, not women; it refers to an attack on women, for panties are intimate, genital-related, delicate, hidden garments with the potential to provoke men erotically. In our culture, the public was expected to believe panty raids were simply manifestations of exuberance in masculine, middle-class, collegiate youths, silly but cute adventures in anticipation of more serious commitments to be fulfilled later. High spirits and good-natured frivolousness were excusable, for the young men were heterosexual, and they mean no real harm.

To steal women's underwear was to promise society that its future men—fathers and citizens—would turn out just fine. No one was hurt. It was a good joke.

There are in this title, then, built-in safety factors, information that tells the transvestite that, though in reality he is masturbating, he has split away a part of himself, who is the man in the story. And what *that* fellow is doing is socially approved, manly, cute, and perhaps even a bit lovable. Were the real man to feel anxious, guilty, or disgusted, he could not so easily buy the booklet.

Below the title are two boxes with clean, neat print. One tells of "other stories of transvestism and female impersonation" within. The other says "No.C–18." The latter, without substantive meaning, puts the publication in the mainstream of orderly, accountable publishing, free from dirtiness. At the bottom, after the announcement, are the words "includes actual correspondence from transvestites."

What about the main feature, the drawing? Let me emphasize a few points only. It depicts three people, two women and a man. The women are clearly, extravagantly, female. They are, with all their femaleness and femininity, powerful, dangerous, cruel. They overpower but not by brute strength. They do have physical threat available, for whips are depicted. But, once again, the man could escape easily enough, if the women's inner power did not hold him captive.

The young man is the center of the picture. A tear runs down his face. He is certainly unhappy in his lovely lingerie. The women have overpowered him and, I suspect, humiliated him. He is forced to do something he does not like. We cannot fill in all the details from the text, for it describes no scene quite like that on the cover. Nonetheless, you will find in all samples of this genre of transvestite pornography that the fundamentals are the same: the heterosexual young man, unquestionably totally male, innocent, is captured by females who do so not by physical power but by the mysterious power inherent in femaleness and femininity. Humiliated, he is forced by them into women's clothes. That is the essential story, and that is what the cover promises the transvestite. For him the story is a winner. For the rest of us it is uninteresting. If we even wondered about it, we would only be puzzled how this could be erotic.

TRAUMA AND HUMILIATION

How can humiliation excite? Even when the text shows that the women have forced him to question the solidity of his masculinity and maleness, we are hardly enlightened. But the cover does not tell all; it only shows trauma. There is a happy ending: with the women's help, the man's humiliation is changed to a pleasurable, nonerotic state when the women openly accept him as a man and a male who has remained a man, but one who looks pretty and graceful in women's clothes. To the outsider, it hardly sounds like the stuff of excitement. Why is this so compelling that it is repeated over and over in transvestite pornography?

Transvestites report, far more than any other group of men (including those with the other perversions), that they were put into women's clothes—usually by girls or women—as children. I do not believe, however, that a single episode of cross-dressing produces transvestism. Other boys given this treatment are not thus damaged. I presume that only a boy who is already susceptible—through some special uneasiness of gender development in the first two or three years of life—will need the perversion structure in order to preserve identity.

"To preserve identity." Against what? Against humiliation. And humiliation is, of course, a matter of identity, an attack on one's self-respect, the dictionary tells us. Only those strong enough to trust will let others in, allow intimacy. But if we have reason to feel unsafe (for instance, if we were regularly humiliated in the first years of life), we shall be on guard, fearful of what others may find, were we to let them in, and how they will use what they find. So we seal ourselves off, a process that dehumanizes us (Khan, 1979). Then, to be doubly safe, we dehumanize *them*. They convert to fetishes. To those who do not fear dissolution, intimacy is a joy, but for those who do, there is an even more primitive threat: if I let others in, if I thereby merge with them, may they not, like evil spirits, possess me, take me over entirely? Then, the great terror: I shall lose myself. It is against such fundamental menace that perversion is invented.

Note how the perversion preserves the trauma in its structure. In that regard, perversion is audacious. That is not entirely accurate; the exact wording should be that perversion seems to be audacious. One seems to take a risk in approaching the old danger. This is a central part of exciting experiences: the uncertainty, the tense hum between the possibility of triumph and the possibility (memory) of trauma, of failure.

We saw this mechanism at work with the character in the transvestite pornography, and we saw that the danger is real for the fictional character, and fiction for the real character. The transvestite simulates risk when he reads the story of Bruce King's trauma with the sorority girls. His excitement, as in all daydreams, is theater, inasmuch as he knows the excitement only by identifying with a depicted character.

Suppose we try to disprove the thesis. Consider the exhibitionist. Does he not risk his reputation, his safety, his future, when, in the real world, he puts himself at risk of arrest? Of course he does. But, if my explanation is correct, he openly seeks that real risk, because it measures his success in avoiding what is unconsciously for him an even greater risk, namely, humiliation. The business of defensive risk-taking is familiar. We all know people who build active danger into their lives—bullfighters, football players, professional soldiers, swindlers, and so forth—to bolster their identities and try to prove themselves intact and strong (by means of the applause of the world). The more violent manifestations of masculinity some men demand of themselves also exemplify this mechanism.

Once aware of this device, one finds it anywhere. A is a transvestite whom I have known for years. One day, at a resort, during a scientific meeting he also attended, I heard my name called as I was lying on the beach. Looking up, I saw, rising from the water, a vision in pink: pink bathing suit and pink hat on a fiftyish woman, who was living dangerously to be so pinkified. It was A; and from the way he was yelling and displaying himself, as on a stage before the audience of sunbathers, no one could question he was calling attention to himself. He looked like a woman (a histrionic one, of course), but with one bizarre element. In the crotch of "her" bathing suit were several large, pointed, protuberances that looked like a penis shrub. Approaching me and the watching public, "she" reached into "her" bathing suit and removed coral pieces "she" had stashed therein. It was some display.

Here is another example, also from transvestites, that exemplifies the same dynamic. When transvestite men sit cross-dressed in my office, they typically manage their legs to reveal upper thighs and a flurry of frilly, fluffy underwear emplaced thereon.

These two behaviors—A on the beach and B, C, D in my office—have, I believe, the same function: the transvestite stages the question, "When I am like a female, dressed in her clothes and appearing to be like her, have I nonetheless escaped the danger? Am I still a male or did the women succeed in ruining me?" And the perversion—with its exposed thighs, ladies' underwear, and coyly covered crotch—answers "No, you are still intact. You are a male. No matter how many feminine clothes you put on, you did not lose that ultimate insignia of your maleness, your penis." And he gets excited. What can be more reassuringly penile than a full and hearty erection?

Were we to study the role of humiliation in provoking psychopathology, we would find it at work wherever sadism and masochism appear; for instance, in paranoid (sadistic) or depressive (masochistic) responses. My guess is that humiliation shapes erotic life only when the attack is aimed at those parts of the body/psyche concerned with erotic or gender behavior.

DYNAMICS

Let me review the dynamics, the interplay of wishes, motives, interpretations, scripts and meanings, I extract from the data of perversions, such as in the descriptions above.

Perversion is theater, the production of a scenario, for which characters are cast in the form of people, parts of people, and nonhuman (including inanimate) objects. The performance is played before an audience, the crucial member of which is the perverse person viewing himself or herself performing (either in reality, or with mirrors, with photographs, or in fantasy). Transforming an erotic act into a performance serves to protect one's excitement from being ruined by anxiety, guilt, or boredom, and to allow the creator to simulate reality without running the risks we all face unless we manipulate reality, especially real people. Perversion is a detour that, at best, leads asymptotically to intimacy: it never arrives. The dangers of intimacy in reality are too great. That, I think, has always been the experience, and therefore the expectation, of the perverse person. Pain and frustration of earlier times live on, unresolved, carried within, always a potential threatening force motivating one to resolutions that never quite work. How exciting it is then, when eroticism—which, in its biologic and psychologic fullness, leads to the greatest intimacy—is a defense against intimacy: the risk is surmounted.

Why do these perversions—attempts at cure—fail? Because they are scripted to harm the desired object, to bring restitution by revenge. It is not easy to get to a safe and loving intimacy by means of anger and the desire to harm. How can one reach another person if one transforms him or her, by means of one's scripts, into something he or she is not, something less than his or her full personhood? Even the pornographer's seemingly trivial airbrush removes the truth, the little "blemishes" that are unbearable, unaesthetic.

This is dehumanization. Because we cannot stand the revelations of intimacy, we deprive others of their fullness. We see them only as members of classes or as the mere possessors of selected parts or qualities. We anatomize them. And if even that is too intimate, we turn from humans to inanimate objects, such as garments, granting them a certain amount of humanness while not needing humans. By doing this, in fantasy, for a moment, as long as we can write, direct, and produce the show, we avoid anxiety or, even worse, despair.

I have emphasized how one dehumanizes his or her object in order to feel safe enough to get excited. There is a price: doing so dehumanizes the dehumanizer—and that knowledge is not always unconscious.

The trauma in each perversion script—whether the story is told as a daydream, pornography, or performance in reality—is converted to a triumph. The attackers of earlier times are defeated, undone, unable to persist in their attack. Now, each new episode of the trauma is constructed so that the victim is not defeated, though the experience is carried out by using the same essentials that had earlier led to the disaster. Now the victim is the victor, and the trauma is a triumph, the crazy optimism of a full erection. If the story is well constructed, one feels guiltless and without anxiety. (Consciously so; that is, the guilt and anxiety are outside awareness, or, if still felt, are attributed to more acceptable causes. This latter is rationalization and can, for instance, change sinner to saint or fanatic and can convert the infant, guilt-ridden patricide into the adult, proud regicide.) In this brilliant replay lies the idea that the old attackers have been thwarted and thereby humiliated—and humiliation is the fundamental experience that is exchanged in these episodes. By humiliation, one gets revenge.

REFERENCES

Gillespie, W. H. (1956), The general theory of sexual perversion. *Internat. J. Psycho-Anal.*, 37: 396–403.
Khan, M.M.R. (1979), *Alienation in Perversions*. London: Hogarth Press.
Krafft-Ebing, R.V. (1906), *Psychopathia Sexualis*, trans. F.J. Rebman. Brooklyn, NY: Physicians and Surgeons Book Co., 1932.
Stoller, R.J. (1975), *Perversion*. New York: Pantheon.
———. (1979), *Sexual Excitement*. New York: Pantheon.

IV OBJECT RELATIONS AND THE UNCONSCIOUS: A METHODOLOGY

12

The Empirical Study of Controversial Clinical Issues in Psychoanalysis: Investigating Different Proposals for Treating Narcissistic Pathology

Eric Mendelsohn
Lloyd Silverman

Since the time of Freud there has been a troubling contradiction within the psychoanalytic community. On the one hand, the great majority of psychoanalytic clinicians and theoreticians have regarded our discipline as a science; on the other, we have not established a strong tradition of scientific inquiry nor developed accepted, objective means of theory validation. In making these assertions, we are using the term "science" broadly; that is, we do not restrict it solely to the use of controlled experimental methods, but rather we refer to the systematic classification of observations about behavior and natural phenomena and the development of trustworthy methods for the validation of proposals within this domain.

As a corollary to our failure to establish a scientific tradition, our professional behavior has often not been that of scientists. Historically, our interest has been more in expanding and updating the domain of psychoanalytic inquiry than in systematically testing theoretical formulations. A lack of generally accepted methods for resolving disagreements for evaluating new contributions has often led to factionalism, acrimony, and intellectual combat based on unfounded assertions rather than verifiable conclusions. As Fisher and Greenberg (1978) observed, "The avoidance of questions of scientific validity has hurt the psychoanalytic enterprise by encouraging dogmatism" (p. 6). At times clinicians and theoreticians who strongly disagree react to each other much as competing religious factions do. Each camp considers itself to be the "true" exponent of psychoanalytic theory and regards the other as rigidly reactionary or misguidedly revisionistic. "In" and "out" groups are often set up, with traditionalists and innovators extolling themselves and demeaning or ignoring the other. In

237

some cases, there are attempts to address opposing views, but often these are on the level of simple assertions, often buttressed by unconfirmable references to "clinical experience." In such an atmosphere, changes in theory and clinical practice may come about more as a function of the "power status" or "persuasive fluency" of exponents of particular views than as a result of the validity of the theories they espouse. It is rare that proposed revisions of psychoanalytic theory and practice are accompanied by calls for their systematic study. As a result, "the selection of what is to be considered valid or invalid has been left to a process whose nature is vague and really impossible to specify" (p. 7).

Silverman and Wolitzky (1982) have enumerated the minimal requirements of any discipline, including psychoanalysis, that aspires to attain scientific status and seeks to establish a tradition of impartial and systematic inquiry. These include the following: (1) The raw data of observation must be made available to independent observers; (2) the basic tenets of theory and clinical practice must be formulated as clear and falsifiable hypotheses; and (3) rigorous means of verifying or disconfirming these hypotheses must be developed. As a corollary to the last requirement, it is necessary that the investigative methods which are established be accepted and utilized by a broad spectrum of workers in the field. If this were accomplished, evidence produced by such methods would "pass muster" and be considered authoritative and substantive. Alternatively, in the absence of agreed upon investigative methodologies (as is currently the case), research findings can be readily dismissed by those whose views the findings challenge, while the scientific merits of the research are unlikely to be adequately assessed.

Though in recent years some modest attempts have been made by psychoanalytic investigators to meet the first two requirements (e.g. Gill, Simon, Fink, Endicott, and Paul, 1968; Sampson, Weiss, Mlodnosky, and Hause, 1972), there has been a relative failure to address the third, that is, to develop methods to verify or disconfirm controversial theoretical and clinical formulations. Under the best of circumstances, proponents of a controversial view may present clinical evidence to support their position—with the evidence varying considerably in terms of how compelling it is. It is rare indeed for such evidence to be sufficiently persuasive to have an impact on those who favor an opposing position. In order for arguments based on clinical evidence to have such an effect, the clinical material must be extensive, detailed, and subject to a careful, logical analysis to demonstrate why it supports one position better than another. However, even if such arguments and analyses are undertaken, this way of proceeding can only be considered an initial step in resolving clinical and theoretical controversies. The step that should then follow is to address the controversies and seek their resolution through an objective and systematic seeking of relevant data. The goal of such a program of study would be to enable psychoanalytic investigators to determine which of two or more competing formulations was most valid or, at least, to specify the conditions under which each formulation held true.

What we attempt in this chapter is to describe concretely how such a program of objective study could be undertaken, using for illustrative purposes one of the most controversial issues currently confronting the psychoanalytic community. We are referring to the differing proposals of Heinz Kohut, Otto Kernberg and others regarding the understanding and treatment of individuals said to be suffering from narcissistic disorders. Our plan for the chapter is as follows. The clinical and theoretical understanding of narcissistic pathology and the resultant treatment recommendations of four clinical writers—Heinz Kohut, Otto Kernberg, Arnold Rothstein, and James Masterson—will be briefly presented and contrasted. These four clinicians were chosen because they have presented well-articulated proposals that have important areas of convergence—and are thus comparable—but which also differ in clear and substantial ways. In addition, the writers chosen have to varying degrees, attained an influential status within the psychoanalytic community, and their views have been the subject of considerable debate. In summarizing the clinical understanding and treatment recommendations of these writers, the following four areas will be highlighted: (1) diagnosis and description, (2) the core understanding of narcissistic pathology, (3) treatment recommendations, and (4) outcome criteria. Following these brief synopses, we will present our general research proposals. Our method involves combining the results of several types of studies and these will be briefly described. Having done this, we will return to the proposals of the four clinical writers and show how they could be studied using the various research methods we described. We will conclude by briefly discussing the strengths, difficulties, and limitations of such an empirical approach.

THE DIFFERENT VIEWS OF NARCISSISTIC PATHOLOGY

In recent years there has been increasing interest among psychoanalytic clinicians in the etiology, phenomenology, psychodynamics, and treatment of narcissistic disorders. This is most likely the result of several factors: (1) a general and, by now, well-established trend toward expanding the purview of psychoanalytic study and therapeutic technique to include the more serious character disorders, as well as the borderline and psychotic conditions (e.g. Knight, 1954; Rosenfeld, 1965; Searles, 1965; Kohut, 1971; Kernberg, 1975; Pao, 1979; Little, 1981); (2) related to this, the development of interest in the preoedipal era (e.g. Mahler, Pine, and Bergman, 1975; Pine,

1985; Stern, 1985); and (3) sociocultural changes that may have affected the expression, visibility, and prevalence of narcissistic pathology (e.g. Lasch, 1978). The most frequently cited and influential theories of narcissistic disorders and their treatment are similar enough to be compared. However, important differences exist in diagnostic understanding, the core conceptualization of narcissistic pathology, treatment recommendations, and outcome criteria. The following brief summary of the views of Kohut, Kernberg, Rothstein and Masterson is undertaken with the goal of highlighting fundamental areas of disagreement and clarifying which issues would be most important to address empirically.[1]

Kohut

Heinz Kohut and his colleagues have written extensively about theoretical and clinical issues in narcissism. For our current purposes, we will confine ourselves to the views presented in Kohut's 1971 monograph and 1977 book.

Diagnosis and description

Kohut differentiates narcissistic personalities from schizophrenia and depressive disorders as well as from "borderline states" (which he views,

---

[1]The development of an ideal research program would require that each of the four sets of proposals be comprehensive and explicit. Under the best of circumstances answers to each of the following questions would be available. (1) As regards diagnosis: What diagnostic terms are used? How are narcissistic patients described? What are the diagnostic schemas of each author? Where are narcissistic patients located within these more general schemas? (2) As regards the core conceptualization: How is narcissistic pathology understood? What factors are relevant to etiology and pathogenesis? How is narcissistic pathology maintained and exacerbated in the "here and now"? What dynamic and structural features characterize narcissistic personalities? What are the relative roles of conflict and developmental faults? What is the role of aggression? (3) As regards treatment: What is the author's general theory of therapeutic change? How does the recommended treatment for narcissistic disorders fit in with the more general schemas? When is psychoanalysis recommended? Psychotherapy? No treatment? What additional personality features will influence therapeutic approach (e.g., presence of antisocial features, negative therapeutic reaction, etc.)? Are there general technical recommendations? If so, what are they? What types of interventions are emphasized? Are there interventions that can be said to represent the essence of the approach? (4) As regards outcome: What are the criteria for successful outcome? What descriptors are applied to successfully treated cases? What is the predicted course of a treatment? What developments are likely to occur concurrently in the person's life? As we shall see, because it is not always possible to answer each of these questions from the writings of the four clinicians we are comparing, the research hypotheses we can currently envision and the studies we can propose may lack the precision and specificity that would ultimately be desirable. Since, however, in this chapter, we are examining these four sets of proposals as an exercise, to illustrate an empirical approach to controversial issues in psychoanalysis, we do not, for the moment at least, have to confront the difficulties posed by such an absence of specificity.

for the most part, as prepsychotic conditions). Narcissistic personalities are grouped with "personality disturbances of lesser severity whose treatment constitutes a considerable part of present day psychoanalytic practice" (1971, p. 1). The general description of these patients is that they often show, on the surface at least, relatively good social functioning, though on closer inspection they may have difficulty forming and maintaining close relationships. They may also be active and talented, but their capacity to work to capacity and to maintain feelings of well being is impaired. They often describe experiences of emptiness, depression, depletion, and ennui. They experience wide fluctuations in self-esteem, with extreme sensitivity to criticism or lack of recognition, and active searching for admiration and approval. They are subject to rage episodes as a consequence of narcissistic injuries, and can be haughty, arrogant, demanding, humorless, unempathic, and controlling. During analytic treatment, there may be temporary regressive episodes with psychotic-like symptoms but these tend to be short-lived and can almost always be resolved with the use of "proper analytic technique." According to Kohut the differential diagnosis between narcissistic personality and borderline and psychotic disorders on the one hand, and the neuroses on the other, is best made during a trial analysis rather than being based upon presenting symptoms. The critical differential diagnostic criterion is the establishment of one of the stable, prototypical narcissistic transferences.

Core understanding

Narcissistic personalities are viewed as suffering from a deficit state resulting from arrests in the development of critical psychological capacities. Failures of parental empathy and responsiveness are thought to play an important etiologic role. In the "here and now," narcissistic pathology may be exacerbated by empathic failures, slights, and separations. Narcissistic rage is understood as being reactive, and aggression is thought to be a secondary rather than a primary aspect of the character pathology. Controlling, imperious, and coercive interpersonal behavior is understood primarily as a defensive adaptation to a deficit state rather than deriving from aggressive "object-instinctual" wishes. Separate lines of development are proposed for narcissism and object relations, and, to some degree, mature forms of object relations are thought to be possible even in the presence of significant narcissistic pathology.

Treatment recommendations

Kohut recommends "psychoanalysis" as the treatment of choice for narcissistic personality disorders. The goal of technique with such patients is to permit the unfolding and full development of either or both of the mirroring or idealizing transferences which are viewed as transference expressions of thwarted narcissistic development. The analyst is cautioned against prematurely pointing out the unrealistic aspects of the patient's expectations of the analyst and is counseled to interpret the resistances to the development of these transferences while conveying an attitude of empathic appreciation and tolerance of the analysand's entitlement and demandingness (mirror transference), or his exaggerated admiration of the analyst (idealizing transference). The principal interventions are interpretations and reconstructions, and these are to be conveyed "empathically," that is, in a way designed to convey to the patient that the analyst can understand and appreciate his feelings and state of mind. Reconstructions of early childhood experience and the recovery of early memories bearing on narcissistic trauma play an important role once the transference has been consolidated. The analyst is cautioned against adopting a gratifying stance and becoming an "activist." Rather, the analyst's neutrality and interpretations, combined with the recognition and acceptance of previously thwarted narcissistic needs, are seen as fostering an atmosphere of optimal frustration leading to the gradual transformation of primitive to mature narcissism.

Outcome criteria

According to Kohut, analytic treatment should engender a gradual movement toward more adaptive means of self-esteem regulation. Kohut discusses changes occuring primarily and specifically in the narcissistic sphere and secondarily and nonspecifically in the realm of object relations. In terms of the former, the following changes are likely to occur in successful treatment: (1) more controlled and adaptive expression of impulses and affects; (2) the consolidation, internalization, and articulation of goals and ideals, along with increased vitality and the desire to pursue these; (3) greater stability and continuity of self-experience; (4) a movement toward more mature means of attaining approval and self-confirmation; (5) greater creativity and sensitivity; and (6) the growth of humor and sound judgment. In terms of object relations, as a result of these improvements, there may likely be a greater interest in and capacity for mature, lasting involvements with others.

Kernberg

We have summarized Kernberg's views as presented in his 1974 paper and 1975 book. As we did in our summary of Kohut, we will focus on central and distinguishing aspects of Kernberg's position.

Diagnosis and description

Kernberg places narcissistic personalities along a continuum from moderate to severe psychological disturbance. Relatively few patients with narcissistic features are considered narcissistic personalities proper. As with borderline patients, there are prominent oral aggressive conflicts and a reliance on "primitive" defensive operations. In contrast to borderlines, however, most narcissistic personalities show relatively good social functioning, better impulse control, and a capacity to work successfully (though not up to capacity) in some areas. These differences reflect the fact that narcissistic personalities have a relatively more stable (though highly disturbed) experience of self than do borderlines. Three subtypes of narcissistic personality are described, the most disturbed being patients who function on a manifestly borderline level. Kernberg's clinical description of narcissistic patients is in many respects similar to Kohut's. However, he places greater emphasis on the narcissistic personality's coldness, ruthlessness, superficiality, predilection to devaluation and extractiveness, and susceptibility to rage. In addition, Kernberg emphasizes the incapacity to feel true sadness or depression, the general shallowness of emotional life, and the tendency to be self-referential in interaction with others.

Core understanding

Kernberg's model of pathological narcissism emphasizes the role of intrapsychic conflict, particularly conflicts involving oral rage and envy. He rejects the notion of separate lines of development for narcissism and object relations and states that in order to understand pathological narcissistic development one must look ultimately to pathology in the realm of early object related libidinal and aggressive strivings. Grandiosity, coldness, and predilection for devaluation are seen as primarily reflecting a need to attack loving and graftifying objects in order to remove sources of envy. Paranoid trends are associated with the tendency to project aggression, and aloofness and grandiose self-sufficiency may be understood as defenses against the threat of retaliatory attack. Thus, unlike Kohut, Kernberg understands the tendency to grant significant others (including the analyst) only a "satellite existence" as reflecting defenses against conflicts associated with aggressive wishes and "primitive" object relations. As regards the activation of narcissistic pathology in the "here and now," Kernberg places great stress on the mobilization of aggressive reactions following failures to control the actions of others. Kernberg does not stress the destabilizing effects of separations from significant others on the functioning of narcissistic personalities; rather, he maintains they frequently "forget" the analyst during vacations and, until significant change has occurred, show little response to separations.

Treatment recommendations

"Psychoanalysis" is the treatment of choice for most narcissistic personality disorders, though supportive psychotherapy (with some limited exploration) is recommended for narcissistic patients functioning on a manifestly borderline level. In keeping with his emphasis on the role of intrapsychic conflict and aggression, Kernberg is highly critical of Kohut's technical approach. He maintains that full activation and resolution of narcissistic transferences is best achieved by systematic analysis of both positive and negative aspects of the patient's transference claims rather than through their "acceptance." He believes that Kohut's approach prevents full development of the negative transference by failing to highlight the wishes for omnipotent control underlying the patient's grandiose expectations. As a result, the patient remains frightened of the effects of his rage and envy, and, ultimately, fails to resolve central dilemmas. Deep and lasting personality change (as opposed to merely a "toning down" of pathology, which Kernberg believes the Kohutian approach produces), can occur only if the aggressive controlling wishes underlying narcissistic idealizations are clarified and interpreted. At the same time, the patient's capacity for realistic appreciation of the analyst's efforts must also be explored. In short, the emphasis is on the vicissitudes of object-related strivings and intrapsychic conflict. Confrontation and interpretation are the major technical tools, with genetic reconstructions eschewed until late in treatment. Kernberg, unlike Kohut, does not favor "empathic communications"; rather, he maintains the stance of an outside observer.

Outcome

Kernberg anticipates improvements both in the areas outlined by Kohut and in the realm of object relations. As primitive aggressive wishes are analyzed and worked through, there are likely to be crises involving intense paranoid fears and, later, guilt and depression in response to the recognition of previous aggressiveness. Eventually there should be shifts toward more flexible and adaptive defenses, greater object constancy, and a capacity for ambivalence. If the analysis goes well, the patient eventually comes to experience the analyst as truly separate, and develops greater concern for the analyst and others, along with an increased capacity for commitment, loyalty and dependency.

Rothstein

For the purposes of our illustrative exercise, the summary of Rothstein's position (and that of Masterson that follows) will be somewhat briefer than those of Kohut and Kernberg. We will highlight those aspects of his views that distinguish him from the other writers (particularly his emphasis on oedipal issues in narcissistic pathology), while acknowledging that we are not presenting a full account of his position. The views summarized here are presented in his 1979 paper and 1980 book.

Diagnosis and description

Rothstein considers narcissistic concerns and strivings to be ubiquitous. He classifies narcissistic disorders according to the major mode of narcissistic investment (in the self- or object representation) and the state of structural integration of narcissism (and the personality). Narcissistic personality disorders vary in severity of disturbance, with no one description deemed "typical." For our purposes we will focus on Rothstein's descriptions of those narcissistic personalities for whom oedipal issues figure prominently. Among such patients, infantile grandiosity, weakness of internal standards and controls, a strong tendency to act out, and a compulsive need for self-punishment are frequently noted.

Core understanding

Rothstein, like Kernberg, adheres to a conflict model. While maintaining that a range of preoedipal and oedipal conflicts are implicated in pathogenesis, in contrast to Kernberg, he stresses the important role of oedipal wishes. For the subgroup of male narcissistic personality disorders we are focusing on, grandiosity, deficiencies in self-control, and self-destructiveness are rooted in the self-inflation, castration anxiety, and guilt engendered by the feeling of having come close to an actual oedpial victory. In all cases, preoedipal factors, especially disturbances in the relationship with the preoedipal mother, are deemed important, but the centrality of these, in comparison to oedipal conflicts, varies. Rothstein also believes that, because it is often externalized, the capacity of narcissistic personalities for guilt is often underestimated. In the "here and now," narcissistic injuries can provoke temporary regressions to more "primitive" levels of personality integration. Feelings of emptiness and boredom are thought to reflect failed efforts to restore feelings of perfection and mastery (defense), rather than reflecting a deficit state.

Treatment recommendations

For narcissistic personalities in the neurotic or neurotic-to-borderline range, Rothstein recommends "psychoanalysis" as the treatment of choice. For those with antisocial or addictive features, he recommends psychotherapy, where "transmuting internalizations" deriving from unanalyzed identifications with the analyst can lead to stable, adaptive behavior change. The general task of analysis is to identify and resolve those narcissistic investments which are maladaptive and contribute to suffering. For the results to be complete, both preoedipal and oedipal issues must be analyzed; and, for certain patients, core oedipal dynamics—including wishes related to feelings of oedipal triumph—must eventually be interpreted if infantile grandiosity is to be resolved. The analyst is counseled to work interpretively and to avoid "gratifying" the patient's wish that he fill the role of an idealized parent figure. As is the case for Kernberg, empathy is a means of understanding rather than a communicative mode.

Outcome

Successful analytic work leads to more realistic and successful means of achieving narcissistic aims. General tolerance for conflict, insofar as conflict is associated with narcissistic injury, increases and there is less of a regressive potential. Others come to be treated in a less controlling and more concerned manner. Personal limitations can be better accepted, and, in general, the capacity for love and relatedness increases. For those with significant oedipal dynamics, there is a resolution of infantile grandiosity, more mature and modulated means of impulse expression and affective regulation, and a reduction in the compulsive need for self-punishment. For more disturbed patients in psychotherapy, the transference may be used to foster improved adaptation, while less insight is engendered.

Masterson

Our summary will focus on the specific developmental fixation Masterson believes characterizes narcissistic personalities and the implications of this for treatment. Our discussion is derived from Masterson's 1981 book.

Diagnosis and description

Masterson locates narcissistic personality disorders in the more severe range of character pathology. They may function more stably than patients he classifies as borderline, but their development in certain crucial respects has not proceeded as far. Like the other writers, he believes narcissistic personalities vary greatly in severity of disturbance. His descriptors include grandiosity, self-centeredness, lack of empathy and concern, a need for admiration and approval, and feelings of emptiness and rage.

Core understanding

Masterson, like Kohut, links pathological narcissism to a developmental arrest. Masterson, however, uses a model derived from Mahler's psychoanalytic developmental psychology, and posits a specific fixation point prior to the resolution of infantile grandiosity (prior to the consolidation of self-other boundaries). Experiences of emotional abandonment are thought to occur at crucial points in the second year of life. Strivings toward individuation are discouraged as the mothers of these patients fail to relinquish their sense of oneness with their narcissistically regarded children. The infantile experience of fusion with mother thus remains unresolved and reinforced. As a result, experiences of intense dysphoria ("abandonment depression") or experiences of fragmentation can occur for such patients in the "here and now." These may be brought on when others fail to meet their needs and expectations. Alternatively, these distressing experiences result from their own strivings toward individuation and self-expression. Narcissistic defenses and character traits come about as a result of this developmental arrest, and (as is the case for Kohut) acgression is seen as secondary and reactive.

Treatment recommendations

Masterson apparently favors psychoanalytic psychotherapy as the treatment of choice for narcissistic personality disorders. He recommends a dual focus in treatment: (1) systematic clarification and interpretation of narcissistic defensive activity, and (2) fostering of the arrested individuation process. Though Masterson stresses the need for tact and a gradual pace, he recommends that the therapist should not "accept" the patient's narcissistic expectations but, from early in treatment, should interpret the narcissistic vulnerability and the resultant wishes for mirroring. By implicitly taking the position of emphasizing the irrational aspects of these wishes, and by systematically interpreting regressive responses to the expression of autonomous strivings, the therapist supports and encourages the arrested developmental process. According to Masterson, the need to achieve the consolidation of a separate sense of self should always be kept at the forefront. The differentiation between patient and therapist should be reinforced by interpretation, by adhering to a nongratifying stance, and by maintaining a consistent focus on the patient's need to repudiate autonomy. Genetic reconstructions can be formulated in the middle to latter stages of treatment after there has been considerable working through of the narcissistic transferences. Like Kernberg and Rothstein, and unlike Kohut, Masterson advocates maintaining the position of outside observer.

Outcome criteria

Masterson does not specifically discuss outcome, but it stands to reason that in addition to the reduction of maladaptive narcissistic character traits and the development of more mature and stable means of self-esteem regulation, Masterson would expect the following changes in successfully treated cases: (1) the development of talents, skills and interests; (2) increasing assertiveness; (3) greater capacity to accept the separateness of others; (4) a greater capacity for mutuality.

Summary

In this section we have briefly summarized the formulations of four clini-cians regarding the understanding and treatment of narcissistic pathology. Two of the clinicians, Kernberg and Rothstein, agree that intrapsychic conflict plays a central role in the narcissistic disorders but disagree about which are the most crucial conflicts. Kernberg stresses preoedipal conflict, Rothstein oedipal conflict. Kohut and Masterson both view developmental arrests as central to narcissistic disorders but differ in their descriptions of the crucial pathogenic events. According to Kohut, parental unavailability and failures of empathy lead to arrests in the development of key psycho-logical capacities. For Masterson, it is specifically the failure of the mother to accept and encourage individuation that leads to difficulties in moving toward autonomy. In addition, Kohut and Masterson differ greatly in treat-ment approach, with Kohut allowing a full development of the narcissistic transferences, while Masterson adopts a more confrontational approach. Schematized in this way, the four formulations lend themselves to com-parative study. As we shall see, some aspects of these formulations can be more readily studied than others using the research methods we propose. In general, we will focus on the validation of the key psychodynamic hypotheses and clinical proposals rather than on the genetic hypotheses.

AN EMPIRICAL APPROACH

In order to go beyond the initial step of critical logical analysis and under-take a program of empirical study in this area, a multifaceted research approach is necessary. Several types of studies, each designed to address a different set of research questions, could be carried out in order to consider the relative merits of the four formulations presented above. The goals of such a program would be to compare the efficacy of the different treatment approaches, to determine when, how, and for whom they work, and to validate or disconfirm key dynamic hypotheses.[2]

What kinds of objective and systematically collected data would have bearing on these clinical and theoretical propositions? In a recent paper, Silverman and Wolitzky (1982) described several research paradigms that could produce data relevant to controversial psychoanalytic treatment is-sues. These were characterized as ranging from most to least "naturalistic," a continuum reflecting the degree of departure of the approach from the

---

[2]The clinical theory of psychoanalysis consists of "genetic" and "dynamic" propositions. The former concern the origins and development of psychopathology, while the latter refer to factors affecting the severity (exacerbation or reduction) of psychological disturbance. "Ge-netic," or etiological, hypotheses cannot be tested by the research methods presented in this chapter. Prospective, longitudinal studies would be required to validate or disconfirm "genet-ic" propositions.

typical psychoanalytic or psychotherapeutic treatment situation. The dilemma researchers face in undertaking empirical study of clinical issues is that the greater the methodological rigor of the study, the more likely it is that the experimental situation will differ from the naturalistic treatment situation, making generalizations about such situations hazardous. On the other hand, the closer the research situation is to treatment as it is typically conducted, the fewer the controls that can be instituted and the more tentative the inferences that can be drawn. The solution to this dilemma which was proposed by Silverman and Wolitzky (1982) and which we advocate here, is to combine research approaches that range from naturalistic to experimental. In this way, within one comprehensive research program, the needs for relevance and generalizability on the one hand and experimental controls on the other can be met. Data generated from such a program of study can be considered converging lines of evidence bearing on the issues at hand.

The two most naturalistic designs we propose seek data from psychoanalytic or psychotherapeutic treatment as it is ordinarily conducted. Both involve outcome studies in which objective comparisons are made of the results of treatment conducted by clinicians who adhere to the different treatment proposals summarized earlier. The first of these paradigms utilizes a different therapist for each of the four approaches. In this design the results of treatment conducted by followers of each of the four clinicians earlier cited would be compared using appropriate outcome measures. The second naturalistic design would be similar to the first, but instead of comparisons being made between groups of clinicians, they would be made between sets of cases treated by one group of clinicians. In this design *each* clinician would conduct treatment with four patients, one of the four being treated in the manner prescribed by Kohut, one according to Kernberg's guidelines, and so forth. This variation in design has the advantage of controlling (or at least partially controlling) for confounding therapist variables. However, it poses a practical problem: the clinicians involved would have to be willing and able to conduct treatment from four different perspectives. For this to be feasible, the participating therapists would in all likelihood have to be neophyte clinicians, not set in their ways and closely supervised by experienced adherents of each viewpoint.[3]

The results of such outcome studies, properly designed and controlled, would provide information about the relative efficacy of the four therapeutic approaches to narcissism. However, other issues, such as the question of what aspects of a given clinical approach account for its success, could not be answered by outcome studies alone. Further, key dynamic propositions that reflect each writer's understanding of narcissistic pathology would

---

[3]We are aware of the practical difficulties of such an endeavor. In practice some modification of this suggestion would in all likelihood be necessary.

remain unexamined. In order to address these issues, studies of therapy process, utilizing transcripts of actual treatment sessions, would be necessary. Through such studies, patients' responses to specific therapeutic interventions could be observed and systematically coded. Further, the intensification or diminution of narcissistic pathology could be related to specific psychodynamic and therapeutic contexts. In this manner, the relevance and efficacy of specific recommendations, and the "goodness of fit" between core formulations concerning narcissistic pathology and dynamic sequences occurring in the treatment setting, could be determined. The specific procedure-oriented studies we propose will be described later.

To complement the essentially correlational data that would be derived from process oriented studies, we further propose that the comprehensive research program include a third aspect: experimental studies, specifically ones designed to manipulate psychodynamic variables in a controlled manner. Since such studies can involve considerably larger samples than clinical studies, they can enhance the generalizability of findings from the studies just described as well as provide more rigorous tests of specific psychodynamic formulations. One technique currently available to achieve these goals is the subliminal psychodynamic activation method. This will be described in detail at a later point.

The foregoing is a brief summary of our proposed research program. We will now describe the different aspects of the program in more detail as we consider how these studies could address the controversies related to the treatment and understanding of narcissistic pathology. We will also discuss some of the considerable practical and methodological problems that would confront researchers undertaking such a program of study.

The first question to consider is that of subject selection. Before undertaking the outcome, process, or experimental studies outlined above, it is necessary to arrive at criteria for the diagnosis of narcissistic personality disorder. Our review of the diagnostic schemata employed by Kohut, Kernberg, Rothstein, and Masterson suggest that this would be no simple matter. There are substantial differences between these writers as regards: (1) the relative severity of the disorder; (2) how homogeneous or heterogeneous a designation it is; and (3) the behavioral traits deemed most specific to the disorder. Moreover, each writer identifies (whether formally or informally) subgroups with relatively intact social and vocational functioning and those whose adaptations are more overtly and severely compromised.[4]

---

[4]Kohut (1977) distinguished narcissistic personality disorders from "narcissistic behavior disorders." The latter subgroup is descriptively close to the more disturbed subgroups described by other writers.

What implications do these issues have for our proposed research program? One key question is whether Kohut, Kernberg, and the others have sampled the same or different groups of patients. Is there a group of potential research subjects that all four writers would agree merits the diagnosis "narcissistic personality disorder"? When one considers the differences in diagnostic description, along with the observation that narcissistic pathology is understood and treated in such different ways, the possibility arises that differences in understanding and treatment recommendations reflect differences in the groups of patients themselves. That is, it is possible that in his clinical work each writer has tended to select from different subgroups of narcissistic patients. If this is the case, the formulations of each writer might be applicable, or most applicable, to that particular subgroup, while having no (or limited) relevance to patients described by other writers. A second possibility is that patient differences have arisen iatrogenically. That is, each writer in his clinical work may have sampled initially from an equivalent pool of subjects, but then differences in therapeutic technique may have led to the amplification and highlighting of different aspects of narcissistic pathology (cf. Ornstein, 1974). If this is true, it may be that differences in theoretical understanding have come about as an artifact of differences in technical approach. Another possibility is that a process akin to observer bias has operated. According to this scenario, equivalent subjects have been sampled but diverging (theoretical) expectations have led the different authors to describe their patients' symptomatology and experiential worlds in different terms.

As can be readily seen, these different alternatives bear crucially on the feasibility of undertaking the research program we propose. If it could be determined that each writer has selected from an equivalent group of patients, and that descriptive differences have resulted from observer bias or from differences in technical approach, then it would not only be possible to pursue experimental and process-oriented studies, but direct comparisons of the efficacy of the different approaches to treatment (outcome studies) could be undertaken. However, if it turned out that initial subject differences are responsible for the different descriptions and formulations of the four writers, a different situation would arise. In this case, process-oriented and experimental studies could still be carried out, and the goals of validating dynamic formulations as well as systematically studying the effects of therapeutic interventions could still be pursued. However, the goal of determining the relative efficacy of the four approaches by pitting them against each other in an outcome study could not be met; subject differences would, of course, confound the results.

How could these questions be answered and a subject sample selected? One possible method would be for knowledgeable adherents of the four positions to develop manuals with explicit, clear inclusionary and exclusionary diagnostic criteria. These would then be exchanged among the participants and areas of apparent discrepancy discussed. Revised diagnostic manuals would then be developed and distributed for further discussion. The goal would be to develop a prototypical diagnostic profile (probably defining a narrower sample than that designated by any individual writer) that all four adherents would agree matched their criteria closely enough to be considered "narcissistic personality disorder." A variation of this method would involve presenting case histories and interviewing patients at case conferences attended by adherents of the four viewpoints. Only patients who all four clinicians agreed met their criteria for narcissistic personality disorder would be included in the study.

As noted earlier, it is possible that one or more of the four writers based his views on experience with different groups of patients. If this is the case, then it is likely that these differences would clearly emerge in the course of joint case conferences or in the process of developing a consensus diagnostic manual. If it turned out that the diagnostic criteria of one or more writers did not fit sufficiently with the others, the proposals of those writers could not be evaluated in comparative outcome studies. However, the opportunity to clarify this issue would itself greatly assist psychoanalytic clinicians in better evaluating the different proposals presented by these writers.

Let us assume that diagnostic consensus proved obtainable and comparative outcome studies feasible. What other considerations would be relevant to the design of such studies? For a meaningful comparison of the efficacy of different treatment approaches, it would be necessary to control for potentially confounding therapist and patient variables. It will be recalled that two naturalistic treatment paradigms were proposed. The first would involve assessing the outcome of the psychoanalytic treatment of narcissistic personality disorders by groups of therapists representing each of the four contrasting positions. For this paradigm to advance knowledge substantially, each of the positions would have to be represented by a sizable number of clinicians—with the analysts in the four groups equated for years of experience. The patients assigned would also have to be matched for overall severity of pathology as well as for other potentially significant subject variables affecting outcome—age, socioeconomic status, education, marital status, and so on. Posttreatment evaluations would have to be made by independent clinicians who were blind to the particular treatment approach each patient had received.

The second research paradigm, cited earlier, would allow for an outcome study in which each of a group of neophyte therapists would treat four patients under the close supervision of seasoned clinicians representing the four approaches. As with the first paradigm, a sizable number of clinicians would need to be involved, similar controls for confounding patient and therapist variables built in, and posttreatment evaluations conducted blindly.

Recently it has become standard practice to develop treatment manuals for studies of therapy outcome and process. Such manuals provide guidelines for participant therapists and help ensure that the treatment programs being studied are being accurately applied and that each therapist is working in more or less the same way. Though manuals providing precise and thorough guidelines for the timing and content of therapeutic interventions are most applicable to the briefer, focal therapies, some version of a treatment manual would need to be developed for each of the four viewpoints. These manuals would articulate the goals and major strategies of treatment, describe the expected transference developments, provide guidelines and case examples pertaining to management and mode of intervention, and clarify the recommended therapeutic stance. Tape recorded transcripts could then be periodically reviewed to determine if the analyst was adhering to the guidelines set forth in the manual.

Finally, to compare the effectiveness of these different treatment approaches, it would be necessary to define outcome measures that all four writers would deem acceptable and relevant. Since different writers look for improvement in different areas, it would be prudent to select a range of outcome measures. Such a sampling of measures could include symptomatic, personality, and life adjustment measures, as well as self-ratings and ratings by significant others of important characterological variables. In addition, the outcome measures could include ones germane to the views of each theorist. By using such a variety of measures it might be possible to answer the following questions: (1) Are different types of analytic treatment likely to produce different outcomes, or do seemingly divergent treatments produce more or less the same results? (2) What is the relationship between reductions in narcissistic pathology and changes in object relations? (3) Are improvements likely to occur in areas not specifically made the focus of analytic inquiry? It would also be valuable to collect follow-up data at intervals after the conclusion of treatment as a way of assessing stability of change.

In our view, the two types of outcome studies we propose would provide complementary kinds of data. Paradigm (1) allows for a direct comparison of the efficacy of different therapeutic approaches as they are commonly practiced, while paradigm (2) controls for therapist differences that might account for differential efficacy. However, even when considered together, the data from these two types of studies, regardless of how they turned out, would have to be supplemented with data from other research paradigms. The reason for this is that outcome studies alone cannot determine what factors within a complex treatment are responsible for its effects. Not knowing this would leave many crucial issues unanswered.

Consider the following hypothetical scenario. Suppose that in both outcome studies the Kohutian treatment proved more efficacious than the
other three approaches. As suggestive as these findings might be, they
would provide no clue to which aspects of a complex and multifaceted
treatment approach had produced a superior outcome. It might even be
that the superiority of this approach was unrelated to Kohut's specific
treatment recommendations. For example, because this approach is new
and quite different from traditional psychoanalytic approaches, it may be
that those using it (including young, "nonaligned" therapists under supervision) view themselves as pioneers. In keeping with some of the literature
on nonspecific treatment effects (e.g., Shapiro and Morris, 1978), the enthu-
siasm accompanying such a self-image might be the critical factor in making it more effective. Of course, this is just one among a multitude of
possible scenarios; the point is that the results of outcome studies could
not, by themselves, provide validation for key dynamic propositions or
confirm the effectiveness of specific technical recommendations. Thus,
other types of studies would be needed that allow for a more direct examination of the variables that are at the heart of the various clinical formulations. We have in mind process-oriented studies using tape recorded
transcripts of actual treatment sessions.

Two clinical research methods have been developed that could be used
to study the clinical formulations and treatment recommendations of the
four writers. The first is Luborsky's symptom context method (e.g.
Luborsky and Auerbach, 1969). This method enables investigators to test
hypotheses about the unconscious motives associated with particular behaviors by examining the context in which the behaviors emerge in treatment sessions. The method could be adapted to the study of narcissistic
pathology, in particular, the motives underlying its exacerbation and diminution within a session. The first task would be to identify key aspects
of narcissistic pathology to be targeted for study. The focus would be on
aspects of the behavior of subjects that could be reliably viewed as either
direct or transference expressions of their narcissistic pathology. For example, grandiosity, exhibitionism, use of the analyst as an extension of the self
through demands for mirroring, or a rage response following an objectively
minor oversight, would be instances of such targeted behaviors. Luborsky's
method would call for a group of judges reading the material from a large
number of recorded sessions. The judges would be asked to identify each
instance a targeted behavior appeared. Several judges would have to be
utilized so that the reliability of judgments could be determined. Adequate
reliability would then allow for pooling the ratings of the different judges.

Sessions in which the targeted behaviors could be found would be designated the "experimental sessions." For present purposes, an adequate number of such sessions would have to be identified. Then a "control session"

would be selected to match each "experimental session," one occurring during the same period of treatment but in which no targeted behavior appeared. The next step would be to select portions of the experimental sessions that provide the context for the targeted behaviors, that is, the patients' associations or the analyst's interventions[5] just before and after the targeted behavior occurred. Sequences from parallel segments of the control sessions would also be selected. Then the sequences for both the experimental and control sessions would be submitted to a second group of judges, who would rate them for the degree to which they reflected motives that each of the four writers views as linked to narcissistic behavior in narcissistic personality disorders. Both sets of judges would, of course, need to be blind to the hypotheses of the study, and the second group of judges blind to whether the contextual sequences came from experimental or control sesssions.

Let us illustrate how this method could be applied to the study of key aspects of each writer's formulation. According to Kohut's theory, narcissistic character pathology might be exacerbated in response to a narcissistic slight or disappointment experienced either within or outside the transference. For Kernberg, the hypothesis would be that such pathology might follow the activation of conflicts over oral rage and envy. According to Rothstein, the same behavior might be expected to be linked to an oedipal conflict. Finally, Masterson would predict that exacerbations of narcissistic character pathology might follow the expression of autonomous strivings. The question that this method would allow investigators to address is whether any of the four types of material was regularly more prominent in the contextual material of the experimental sessions, with the contextual material of the control sessions serving as the point of comparison. Obviously, large numbers of comparisons would have to be made in order for meaningful results to emerge. Since all complex human behavior is multiply determined, no single sequence of antecedent and behavior change would be definitive. Moreover, in some areas, there is sufficient overlap between the different formulations (for example, Kohut, Kernberg, Rothstein, and Masterson might all expect reductions in narcissistic behaviors when the analyst provides a mirroring response) that certain linkages would not be more confirming of one viewpoint than another. However, if large numbers of examples were selected from nu-

---

[5]Luborsky and Auerbach (1969) used segments consisting solely of patient associations. We recommend a modification of this procedure. We believe that the usual distinction that is made between the analyst "intervening" (e.g., via a question, clarification, interpretation, etc.) and "not intervening" (via silence) is artificial since both speaking and remaining silent are behaviors that have an impact on the patient. Therefore we recommend including sequences containing analytic "interventions."

merous treatments, it should be possible to demonstrate whether the findings were more consistent with one position than another. Moreover, this method would enable investigators to determine whether *some* manifestations of narcissistic pathology occur more in accord with one theory while *other* manifestations occur more in accord with another. Further, this method could be adapted as a modified outcome study; the relative frequency of targeted narcissistic behaviors within sessions could be determined at different points in treatment. Finally, changes observed during the course of treatment, and the relative severity of pathology observed in sessions, could be compared to final outcome.

The second type of process study we propose is based on the work of Sampson, Weiss and their coworkers (e.g. Sampson et al., 1972). These investigators examined, in a systematic and controlled fashion, patients' responses to particular statements and behaviors of the therapist. With their methods, the specific recommendations of the four writers could be subjected to objective study. Again, tape recorded transcripts of treatment sessions would be used. Therapist interventions would be rated by blind, independent judges for the degree to which they address certain preselected issues. For example, ratings could be made of the degree to which interventions, especially interpretations, addressed issues associated with a deficient sense of self (Kohut), preoedipal conflict (Kernberg), oedipal conflict (Rothstein), or separation-individuation issues (Masterson). (Obviously, a reliable coding system for interventions would need to be generated.) A second group of judges, blind to the hypotheses of the study, would then rate the patients' responses to these interventions for indications of what can be termed "psychoanalytic movement." By this is meant such developments as indications of lessening defensive activity (cf. Sampson et al., 1972), or the emergence of relevant memories, or a strongly affective response, or even an "aha" experience.

Through the use of this method the following types of questions could be addressed. What happens when a patient's grandiose attitudes toward the therapist are interpreted as a wish to aggressively control, and as a reaction to primitive envy (Kernberg)? What happens when this same grandiosely conveyed expectation of a mirroring response is acknowledged and merely noted rather than interpreted (Kohut—early states of treatment)? Or suppose the same behavior is interpreted as a reflection of the patient's enmeshment with the therapist, an involvement designed to prevent his feeling more autonomous (Masterson)? Or, finally, what if the same behavior is interpreted as a legacy of certain oedipal experiences and is seen as designed to prevent open competition with a paternal figure (Rothstein)? It is possible to select any number of key analytic interventions representative of each viewpoint and study their immediate effects within sessions.

A similar study could be carried out in which a comparison would be made between interventions that qualify as empathically communicated

(Kohut) and those formulated from the vantage point of an outside observer (Kernberg, Rothstein, and Masterson). Again, indicators of psychoanalytic movement would be the dependent variable. Combining the results of these two types of studies would enable investigators to determine whether psychoanalytic movement is more associated with the interpretive addressing of one type of content or another, and if there is an advantage to employing "empathic" as opposed to more neutrally framed interventions.

We are well aware that process-oriented studies of this kind are by nature reductionistic. That is, the very focus on discrete interventions runs counter to certain central characteristics of analytic treatments, namely, that they are complex, multifaceted, and lengthy. It is likely that the effects of interventions and the adoption of particular stances by the therapist are primarily expressed cumulatively rather than immediately and discretely. However, considering the cumulative effects of a technical approach amounts to conducting an outcome study and leaves the investigator unable to determine what factors in a treatment account for its efficacy. It is to be hoped that the discrete sequences studied would be pertinent, representative, and nontrivial. It is also important to keep in mind that the results of this type of process-oriented study would be combined with many other kinds of data, and the results could then be viewed in a broad, enriched context.

The results of the studies just outlined would complement the findings from the treatment outcome studies. Among other things, it would be of interest to see what relationship there is, if any, between signs of psychoanalytic movement within sessions (process studies) and changes observed at the end of treatment and at follow up (outcome studies). The findings from these two kinds of studies, as well as the relationship between them, might be found to vary from one subtype of narcissistic disorder to another, or conceivably from one patient to another. With a wide sampling of narcissistic patients studied in this manner it would be an empirical question whether generalizations could be made about the content and mode of interventions that are most effective with narcissistic personality disorders. It is, of course, the generalizability of the different formulations and approaches, rather than their relevance and effectiveness with any specific patient, that is the basis for the current controversy within the psychoanalytic community. It is this last issue, generalizability, that we will now address by turning to the final type of research paradigm referred to earlier—laboratory experiments.

While laboratory experimentation may seem alien to some psychoanalysts, it is as necessary in investigating clinical psychoanalytic propositions as it is in medical research (see Holt, 1985). The particular advantage of controlled laboratory methods is that they can provide a degree of control over extraneous variables that cannot be exercised in clinical studies and thus permit causal rather than merely correlational relationships to be inferred. (See Silverman, Lachmann, and Milich, 1982, for a detailed account of this position.) Thus, for example, while process-oriented studies could permit investigators to identify "contexts" in which narcissistic pathology may be exacerbated or diminished one could never be sure whether the particular interventions (representing "precipitating events") presumed to have led to changes in behavior were, in fact, instrumental. Experimental methods, on the other hand, by controlling extraneous variables, could yield data from which such causal relationships could be demonstrated.

What experimental methods are currently available that can effectively address psychoanalytic clinical issues? Two, developed in recent years, have proven to be reliable. One involves hypnotic induction (Reyher, 1967; Sommerschield and Reyher, 1973) and the other subliminal stimulation. We will now describe the second of these in some detail and suggest how studies could be undertaken relevant to the issues we have been considering.

The subliminal psychodynamic activation method is built upon early work on subliminal perception by Charles Fisher (1954, 1956) and later investigations stimulated by Fisher's work (summarized in Wolitzky and Wachtel, 1973). The method attempts to utilize the phenomenon of subliminal registration for stimulating psychodynamically relevant motives in order to make a systematic, controlled, and precise appraisal of their influence on behavior. In over 70 studies that have been carried out to date, both in Silverman's laboratory and others (work summarized in Silverman, 1985), much evidence has been gathered to support the following general conclusion. The subliminal exposure of stimuli with psychodynamic content (i.e., content related to unconscious wishes, anxieties, and fantasies) can affect behavior in ways that the subliminal exposure of neutral content cannot. Moreover, these effects are consistent with certain predictions derived from clinical psychoanalytic theory about the relationship between unconscious motives and psychopathology. The implications of these findings for psychoanalytic theory have been discussed in several earlier reports (Silverman, 1967, 1970, 1971, 1972, 1975, 1976, 1978, 1983, 1985; Mendelsohn and Silverman, 1982; Silverman and Weinberger, 1985).

The following is a description of the experimental design used in many of these studies. Subjects are seen individually for an experimental and a control session, with the order of these counterbalanced (that is, half the subjects are seen first for a control session and half have the experimental session first). At the start of the session, the subject's propensity for the targeted psychopathological behavior is assessed. The subject then receives four tachistoscopic exposures of a subliminal stimulus, either one with psychodynamically relevant content (experimental session) or one with neutral content (control session). Each exposure is four milliseconds. Repeat assessment is then made of the targeted behavior to determine the effect of the subliminal stimulus. In the second session the same procedure is used except that if the psychodynamically relevant stimulus was used in the first session, the subject now receives the neutral stimulus, and vice versa. Both the experimenter and subject are blind to the content of the subliminal stimuli. The evaluation of pathological behavior is also carried out blindly.

The early work using this method addressed the conditions under which psychopathology is exacerbated, that is, the kinds of impulses, wishes, and fantasies which when activated intensify particular forms of pathology. In numerous studies, when subliminal stimuli designed to activate derivatives of conflictual unconscious wishes were compared with neutral stimuli, they were found to intensify pathology in several subject populations, including adult male schizophrenics (summarized in Mendelsohn and Silverman, 1982), stutterers (e.g., Silverman, Bronstein, and Mendelsohn, 1976), male homosexuals (e.g., Silverman, Kwawer, Wolitzky, and Coron, 1973), and depressives (e.g., Dauber, 1984).[6] Data from these studies supported psychoanalytic formulations regarding the relationship between oral aggressive wishes and ego pathology in schizophrenia, anal wishes and stuttering, incestuous wishes and male homosexuality, and aggressive wishes and depression.

A more recent series of studies investigated the conditions under which pathology remits or diminishes. Much of this work has involved the activation of unconscious fantasies of oneness, or what have been referred to as symbiotic-like fantasies. It has been found that the activation of such fantasies often leads to symptom reduction and other adaptive changes in a variety of clinical and nonclinical populations (results summarized in Silverman, Lachmann, and Milich, 1982; and Silverman, 1983). Among the major findings from studies of this type is that schizophrenic men subliminally exposed to the phrase "Mommy and I are one" experience diminished thought disorder and behavioral pathology. That is, when this stimulus was tested against other subliminal stimuli in double-blind studies, it was found to reduce pathology in a way that other stimuli did not. This was the case even when the other stimuli were in certain respects similar, for example, "Mommy and I are alike," "Mommy holds me safely,"

---

[6]Experimental effects in this type of study have typically been mild and short-lived. See Silverman (1977) for a full discussion of ethical issues in this research. It has been further demonstrated that these effects do not occur when the same stimuli are exposed supraliminally. This is consistent with the psychoanalytic view that once a conflictual wish becomes conscious its status as a contributor to psychopathology may be compromised e.g. (Silverman and Spiro, 1967; Lomangino, 1969).

and "Mommy is always with me." The results have been interpreted as lending support to the clinically based formulation that it is especially and specifically symbiotic-like unconscious fantasies (as opposed to other fantasies of wish fulfillment or anxiety reduction) that have an ameliorative potential for schizophrenics (Mendelsohn and Silverman, 1982).[7]

In more recent studies it has been found that the adaptation-enhancing effects of the "Mommy and I are one" stimulus are not limited to schizophrenics; positive effects have been noted in various groups of non-schizophrenics. In one series of studies, where groups of subjects received repeated exposures of the experimental stimulus over a period of weeks, while control groups received neutral stimuli, it was found that the activation of symbiotic-like fantasies enhanced academic performance (Zuckerman, 1980; Ariam and Siller, 1982; Parker, 1982; Hobbs, 1983). Another series of studies with this general design investigated whether the activation of these fantasies could enhance the effectiveness of psychological therapies. Linehan and O'Toole (1982) and Schurtman, Palmatier, and Martin (1983) demonstrated positive results for college students in group counseling, and alcoholics in AA-type individual counseling respectively. In four other studies, the subliminal stimulation of symbiotic-like fantasies proved successful as an adjunct to various behavior therapies including systematic desensitization (Silverman, Frank, and Dachinger, 1974), behavior modification of obesity (Silverman, Martin, Ungaro, and Mendelsohn, 1978), rapid smoking (Palmatier and Bornstein, 1980), and assertiveness training (Packer, 1982). In these four studies when the behavioral interventions were accompanied by the oneness stimulus they proved more effective than when accompanied by a neutral stimulus. (For a fuller discussion of these findings, including the questions of dosage of subliminal stimulation, sex differences in results, and negative findings, see Mendelsohn and Silverman, 1984, and Silverman and Weinberger, 1985.)

In yet another series of studies, attempts were made to assess the effects of stimuli designed to temporarily exacerbate or diminish oedipal conflicts in samples of college students. In one group of laboratory studies with college men engaged in a competitive dart throwing task, the effects of stimuli sanctioning or forbidding the expression of oedipal impulses were assessed. The findings from these studies have been less consistent and more subject to alternative interpretations than the pathology exacerbation and pathology reduction studies reviewed earlier (see Silverman, 1983; Silverman and Mendelsohn, 1984). However, the results clearly indicate the

---

[7]While "Mommy and I are one" is ameliorative for schizophrenic men, it is not for schizophrenic women. For female schizophrenics, "Daddy and I are one" has led to pathology reduction, (Cohen, 1977; Jackson, 1983) but this latter stimulus has not proven therapeutic for schizophrenic men (Kaye, 1975; Jackson, 1983).

usefulness of the subliminal psychodynamic activation method for investigating the influence of oedipally related motives on behavior.

What applicability does this experimental method, and the findings that have emerged, have for the issues we have addressed in this chapter concerning narcissistic pathology? As we indicated earlier, controlled experimental methods enable psychoanalytic investigators to pursue more rigorous tests of clinical formulations than can be accomplished using clinical methods. Process-oriented studies typically produce data that can be characterized as consistent with particular dynamic hypotheses and technical recommendations rather than as directly supportive of them. Without concommitant experimental study, the results from such studies tend to remain merely suggestive because there are serious limitations to the conrols that can be exercised over extraneous variables in process-oriented studies. The subliminal psychodynamic activation method could help address this difficulty. Experiments could be designed to test out the central formulations about narcissistic pathology advanced by each of the four writers.

One possible design is the following. Subjects would be selected for study who met the agreed upon diagnostic criteria for narcissistic personality disorder. Objective measures of the level of manifest narcissistic pathology could be devised; perhaps ratings of degree of grandiosity, devaluation, emptiness, nonrecognition of the separateness of the other, and the like could be made on the basis of a semistructured interview. (We recognize this would be a substantial project in its own right.) Following this baseline assessment of pathology, subjects would be exposed to one of several subliminal stimuli, which would include one with neutral content and others where the content reflected the formulations of the four clinical writers. Stimuli could be devised that would be expected, on the basis of each writer's understanding, to intensify or reduce narcissistic pathology. The goal would be to devise stimuli that represent the essence of each writer's understanding of narcissistic pathology, yet which, as much as possible, distinguish his views from those of the other writers. For example, according to Rothstein's formulation, the stimulus "Winning Mom is okay" would be expected to reduce narcissistic pathology (in men), while the stimulus "Winning Mom is wrong" would result in a (temporary) exacerbation of narcissistic pathology. Likewise, stimuli geared to the formulations of Kohut, Kernberg, and Masterson would reflect the central and distinguishing features of their understanding of narcissistic pathology.

Subjects would be exposed to the experimental and control stimuli in separate sessions (in counterbalanced order), and assessments of narcissistic pathology would be made following exposure to these stimuli. Through experiments of this type, the relative bearing of oedipal and preoedipal conflicts, or of wishes for oneness versus separateness, on narcissistic pathology could be assessed. If certain of the experimental stimuli were found to be especially potent in either exacerbating or diminishing manifest narcissistic pathology, further studies could be undertaken to determine the elements in each stimulus responsible for its effects.[8] In this way, through a series of studies of increasing specificity and focus, the various formulations proposed to account for narcissistic pathology could be compared, evaluated, and refined. It is also possible that different subgroups of narcissistic patients could be identified on the basis of differential responses to these stimuli. It would then be valuable to determine if such subgroups corresponded to subgroups responding differentially to the different treatment approaches.

How else might the subliminal psychodynamic activation method be adapted for study in this area? Let us tentatively propose the following. As we reviewed earlier, one key aspect of Kohut's technical approach, and one that distinguishes it from those of Kernberg, Rothstein, and Masterson, is his advocacy of the use of "empathic communications." Since empathic communication, as we defined it earlier, involves the therapist's conveying that he is viewing matters from the patient's perspective—that the therapist is, to some degree, sharing the patient's experience—it does not seem unreasonable to suppose that such communications inadvertently activate unconscious oneness fantasies. Thus, if it should turn out that these communications have the therapeutic promise Kohut claims (and it may be added that years ago Carl Rogers [1951] made similar claims) the studies we reviewed earlier of the pathology-reducing and adaptation-enhancing effects of the "Mommy and I are one" stimulus suggest which aspects of such communications are responsible for their efficacy—their ability to activate oneness fantasies.

To study the possible connection between the findings from the oneness studies and Kohut's claim that empathic communications are especially useful in the treatment of narcissistic personalities, the following investigations could be undertaken. One could evaluate subjects in future subliminal stimulation studies where the adaptation-enhancing effects of the oneness stimulus are being examined for the degree of narcissistic pathology in evidence. To date this has not been done, with subjects chosen simply on the basis of group characteristics, for example, smokers' trying to give up smoking or alcoholics seeking to reduce alcohol intake. Since there have been wide variations in all such studies in terms of how different subjects have responded to the oneness stimulus, it could be those subjects with notable narcissistic pathology who carry the positive group

---

[8]See Silverman and Weinberger (1985) for an account of how this stategy was used to determine which elements in a frequently used subliminal psychodynamic stimulus (Mommy and I are one) were responsible for its effects.

effect. One could then say that it is those persons most in need of a maternal selfobject (to use Kohut's language) who can profit from the activation of symbiotic-like fantasies.

Of course, Kohut's advocacy of the use of empathic communications with narcissistic personalities does not stem from his belief that this would directly ameliorate pathology. Rather, he views these communications, as well as his approach in general, as furthering the psychoanalytic process. On the other hand, some of Kohut's critics, including Kernberg (1974), have challenged this assertion and have maintained that his approach prevents rather than fosters analytic exploration. Of course, the outcome and especially the process-oriented studies described earlier, in which treatment sessions are taped and movement within sessions evaluated, would bear on these opposing claims, but so might further studies using subliminal exposures of oneness stimuli. It should be possible to carry out an experimental study in which methods are first devised for tapping a person's potential for psychological mindedness (adaptations of the TAT could be used for this purpose). Evaluations could then be made of this variable after both the "Mommy and I are one" and control conditions for subjects of varying personality types. An hypothesis that could be tested is that subjects meeting the diagnostic criteria for narcissistic personality disorder would show increased psychological mindedness after the oneness condition.

In addition to studies employing subliminal activation of unconscious motives, studies using hypnotic induction could be applied to investigations in this area. Hypnotic induction has the advantage of enabling investigators to devise complex and specific scenarios that can be presented to subjects outside of their awareness. Inductions could be devised to represent key aspects of the formulations of each writer. For example, an induction designed to sanction the gratification of certain oedipal wishes could be given to subjects as a test of Rothstein's views. Similarly, inductions designed to sanction the gratification of aggressive wishes (Kernberg), expose subjects to empathic maternal responses (Kohut), or to accepting, nonpossessive maternal behavior (Masterson) could be presented to subjects and their effects upon narcissistic pathology compared. If one type of induction were clearly more effective than the others in reducing narcissistic pathology, the results would lend support to the one formulation to which it corresponded.

Obviously no single study, whatever its results, would be decisive in resolving a controversy as complex and multifaceted as the one under discussion. Many experiments of different types carried out at a number of laboratories are called for, and these need not be limited to the subliminal psychodynamic activation method or to hypnotic induction. Any other experimental manipulation that proves effective in activating psycho-

264 MENDELSOHN AND SILVERMAN

dynamic processes could be used in complementary experiments. And, as we said earlier, experimental data bearing on these issues need to be considered together with findings from outcome and clinical process studies— the converging lines of evidence concept we made reference to earlier.

CONCLUSIONS

What are the advantages, difficulties, and limitations of the empirical approach that we have proposed?

Our approach allows for the objective, comprehensive, and systematic study of different dynamic formulations and treatment proposals. The benefits that could be attained, briefly summarized, are as follows: (1) development of greater diagnostic specificity and reliability; (2) facilitation of meaningful diagnostic subtyping; (3) clarification of the degree to which diagnostic differences have produced differences in the understanding and treatment of narcissistic disorders; (4) determination of the degree to which descriptive differences are artifacts of differences in technique; (5) clarification of the relationship between therapy process and outcome; (6) evaluation of the relative efficacy of different treatment approaches; (7) assessment of the efficacy of specific technical interventions; and (8) determination of the validity of specific psychodynamic formulations regarding narcissistic pathology.

The difficulties that this type of empirical approach would encounter include some that are specific to this area of study and some that would apply to the investigation of other controversial clinical issues as well. As regards the former, the present lack of uniform diagnostic criteria and the apparent differences in diagnostic descriptions might preclude comparative study of the different treatment approaches. In a similar vein, in undertaking experimental studies of key psychodynamic formulations, it may prove difficult to devise subliminal stimuli or hypnotic inductions that *both* represent each position *and* distinguish it from alternate positions. It is quite possible that a stimulus derived specifically from the formulations of one writer would also bear on issues germane to the formulations of other writers. There is a more general problem that such an approach would have to contend with, namely, an unavoidable tendency toward reductionism, especially in process-oriented and experimental studies. The focus on "key" aspects of theory or technique rather than on an overall gestalt would detract from the validity and applicability of any one study. However, as stated earlier, the strategy of combining several empirical approaches significantly reduces the possibility that this factor will limit the interpretability of findings.

The limitations of the research program we are proposing are that those aspects of each writer's core understanding that bear on etiology and

pathogenesis would not be addressed, while only psychodynamic propositions (variations in narcissistic pathology in the "here and now") would be
investigated. To undertake studies of etiology and pathogenesis, prospective, longitudinal, and perhaps even epidemiological studies would be required. Discussion of these is beyond the scope of this chapter, but suffice
it to say, the practical difficulties confronting potential investigators in
these areas would be considerable. In addition, the process-oriented studies
we have proposed lend themselves to the study of discrete interventions,
for example, interpretations of one type of content or another. Study of the
effects of therapist stance, activity level of the therapist, and the use and
timing of reconstructions could not be accomplished by the methods we
have proposed.

Despite the problems and limitations of our proposed research program,
despite the numerous salient questions that would be left ambiguously
answered or totally unaddressed, we maintain that the benefits of such an
approach would be considerable and would justify the effort of such an
undertaking.

In 1976 Philip Holzman wrote:

> It is noteworthy that our 80-year-old discipline never developed canons for
> . . . judging the worth of contributions. . . . New ideas in psychoanalysis
> provoke some essays for and against but these are not sufficient. Unlike . . .
> literary criticism, we require much more than such essays. We need proposals
> to test ideas systematically and unfortunately there are too few calls for such
> tests [p. 269].

This chapter is intended as one such call. The contrasting views on the
understanding and treatment of narcissistic pathology are too important to
be left to what Merton Gill referred to as "waves of fashion." (Gill, 1979) If
with regard to this controversy as well as the many other controversies in
the psychoanalytic community, we are to weed out the invalid from the
valid and develop a clinical theory that can attain a reasonable consensus
among us, business cannot proceed as usual. The essays for and against, as
Holzman calls them, must be replaced by a concerted effort to address
differences thoroughly, rigorously, objectively, and with scientific safe-
guards.

REFERENCES

Ariam, S., & Siller, J. (1982), Effects of subliminal oneness stimuli in Hebrew on academic
    performance of Israeli high school students: Further evidence on the adaptation enhancing
    effects of symbiotic fantasies in another culture using another language. *J. Abn. Psychol.*, 91:
    343–349.

Cohen, R. (1977), *The Effects of Four Subliminally Introduced Merging Stimuli on the Psychopathology of Schizophrenic Women.* Unpublished doctoral dissertation, Columbia University.

Dauber, L. (1984), Subliminal psychodynamic activation studies of autonomy issues in depressed women. *J. Abn. Psychol.*

Eissler, K. R. (1953), The effects of the structure of the ego on psychoanalytic technique. *J. Amer. Psychoanal. Assn.*, 1:104–143.

Fisher, C. (1954), Dreams and perception. *J. Amer. Psychoanal. Assn.*, 2:389–445.

——— (1956), Dreams, images, and perception: A study of unconscious-preconscious relationships. *J. Amer. Psychoanal. Assn.*, 4:5–48.

Fisher, S., & Greenberg, R. P. (1978), *The Scientific Evaluation of Freud's Theories and Therapy.* New York: Basic Books.

Gill, M. M. (1979), The analysis of the transference. *J. Amer. Psychoanal. Assn.*, 27:263–288.

——— Simon, J., Fink, G., Endicott, N. A., & Paul, I. (1968), Studies in audio-recorded psychoanalysis: I. General considerations. *J. Amer. Psychoanal. Assn.*, 16:230–244.

Hobbs, S. (1983), *The Effects of Activated Oedipal and Symbiotic Fantasies on Prejudiced Attitudes.* Unpublished doctoral dissertation, New York University.

Holt, R. R. (1985), The current status of psychoanalytic theory. *Psychoanal. Psychol.*, 2:289–315.

Holzman, P. S. (1976), The future of psychoanalysis and its institutes. *Psychoanal. Quart.*, 45(2):250–273.

Jackson, J. (1983), The effects of fantasies of oneness with mother and father on the ego functioning of male and female schizophrenics. *J. Nerv. & Ment. Dis.*, 171:280–289.

Kaye, M. (1975), *The Therapeutic Value of Three Merging Stimuli for Male Schizophrenics.* Unpublished doctoral dissertation, New York University.

Kernberg, O. (1974), Further contributions to the treatment of narcissistic personalities. *Internat. J. Psycho-Anal.*, 55:215–240.

——— (1975), *Borderline Conditions and Pathological Narcissism.* New York: Aronson.

Knight, R. P. (1954), Borderline states. In: *Psychoanalytic Psychiatry and Psychology*, ed. R. P. Knight & C. R. Friedman. New York: International Universities Press.

Kohut, H. (1971), *The Analysis of the Self.* New York: International Universities Press.

——— (1977), *The Restoration of the Self.* New York: International Universities Press.

Lasch, C. (1978), *The Culture of Narcissism.* New York: W. W. Norton.

Linehan, E., & O'Toole, J. (1982), The effect of subliminal stimulation of symbiotic fantasy on college students' self-disclosures in group counseling. *J. Counsel. Psychol.*, 29:151–157.

Little, M. I. (1981), *Transference Neurosis and Transference Psychosis.* New York: Aronson.

Lomangino, L. (1969), *Depiction of Subliminally and Supraliminally Presented Aggressive Stimuli and Its Effects on the Cognitive Functioning of Schizophrenics.* Unpublished doctoral dissertation, Fordham University.

Luborsky, L., & Auerbach, A. H. (1969), The symptom-context method: Quantitative studies of symptom formation in psychotherapy. *J. Amer. Psychoanal. Assn.*, 17:68–99.

Mahler, M. S., Pine, F., & Bergman, A. (1975), *The Psychological Birth of the Human Infant.* New York: Basic Books.

Masterson, J. F. (1981), *The Narcissistic and Borderline Disorders.* New York: Brunner/Mazel.

Mendelsohn, E., & Silverman, L. H. (1982), The effects of stimulating psychodynamically relevant unconscious fantasies on schizophrenic psychopathology: A review of research findings. *Schiz. Bull.*, 8(3):532–547.

——— & ——— (1984), The activation of unconscious fantasies in behavioral treatments. In: *Psychoanalysis and Behavior Therapy: Is Integration Possible?*, ed., H. Arkowitz & S. Messer. New York: Plenum.

Ornstein, P. H. (1974), A discussion of Otto F. Kernberg's "Further contributions to the treatment of narcissistic personalities." *Internat. J. Psycho-Anal.*, 55:241–247.

Packer, S. (1982), *The Effects of Subliminal Psychodynamic Activation on Behavior Assertiveness Training in Women.* Unpublished doctoral dissertation, New York University.

Palmatier, J. R., & Bornstein, P. H. (1980), The effects of subliminal stimulation of symbiotic merging fantasies on behavioral treatment of smokers. *J. Nerv. & Ment. Dis.,* 168:715–720.

Pao, P. N. (1979), *Schizophrenic Disorders: Theory and Treatment from a Psychodynamic Point of View.* New York: International Universities Press.

Parker, K. A. (1982), The effects of subliminal symbiotic stimulation on academic performance: Further evidence for the adaptation-enhancing effects of oneness fantasies. *J. Coun. Psychol.,* 29:19–28.

Pine, F. (1985), *Developmental Theory and Clinical Process.* New Haven: Yale University Press.

Rehyer, J. (1967), Hypnosis in research on psychopathology. In: *Handbook of Clinical and Experimental hypnosis,* ed. J. E. Gordon. New York: Macmillan.

Rogers, C. R. (1951), *Client Centered Therapy.* Boston: Houghton Miflin.

Rosenfeld, H. A. (1965), *Psychotic States: A Psychoanalytic Approach.* New York: International Universities Press.

Rothstein, A. (1979). Oedipal conflicts in narcissistic personality disorders. *Internat. J. Psycho-Anal.,* 60:189–199.

——— (1980), *The Narcissistic Pursuit of Perfection.* New York: International Universities Press.

Sampson, H., Weiss, J., Mlodnosky, L., & Hause, E. (1972), Defense analysis and the emergence of warded off mental contents. *Arch. Gen. Psychiat.,* 26:524–532.

Schurtman, R., Palmatier, J. R., & Martin, C. (1983), The effect of psychodynamic activation of symbiotic gratification fantasies on involvement in a treatment program for alcoholics. *Internat. J. Addiction.*

Searles, H. F. (1965), *Corrected Papers on Schizophrenics and Related Subjects.* New York: International Universities Press.

Shapiro, A. K., & Morris, L. A. (1978), The placebo effect in medical and psychological therapies. In: *Handbook of Psychotherapy and Behavior Change* (2nd ed.), ed. S. L. Garfield & A. E. Bergin. New York: Wiley & Sons.

Silverman, L. H. (1967), An experimental approach to the study of dynamic propositions in psychoanalysis: The relationship between the aggressive drive and ego regression: Initial studies. *J. Amer. Psychoanal. Assn..,* 15:376–403.

——— (1970), Further experimental studies on dynamic propositions in psychoanalysis: On the function and meaning of regressive thinking. *J. Amer. Psychoanal. Assn.,* 18:102–124.

——— (1971), An experimental technique for the study of unconscious conflict. *Brit. J. Med. Psychol.,* 41:17–25.

——— (1972), Drive stimulation and psychopathology: On the conditions under which drive-related external events evoke pathological reactions. In: *Psychoanalysis and Contemporary Science* (Vol. 1), ed. R. R. Holt & E. Peterfreund. New York: Macmillan.

——— (1975), On the role of laboratory experiments in the development of the clinical theory of psychoanalysis. *Internat. Rev. Psychoanal.,* 2:43–64.

——— (1976), Psychoanalytic theory: The reports of my death are greatly exaggerated. *Amer. Psychol.,* 31:621–637.

——— (1977), *Ethical considerations and guidelines in the use of subliminal psychodynamic activation.* Unpublished manuscript, Research Center for Mental Health, New York University.

——— (1978), The unconscious symbiotic fantasy as a ubiquitous therapeutic agent. *Internat. J. Psycho-Anal. Psychother.,* 7:562–585.

——— (1982), A comment on two subliminal psychodynamic activation experiments. *J. Abn. Psychol.,* 91:126–130.

——— (1983), The subliminal psychodynamic activation method: Overview and comprehensive listing of studies. In J. Masling (Ed.), *Empirical Studies of Psychoanalytical Theories*. (Vol. 1), Hillsdale, NJ: Lawrence Erlbaum Associates.

———, Bronstein, A., & Mendelsohn, E. (1976), The further use of the subliminal psycho-dynamic activation method for the experimental study of the clinical theory of psycho-analysis: On the specificity of relationships between manifest psychopathology and unconscious conflict. *Psychother.: Theory, Res. Prac.*, 13:2–16.

——— Frank, S., & Dachinger, P. (1974), Psychoanalytic reinterpretation of the effectiveness of systematic desensitization: Experimental data bearing on the role of merging fantasies: *J. Abn. Psychol.*, 83:313–318.

——— Kwawer, J. S., Wolitzky, C., & Coron, M. (1973), An experimental study of aspects of the psychoanalytic theory of male homosexuality. *J. Abn. Psychol.*, 82:178–188.

——— Lachmann, F. M., & Milich, R. H. (1982). *The Search for Oneness*. New York: Interna-tional Universities Press.

——— Martin, A., Ungaro, R., & Mendelsohn, E. (1978), Effect of subliminal stimulation of symbiotic fantasies on behavior modification treatment of obesity. *J. Consult. Psychol.*, 46: 432–441.

——— & Spiro, R. H. (1967), Some comments and data on the partial cue controversy and other matters relevant to investigations of subliminal phenomena. *Percept. & Motor Skills*, 25:325–338.

———, and Weinberger, J. (1985), Mommy and I are one: Implications for Psychotherapy. *Amer. Psychol.*, 40:1296–1308.

——— & Wolitzky, D. (1982), Toward the resolution of controversial issues in psychoanalytic treatment. In: *Curative factors in dynamic psychotherapy*, ed. S. Slipp. New York: McGraw Hill. p. 321–348.

Sommerschield, H. & Rehyer, J. (1973), Posthypnotic conflict, repression and psychopathol-ogy. *J. Abn. Psychol.*, 82:278–290.

Stern, D. (1985), *The Interpersonal World of the Infant*. New York: Basic Books, Inc.

Wolitzky, D., & Wachtel, P. F. (1973), Personality and perception. In: *Handbook of general psychology* (pp. 826–857), ed. B. Wolman. Englewood Cliffs, NJ: Prentice Hall, pp. 826–857.

Zuckerman, S. (1980), *The Effects of Subliminal Symbiotic and Success-Related Stimuli on the School Performance of High School Underachievers*. Unpublished doctoral dissertation, New York University.

Author Index

Subject Index

A

Abused children, 46–47

Action disposition, unconscious processing and, 204–6

Aesthetic notions, 128–29

Affectionless psychopath, 31

Affective disorders, 24

Affective memory, 8–9

Affects
development of consciousness and, 7–12
in infant-mother interaction, 7–9
peak affect states, 8–9, 10, 20, 24
subjective quality of, 8–9

Affordances, concept of, 207

Aggression, 23

Agoraphobic patients, pathogenic beliefs of, 167–68

Alternatives, assessment and utilization of, 126

Altruism, 54–56

American Psychiatric Association, 222

Ames room perceptual distortions, 170n

Analysis by synthesis, 201

Antisocial personality disorders, superego pathology in, 14–15

Anxiety
castration, 166–67, 169n, 177–78
separation, 35

Archaeology of human relationships, 27–39
achievement of identity and object constancy, 36
attachment process, 31–32
identification and emotional autonomy, 37
normal symbiosis stage, 32–33
oedipal period, 37
practicing period, 33–34
preattachment stage, 30–31
rapprochement phase and crisis, 34–36
separation-individuation, 10–11, 33–34

Archaic introject, 181–82

Assumption, identity, 163, 164–65

Attachment, 29
failure of, 44–45
process of, 31–32

Attention, selective, 199–202

Attenuation theory of selective attention, 200

Attribution error, fundamental, 73

Authentic personal freedom, 17

Autism, infantile, 30–31

Autonomy, emotional, 37

B

"Basis trust," 31

Beliefs, pathogenic, 166–69, 173–74, 177, 181, 183

Benzene ring, discovery of, 85–87